# The Craft
# of
# Pitching

by
## Larry Jansen
with
## George A. (Al) Jansen, M.D.

## Illustrations by
## Karl Van Loo

MASTERS PRESS

*A Division of Howard W. Sams & Company*

Published by Masters Press
A Division of Howard W. Sams & Company
2647 Waterfront Parkway, E. Drive
Suite 100
Indianapolis, IN 46214

97 98 99 00 01 02          10 9 8 7 6 5 4 3 2 1

**Library of Congress Cataloging in Publication Information**

Jansen, Larry, 1920-
   The craft of pitching / by Larry Jansen and George A. (Al) Jansen,
      p. cm.
   ISBN 1-57028-151-3
   1. Pitching (Baseball)      I. Jansen, George A., 1932-   . II. Title.

GV871.J35      1997
796.357'22--dc21
                                        97-25260
                                              CIP

# Acknowledgments

The technical, tactical and reminiscent material are my product, supplemented by Doctor Jansen. "Doc" also composed nearly the entirety of the written text, and, of course, authored the chapters on physiology and injuries. My loving wife, and dearest friend of 56 wonderful years, Eileen, wrote and edited her memoirs – located in Chapter 10. Karl Van Loo created the illustrations. Although he possessed but a modicum of baseball knowledge at the outset, Karl has since become an enthusiastic baseball aficionado. Doctor Jansen's wife of 32 years, Jeanne, demonstrated an immense amount of patience with her husband whose eyes and head were increasingly buried in the preparation of this work – when he could free himself from his medical duties. To her, we owe an enormous debt of gratitude. To her, and to Eileen, our love and admiration.

Eva Walden-Krois, former Little League manager, ("the only lady manager in the league, and in high heels and mini-skirt at that!") typed every last word and set up the text in a manner that meets the highest standards of professionalism. To her we are deeply grateful.

We much appreciate the intense review and pertinent suggestions related to Chapter 7, **Pitching Injuries**, provided by Harry A. Khasigian, M.D., FACS, orthopedic surgeon and chief, Occupational Orthopedics and Sports Medicine Clinic, Sacramento, California, and by Laura Timmerman, M.D., Team Orthopedist, University of California, Berkeley, Associate Clinical Professor Orthopedic Surgery, University of California, Davis. Our gratitude is also due to Curtiss Brown, strength and conditioning specialist, certified by the National Strength and Conditioning Association, and member of the American College of Sports Medicine, for his review and assistance with Chapter 8, **Pitching Physiology**.

Finally, a special thanks to Christy Yetter for her superb photographic work from which Karl Van Loo drafted a number of his illustrations.

We believe we have contributed in a substantial manner to our communities and to the game of baseball by showing young men (and women), not only how to pitch and play baseball, but also how to live.

## Credits

Cover Photo©Robert Binder/Lovero Group

Illustrations©Karl Van Loo

Text Layout by Kim Heusel

Cover Design by Phil Velikan

Edited by Kim Heusel

# Table of Contents

# Foreword

Larry Jansen was my first big-league coach. He coached me for 10 years while I was in San Francisco with the Giants.

My first year, 1962, was a tough one for me but I remember that during the playoffs against the Dodgers, Coach Jansen showed me what a great coach is all about. In the second game of the playoffs I pitched in relief. When I came to the mound, Maurey Wills was on second base. The bunt was in order, and when it came I was supposed to throw to third base to get Wills out. I got the bunt but I didn't think I could get to third in time to get Wills out, so I threw the ball to first for the sure out. The Giants lost that game (we won the next game and went to the World Series).

Following the game, Coach Jansen came to me and said something like, "Hang in there. The world hasn't come to an end." He was the only person to speak to me after that game. That's the kind of coach he was – he was with me whether I was good or bad.

In the spring of 1964, Coach Jansen took me aside and said, "You need a slider." With those words, he saved my career. The slider became my best pitch.

Every time I warmed up for a game, Coach Jansen was right there watching me to make sure that everything was working as it should work. He was always in the bullpen – where a pitching coach should be! If he thought I needed help, he signaled me and I knew what to do on the next pitch.

The greatest piece of advice he gave me came in 1964. He said, "You will get your chance. Make sure you are ready." I made sure I was ready, and in the second game of a doubleheader I was the last pitcher in the bullpen. When the phone rang, I knew it was for me. I pitched 10 scoreless innings and got the win. I was ready when my chance came.

Coach Jansen and I had a few more great years together, but after the 1971 season, I was traded to Cleveland. I believe I would have been traded sooner if not for Coach Jansen.

In 1991, I was inducted into the National Baseball Hall of Fame. Coach Larry Jansen was the first coach I thanked that day. He was more than a coach to me. He cared about his pitchers and his pitchers cared a great deal about him. I know I did, and I will always be grateful to him for helping me.

**Gaylord Perry, pitcher**
**Hall of Fame, 1991**
**September 1996**

---

Firsthand, I must say Larry Jansen is a remarkable human being, the kind of person whose advice you would listen to very closely. I always did and I tried to follow it because he always seemed to be right on the money, especially when pitching was concerned.

I am able to say I learned a lot from him and I believe the majority of pitchers who came in contact with Larry during his years as a pitching coach would agree.

A great pitcher in his time, Larry was seen as a "big brother" by his peers. He was always very approachable and understanding, but when he had to be a disciplinarian, well, he sure was. My relationship with him was one of affection and kindness, and mostly, one of respect.

Larry is what you would call a great family man who instilled family values.

To Mr. Larry Jansen (as I would call him), my deepest respect to him and his family. He shall always be in my heart due to his unconditional support in the beginning and throughout my career.

**Juan Marichal, pitcher**
**Hall of Fame, 1983**
**September 1996**

# Introduction

Pitching is an art, a science and a craft. It is at once puzzling and mystifying, cruel and kind, intimidating and inviting. Not without reason is the pitcher's mound located near the center of the baseball diamond, for the mound is the fulcrum about which all baseball action turns. From atop this 12-inch hill of dirt the ball is put into play. How this play develops resides largely in the arm, hands and **mind** of the pitcher.

Pitchers come to baseball with different degrees of physical and mental strength. In the last hundred years of baseball, pitchers have shown repeatedly that extraordinary mental strengths can compensate for physical deficiencies; rarely is the reverse true! In this book, I discuss and demonstrate the **physical** features of pitching – interwoven with the mental processes that drive the physical dynamics. These are the tools of the trade for the craftsman called **Pitcher**.

Because the mental aspects of pitching are so important both in the preparation for and the pitching of a game, the pitcher must constantly study and learn from opposing hitters and pitchers, teammates, pitching coaches, statistics, videos, films – and yes, even from the fans. Pitchers must master ways to surprise, mystify and deceive the hitter – or the base runner. Lew Burdette of the Braves summarized this art form: "I exploit the greed of all hitters." Warren Spahn added: "Hitting is timing. Pitching is upsetting timing."

The pitcher's **mind** drives his tactics as he selects the movement, speed, and placement of the pitch. His physical **talent** fulfills – or fails to fulfill –

the tactical plan. While the pitcher tunes his mind with constant study, he empowers his body with sustained work. Before World War II, pitchers were often the product of a youth filled with long days of difficult physical work: Dizzy Dean picked cotton; Joe Page and Stan Coveleski worked in the coal mines; Bob Feller and Grover Cleveland Alexander labored on the farm – the list is endless. What does hard physical work produce? Endurance, stamina – attributes that carry pitchers to, and beyond, the sixth inning! Does this mean that teenagers need to spend summers descending into coal mines or sweating in farm fields? Not necessarily. Certainly, aspiring pitchers are best served by long days of hard physical work punctuated by breaks during which they throw a baseball; days off are for playing the game! Time on the couch before the television or playing video games does not engender endurance and stamina.

The purpose of this book is to insert the reader into the **mind** and **body** of the pitcher for an intimate examination of this player about whom all action on the baseball field spins. I want the reader to look out on the field from the pitcher's mind and senses – to see, hear, feel what the pitcher perceives, and follow the pitcher's logic and physical dynamics. The audience members are **all** ballplayers, and their coaches, in high school, sandlot, summer/fall, college and little leagues. Also included are young players entering professional ball, the present day legatees of bygone eras – my own included – with who I now share in written form what I taught for many years in the minor and major leagues.

This text is not intended for the sole use of pitchers. "Position players" need to understand pitching logic and dynamics in order to position themselves and to react correctly in response to the opponent's actions. Hitters, too, can benefit from a better understanding of the pitcher.

**Finally, and perhaps most importantly, the book is intended for baseball fans, as well as the wives and families of baseball players. After all, it is they who make it possible for the ballplayer to pursue his occupation.**

The tack here carries us into the mainstream of pitching and launches with a discussion of the preparation and character of the pitcher. From there our course takes us to mechanics, pitch placement, control and movement, rules, tactics, strategy, pitching injuries, baseball physiology and psychology. A special chapter dedicated to the pitcher's wife and a chapter on pitching and coaching careers complete the work.

Deliberately, I refrain from long or frequent recitals of impertinent statistics. Such numbers fascinate a few, but contribute little ballast to our discussion. Inevitably, I will draw upon my experience as a major-league

pitcher and coach, as well as that wisdom and lore given me by coaches, managers, players, friends and family from boyhood, through the minor leagues to the majors, and several World Series.

Doctor Jansen and I have reviewed many of the "classic" works written on the mental and physical aspects of pitching, and we have selected our Hall of Fame references (Appendix B). Other works, not yet anointed with the oils of classicism, but nevertheless authoritative, reliable, peer acclaimed writings, were carefully selected and added to the list.

Baseball language and jargon govern the choice of words and phrases. Baseball is a complicated game; the players engage in complex actions compressed into fractions of seconds. Such a sport lends itself to the expression of ideas in very concise terms, and the most concise English words are those with Anglo-Saxon roots. To complicate baseball concepts with elongated words of Latin or Greek origin is to inflict an injustice on baseball's precise lingo. Only when the Latin root best conveys the meaning intended (or when humor demands it) will such words appear. During the discussion of physiology and psychology, there is often no Anglo-Saxon substitute for the terms used. The most beautiful word a pitcher can hear is "strike." The purest melody is the loud chant from bench and stands to a beaten batter: **"Sit Down!"**

**Larry Jansen, January 1997**
**Forest Grove, Oregon**

# 1

# Preparation and Attitude

## In a Nutshell

1. Prepare mind and body
2. Spring training
3. The battery: Catcher and pitcher
4. Long range preparation
5. Work hard and throw often
6. Attitude is half the game
7. Talent is the other half
8. Perseverance — consistency — honesty
9. Industry and anger control
10. Pitcher: The ultimate competitor

*"Fame in baseball is perverse. Hitters wear the win; pitchers eat the loss."*

**Authors**

So! You want to climb to the top of that little mound out there. It's all really a mirage, you know. That is not a bump squatting on a flat green lawn; it is an enormous mountain. The trail to the top is steep, tedious and littered with slippery, sharp-edged stones. At every bend, huge banks of loosened snow and gravel shift restlessly, ready to tumble and bury the climber in a thundering avalanche. The track demands weeks, months — years, even — of bone-aching physical preparation and mind-numbing study to reach the performance peak. When the weary hiker finally gains the summit, he finds himself teetering on the edge of a precipice. The slightest breeze can send him hurtling down. Such are the fortunes of those who choose the pitcher's path.

This book is a trail guide tailored to the climber. The chasms, cliffs and cataracts are clearly marked, but remember, mountains have minds of their own. The first chapter starts in the foothills where the trekker loads on himself the heavy pack of preparation.

Laborers and professional persons prepare both mind and body to perform their work. Such preparation is both long-range and **immediate**. **Long-range** preparation takes shape during the education years when the worker or professional masters the basic skills of his craft, art or science. Immediate preparation encompasses those activities that occur each day, in the interval just prior to a major effort: the farmer turns the soil before planting, the diamond cutter studies the geometry of an uncut diamond, the lawyer drafts his case. It is to the pitcher's **immediate preparation** that we now turn our attention.

Best we begin with **spring training**. Baseball, in all its forms and levels of skill, begins with some form of preparation in the early spring when the days grow longer after the winter solstice. It is then that special sounds shatter the stillness of the languid, warm morning air: Fresh new balls slap into leather gloves and crackle into flight off swishing bats. Coaches bellow, players shout and spikes clatter across cement dugout floors. Now, serious immediate preparations for the season begin. For the pitcher this is a special time of training. Exactly what constitutes the best kind of preparation?

When I became a major-league pitching coach, I adapted several solid ideas about this preparatory period and condensed them into six routine practices pursued by those who are successful pitchers.

1. **Every day for the first seven days (or so), warm up 10 to 15 minutes. Then immediately throw about 50 pitches to hitters during batting practice.** (There is usually not a game of any kind

during this first week.) A pitcher's muscles, especially those of the arm, shoulder and legs, are strengthened and conditioned by daily throwing.

2. **Throw half these pitches from the stretch**. Nearly 50 percent of pitches thrown in a game come from the stretch. Throwing from this position levies special stresses on the pitcher's musculoskeletal system – stresses distinctly different from those experienced while pitching from the windup.

3. **Hurl the entire personal arsenal of pitches from the first day of spring training, including breaking balls**. Occasionally, coaches advise pitchers to withhold breaking pitches for a week or more in spring training. This advice is unsound. The pitcher who withholds his "breaking stuff" until later in the spring frequently experiences an unpleasant rebound in muscle physiology. The pitcher who starts spring training by throwing both straight and breaking pitches will naturally suffer muscle soreness and stiffness which eventually (in about seven days) resolves. The pitcher who throws only straight pitches also recovers from the initial aches only to experience a reappearance of muscle problems when he blends in his breaking balls. Time to healing is usually another seven days. The math is obvious. The latter hurler has taken 14 days to heal his muscle problem; the former only seven.

In the minor leagues spring training is 30 days; in the major leagues, six weeks. Pragmatism dictates that the pitcher not waste an extra week healing. Even worse, some arm injuries occur in pitchers who delay throwing the breaking pitch because those pitchers have conditioned their arms to throwing fastballs. Consequently, the first curves may be thrown too hard – a potential source of injury (see Chapter 7).

My teammate on the Giants, Sal Maglie, and I were breaking-ball pitchers. We found it important to prepare ourselves in the manner described. **The hardest pitch to control is the breaking pitch**, and the earlier the pitcher starts to throw this pitch, the quicker he gains control of it before the season begins.

4. As a corollary to the third point, **even during the warm-up period** (before throwing the 50 batting practice pitches), **use your entire arsenal of pitches**. During batting practice throw two or three breaking balls to each hitter. The hitters appreciate this kind of service!

Current medical literature in sports medicine fails to support the contention that little-leaguers should not be taught to throw breaking balls. The game must be fun, and youngsters who learn to put a spin on the ball are not irrevocably injuring their arms; they are training muscles. The elbow injuries that do appear in little league curveballers appear not as a result of spinning the ball, but from **overuse of the curve.**\*

5. **During the last five minutes of the warm-up, station a teammate in the batter's box (helmet on!) adjacent to the warm-up plate**. The teammate positions himself first on one side of the plate, then on the other to simulate right- and left-handed hitters. This maneuver serves as a gauge for the accuracy of pitch placement (see Chapter 3). Without this gauge the pitcher may harbor an incomplete and/or inaccurate estimate of his placements. Pitchers who find difficulty with placement (control) **early in a game** should heed this advice. Control problems early in the game are avoidable if the pitcher is willing to undertake proper and adequate preparation. There are other reasons for early control problems, but at least the variable of a hitter standing in place has been addressed. Consult Chapter 3 for additional comments on control.

6. One of the best drills to aid muscle flexibility on days **when not preparing to pitch** is the **pepper game**. In this drill three players stand side by side in a line opposite a hitter positioned 15 feet away. The players throw toward the hitter who hard bunts the ball back toward the three. They must repeatedly bend and stretch to field and throw the ball.

**NOTE**: Little-leaguers should throw only 20 to 30 pitches—two or three times a week – during batting practice after 10 to 15 minutes of warm-up. This advice depends on the age of the little-leaguer, the absence of soreness (see Chapter 7) and the coach's careful assessment of his pitcher.

In summary, at all levels of play, the spring training gets underway while the pitcher works on these six precepts. The particulars for the remainder of the spring event depend on each team's own training policies. The pitching coach actively and continuously monitors his pitchers in spring training and pays close attention to detecting and correcting flawed mechanics. Flawed mechanics (see Chapter 2) in spring training can easily and rapidly lead to serious arm problems (see Chapter 7).

## *The Catcher*

The **battery** is an older baseball expression that means the pitcher and catcher of a baseball team. One dictionary\*\* defines a *battery* as "... group of two... cells connected together to furnish an electric current..." An appropriate description for a pitcher/catcher combination! The electric current these two "cells" provide lights and energizes the game by producing **outs**. The connection between these two players must remain unbroken – one heart, one mind. In a sense, the catcher acts as the pitcher's coach, advisor and "associate" strategist during the game. The catcher knows best what is "working" for a pitcher on a given day. He has perhaps caught the pitcher's last few warm-up throws; he has observed the pitcher's state of mind, and he knows how the pitcher prefers to handle special situations.

Set-up close behind the hitter, the catcher studies the hitter's station in the batter's box, his facial expression, practice swings, glances toward the infield/outfield, attention to base coach signals, and an endless number of details and nuances which accompany the hitter to the plate. Both catcher and pitcher know "the book" on the hitter: strengths, weaknesses, **tendencies** in certain situations. Hopefully the "battery" – before the game – discussed these variables. When the battery goes to work on a hitter, any remaining doubts or questions are resolved either before the first pitch or during a sequence of pitches – depends on the situation. The catcher, from the first day of spring training to the final out in the World Series (hopefully), is an integral part of the pitcher's immediate preparations in spring training.

The wise pitcher starts to work with his catcher(s) from the first day of spring training. He throws the daily batting practice with his catchers, and these sessions provide the catcher an early opportunity to evaluate the pitcher's variety of pitches and placements. When I pitched for the Giants, my regular catchers were Walker Cooper (1947-1949) and Wes Westrum (1949-1954). Both were savvy receivers and helped me tremendously in my major-league career.

**Lastly, the most important concept in throwing to the catcher is to concentrate on his mitt**. During spring training culture this practice and make it a habit. The catcher "sets up" behind the hitter to indicate the general location of each pitch and positions his glove as the bull's-eye. The pitcher must discipline himself to hit the bull's-eye with every pitch. Unfortunately, some pitchers tend to cast their gaze downward toward the ground at some point in their delivery. **This head dipping has no value, and is a mistake**. Concentrate on the catcher's mitt and throw

---

*\*See Sisto, D. J., et al, "An Electromyographic Analysis of The Elbow in Pitching," Am.J.Sports Med., 15:260-263, 1987.*

*\*\*Webster's Ninth New Collegiate Dictionary, (Springfield, Merriam-Webster, Inc.), 1984, page 135.*

strikes. When a person throws darts it is foolish to think that this "dartsman" would look down at the ground while trying to hit the bull's-eye. The earlier in spring training that the pitcher trains himself to concentrate on the catcher, the sooner he makes the control "connection", and the sooner the battery supplies power to "electrocute" batters and produce outs.

# Long-Range Preparation

It is healthy for a young boy to fantasize about becoming a professional pitcher, but at some time (in his youth) fantasy must meet the test of reality. In a word, the boy must have **talent** – talent with sufficient substance to carry him into professional baseball. Lacking that substance the boy must settle on a lesser goal somewhere between little-league pitching up to, perhaps, college ball. **Accordingly, the game must be fun at all levels and it is the duty (sounds solemn, doesn't it?) of parents and coaches to insure that the game is fun.** After all, many of us pursue hobbies and activities just because they are fun. We pursue them for the enjoyment they give us, not because we believe we will ever be a professional bowler, or fisherman, or model builder, or checkers player.

A youth filled with hard physical work and frequent throwing is an established long-range method of developing strong arms and superb stamina. Two products of this methodology faced off in a 16-inning game between the Braves and Giants (1963): Warren Spahn, age 42, and Juan Marichal, age 25. Both men threw more than 200 pitches! Neither pitcher ruined his arm or required physical therapy (or psychotherapy!). I do not mean that pitchers nowadays should be used in this manner; I use this example to illustrate (not prove) a point. Both pitchers had lived boyhoods filled with hard work and frequent throwing of baseballs – and even mud balls, snowballs and stones at fences, bottles and cans.

Much has been written about the values of free weight lifting and various strengthening devices found in gyms. Those who advocate these approaches seem to have provided a sound medical/physiological foundation for their theories. In the absence of readily available laborious jobs for youth, maybe we will have to settle for the gym – and throwing and throwing and throwing. Consult Chapter 8. I advise those who send their ballplayers to the gym to scrutinize carefully the physiological foundations of what they prescribe. This is particularly important now, because fresh conditioning theories and new exercise devices are appearing at frequent intervals.

# *Attitude*

With deliberate forethought, I have left this topic for the chapter's dessert course. This is the time in the meal when everyone has eaten his fill, and now feels satisfied, relaxed and ready to engage in a few philosophical reflections. My **Introduction** set the stage when I promised that we would enter the mind of the pitcher for an examination of what must necessarily reside there. The importance of this topic rests in the fact that we must plumb the pitcher's **attitude toward his work – the major factor in his performance** – because his performance is an essential determinant of game outcome. Some baseball pundits have proclaimed that 80 percent of baseball is pitching. That concept transfers a heavy load of responsibility onto the pitcher, **and, he dare not buckle under the burden**.

The pitcher's mound is really an inverted pressure cooker and the hurler is a brisket of beef stewing in its broth. So tough must be his mind and emotional sinews be that he never satisfies the ravenous appetite of the hitter. The hitter can nibble, chew, rip, tear or cut the brisket, but he must forever find it totally unpalatable and inedible. How does the brisket develop this toughness? How do we know it is tough enough?

We are now addressing the pitcher's **long-range mental preparations**. The first step is out of his hands – genetics. A curmudgeonly baseball coach once said, "A pitcher must pick his ancestors carefully." There is a whiff of wisdom in this cynical observation: the great competitors seem to have entered life filled with **competitive attitudes and talent**. Competition is their life's blood, the air they breathe. These athletes love to compete and are unwilling to ignore a challenge. The **pitcher is the ultimate competitor**. In every game he confronts a protracted parade of nine or more "Stygian" monsters (hitters). The hitter, on the other hand, faces only one or several pitchers in a game – hopefully never nine. Commonly a hitter acquires three or four, rarely five, opportunities to best the pitcher in a contest. In each encounter the pitcher must design a way to frustrate the hitter. If the pitcher hurls a perfect game (rarest of rare events in baseball) he faces only 27 batters. The more common scenario in a **well-pitched complete game** is a confrontation with 36 to 38 batters. This requires that he throw an average of 114 to 142 pitches. Imperfect mental and physical genetic substrate provide a poor start for the pitcher. (Note: As the Giants' coach in 1965, I kept track of starting pitchers' pitches for several months and my starting pitchers averaged 122 pitches per nine innings.)

Although this is not a sermon addressed to mature men, nor a treatise on child rearing, there are several aspects of a boy's upbringing that will, if developed in a healthy manner, mature and polish his congenital competitive talent. By example, and through **teaching with positive reinforcement**, the parent should strive to refine at least the following five attributes: **perseverance, consistency, industry, honesty and temperance**. When these attributes blend into a competitive personality, the total player is more likely to be considered professional material, provided he possesses sufficient native physical **talent**. Without these qualities the mature pitcher is desperately wanting and is unlikely to survive in professional ball.

Our objective is to refine the native talents and character of a fierce competitor. However, the competitive fire burns within – not without – the master pitcher's personality. Some of the most ferocious competitive spirits have resided within the outwardly calm. Two pitchers in this decade who epitomize this paradigm are Greg Maddux and Orel Hershiser. A splendid general was also an example – Robert E. Lee. This is not to say that these men were not tempted by frustration, or did not rise to anger; it is to say that they **controlled their anger**. Nor are we denigrating those many superb human beings in who the competitive fire burns with less heat. Milton, the great English poet/philosopher, said: "They also serve who only stand and wait." Some kinds of work do not require inner competitive ferocity, but the pitcher who lacks this quality best look for other employment.

What about the five special qualities mentioned above? **Perseverance:** "... persistence in ... an undertaking in spite of counterinfluences, opposition or discouragement..." (Webster's Ninth New Collegiate Dictionary). Would you be surprised to learn that Orel Hershiser was cut from his high school team in his freshman and sophomore years, and again from his college team during his freshman/sophomore years? Yet several years later he emerged a *primo* major-league pitcher. What is the explanation? Logic dictates that Hershiser persevered. Another attribute this pitcher possesses is **industry**: "...diligence in an employment or pursuit..." (Webster's). The word connotes persistent hard work. Baseball at all levels requires exacting skills; the litany of these abilities is endless and their mastery requires repetitive, and arduous practice. The antithesis of industry is laziness. How much easier it is to lie in bed – drowsy, restful, peaceful – than to arise, dress and go out to the ball diamond to drill and practice, or go to a job that requires long, hard labor!

**Consistency:** "...free from variation..." (Webster's, after *consistent*.) When used in the baseball community the word connotes reliability. A team can depend on the consistent player to be present for work at every practice, at all games (even during a 162-game schedule) and to perform predictably well on each occasion. Professorial gibberish? More plainly stated, consistency (reliability) means Lou Gehrig, Cal Ripken Jr., or Greg Maddux. My intent is not to imply that a consistent player never experiences "bad" days, commits no errors, never walks a batter, never strikes out or always wins. What is meant is that over the long run the reliable player is invariably available to perform well. The opposite of consistent is **erratic**. I rest my case.

**Honesty**: "...fairness...of conduct...(and) refusal to...steal..." (Webster's). In other words refusal to cheat. The cheater trashes rules to win over other participants who follow the same rules. The cheat is a thief who steals money or honors from the honest. The most reprehensible quality of cheating is that it consists of premeditated, calculated, covert acts intended to deceive. The rules of baseball are the carefully reasoned product of thoughtful men who infuse a sense of equity into the game, and need be followed as written (see Chapter 4, **The Rule Book**).

**Temperance**: (has nothing to do here with abstinence from alcohol). It is "...moderation in action, thought or feeling: restraint..." (Webster's). **Raging fury begets a temporary insanity**, so an old saying goes. Lose your temper and you lose your ability to think clearly. The pitcher cannot afford the luxury of an intemperate outburst. He must retain his poise. The pitcher who accomplishes this end radiates confidence, and confidence is contagious. The entire team constantly observes the pitcher and looks to him for leadership. The leader who "loses his head, loses his crown." Advice on controlling one's temper fills volumes, and I will not presume to fell more trees to pontificate on the subject. Walter Bagehot, a 19th century essayist, talked about "hot heads" and observed that if such men "...were horse(s), nobody would buy (them);" nor will a professional baseball team. Homer (an ancient Greek baseball writer) observed that "Achilles' (the ace pitcher) curs'ed anger ... started a myriad of sufferings for the Achaeans (his team)...and a direful spring (it was early in the season)..." (Iliad I:1)

It has been my observation that those individuals, amateur and professional, who find their work full of **fun**, are less likely to exhibit inappropriate anger. **No human lives a life free of anger; the "self-fulfilling" individual has learned to control his anger.**

# 2

# Mechanics

## In a Nutshell

1.  Throwing is a natural act
2.  Pitchers must throw from a standing start
3.  Mechanics is balance, movement, propulsion
4.  A pitcher is like a catapult and a cannon
5.  A pitcher has a power side and aiming side
6.  The pitcher uses a guidance system
7.  Effective mechanics can distract and deceive
8.  The pitching motion: acceleration and deceleration
9.  Improper mechanics leads to injuries
10. Wildness comes from poor mechanics

---

*A pitcher is not a cloned robotic machine. Billions of cells, all with their own agenda, slosh around inside his bag of skin, and every pitcher's sloshy bag is different.*

**Author**

---

For at least a thousand centuries, man has been throwing things – rocks, spears, darts and balls – to bring down game, or enemies, or just for fun! **Throwing is as natural** as walking, hopping, climbing; some people just do it better than others. Among the primates, throwing is **not** the exclusive property of humans. It is common knowledge among zoo keepers that both the gorilla and chimpanzee are hurlers. The adult gorilla can hurl a five-ounce stone (baseball weight) up to 90 feet with amazing accuracy. Strangely, zoo maintenance personnel are frequently the targets of stone throwing gorillas. Perhaps the gorilla prefers to keep his work area in disarray. Chimpanzees tend to toss softer, "smellier" materials! It is unlikely that any hitter would charge the mound against these guys.

Almost without exception hunters or sportsmen (including baseball fielders) take two or more steps forward before releasing their missiles. Baseball rules restrict the pitcher to **one step forward before releasing the ball**. It was not always this way. Prior to 1887, hurlers were allowed to launch their pitches from a running start which began and ended within the boundaries of a pitching box. The box's forward boundary lay only 50 feet from home plate. At this distance the running start provided the pitcher with a tremendous advantage, even though his run was over level ground. In 1886, Matt Kilroy, a rookie with the Baltimore Orioles, struck out 513 hitters and "Toad" Ramsey of the Louisville team fanned 499 batsmen while launching on the run. The new rules of 1887 forbade the running start and limited the pitcher's delivery to one step forward. In 1893 the rules directed that the start of the pitcher's one-step delivery commence at a pitcher's plate located 60 feet, 6 inches from home plate. The authors of this dictum, mindful of the need to preserve balance in rule making, compensated the pitcher by allowing the pitching plate to be raised. The lawgivers did not define the height until 1903 when it was limited to 15 inches. In 1969 the summit was shaved to 10 inches (maximum) and in 1996 elevated to 12 inches.

Sportsmen, who run to throw, translate momentum (mass times velocity) into propulsion. The resultant propulsion adds distance and speed to the throw. Examine Figure 2-1 (javelin thrower) and Figure 2-2 (shot putter). Unfortunately we lack a video of David flinging a stone at Goliath with his slingshot. That ancient weapon required the hurler to whirl the sling over his head while skipping forward (Fig. 2-3). Fortunate for the baseball hitter, the pitcher cannot enjoy propulsion imparted by a running start. The pitcher must supply velocity, movement and placement to his missile from a standing start and a single step forward.

Figure 2-1

Figure 2-2

Figure 2-3

Recently sports physiologists have generated innovative research projects around pitching biomechanics. This research has enlarged our understanding of the subject. In several such projects, these scientists attach telemetric sensors to the pitcher's trunk and extremities, and link the sensors to computer programs capable of generating line figures at rates up to 1,000 figures per second. The computer product displays torso and extremity movements every one-thousandth of a second. High-speed cameras augment data captured by sensor and computer. Such technology can disclose many, **but not all**, nuances of pitching biomechanics not visible to the naked eye. The information gained is helpful, but few coaches possess the facilities to extract and fully use data of this nature. Furthermore, the human is a physiologically complex, intelligent being whose array of actions cannot be reduced to simple biometric analogs. I prefer to illustrate my concepts with drawings based on actual photos of major-league pitchers in action, supplemented by drawings of a few college and high school pitchers.

To make the act of throwing as effective as the talents of a hurler allow – and the rules of the game permit – is the object of this chapter. **Mechanics is the product of balance and movement.**

# *Terminology*

The side of the pitcher away from the hitter is the **power side**; the side toward the hitter, the **aiming side**. Correct medical terminology for parts of the lower extremity: thigh extends from hip to knee; the leg extends knee to ankle. Lay terminology often refers to the entire lower extremity as "the leg." I do also except when precision requires differently. The context will convey the meaning. Upper extremity: arm extends shoulder to elbow; the forearm: elbow to wrist. Common baseball terminology refers to the entire upper extremity as "the arm." I do also except when clarity requires otherwise.

Through illustration and discussion we pass now to a detailed explanation of pitching mechanics. **Caveat:** What I present here represents a moderate, stylized approach adaptable to a large number of pitchers. The effective coach recognizes that each pitcher is unique in thought and motion. Eventually, the pitcher puts on his mechanics like his clothes – in a habitual manner that works best for him. The coach's role is to show the pitcher how to use physical talents efficiently, to open doors for logic and thought, and to enrich gradually the pitcher's character. Whenever it is appropriate there are interjected examples of **how I departed from the stylized approach** in my career; those departures suited my makeup and made me a better pitcher – and coach. Study Figures 2-23 through 2-29, deliberately positioned at the conclusion of this chapter to emphasize how a coach must take under consideration: (1) what a young pitcher brings with him to the game; (2) what makes this pitcher comfortable; and (3) what, if anything, the coach can do to improve him.

For instructional clarity, the pitching motion can be divided into six **elements**.

1. Balance ................................. Figures 2-4 through 2-6

2. Preparation ........................... Figures 2-7 through 2-10

3. Separation ........................... Figures 2-11 through 2-13a

4. Extension ............................ Figures 2-13b through 2-15

5. Plant and propel .................. Figures 2-17 through 2-19

6. Follow-through .................... Figures 2-20 through 2-22

Further subdivision into **cocking** (elements 3 and 4 above), **acceleration** (5) and **deceleration** (6) **phases** is pertinent to pitching injury analysis (Chapter 7).

**Preparation** consists of those stances, mannerisms and movements in the windup or the stretch which immediately precede the pitcher's arrival at the balance point (Figs. 2-7 through 2-10).

**Balance**, because of its critical importance to the pitching elements that follow, is discussed in this text before preparation. Balance is that instant of momentary pause when the pitcher has gathered together all those parts of his anatomy that – in another fraction of a second – will explode in a burst of kinetic energy. The pitcher arrives at the balance point when his forward knee has elevated to its highest point (Figs. 2-4 through 2-6).

**Separation** refers to those movements which occur during and immediately after that instant when the ball is removed from the glove and the hands separate (Figs. 2-11 through 2-13a).

**Extension** is that element during which the pitcher extends his extremities (Figs. 2-13b through 2-15).

**Plant and Propel** occur as a consequence of the pitcher's act of extension. He first plants his forward foot, then rotates his torso as his throwing arm comes forward and his power foot pushes his body forward. The pitcher's body and arm synchronize in a harmony that allows neither arm nor body to "get ahead" or "trail behind" the other member of the duet (Figs. 2-17 through 2-19).

**Follow-through** (Figs. 2-20 through 2-22) commences the instant the ball leaves the pitcher's hand. Its sole purpose is to permit the arm and body to decelerate in a coordinated manner. The most serious pitching injuries commonly occur during flawed follow-through (Chapter 7, **Injuries**).

# Balance

Balance, because of its critical importance to the pitching elements that follow, is discussed in this text before the preparation element. Balance is that instant of momentary pause when the pitcher has gathered together all those parts of his anatomy that — in another fraction of a second — will explode in a burst of kinetic energy. The pitcher arrives at the balance point when his forward knee has elevated to its highest point (Figs. 2-4 through 2-6).

Study Figure 2-4. **This illustrates the balance point.** This right-handed pitcher has arrived at this point in his motion (if in the windup), by taking a short step back with his aiming (left) foot. Next he turned the power (right) foot to engage the leading edge of the pitcher's plate while simultaneously rotating his aiming (left) side toward the hitter and elevating the left knee. If he started from the set position (in the stretch), he simply lifted his left knee. Here the knee has arrived at the highest point in its lift. **There the pitcher pauses a fraction of a second.** Notice how the left leg hangs straight down below the knee. The leg has not "kicked out" toward you (the reader), nor "floated" back of the rubber. **At this instant he is balanced along two major axes – the frontal axis shown here and the side axis** (Fig. 2-5). The "lubber line"* runs from head and neck through the torso, past the belly button (human center of gravity, or C.G.) into the power (right) leg to the ball of the power foot. The illustration (Fig. 2-4) carries an anatomical error. The arch, not the toes, of the power foot faces you in this figure. This peculiarity allows you to see a side view of the foot. In this view we clearly see the arrival of the lubber line at the ball of the power foot, and a slight elevation of the heel as the pitcher comes up on the ball of that foot. The **correct anatomy** is shown in Figure 2-6. If one were to add up the weights of those body parts on the right and left sides of the lubber line in Figure 2-4, the sums would be about equal. At this instant the pitcher tends to fall neither right or left, and he is in "static" balance along the **frontal axis.**

This pitcher's shoulders in Figure 2-4 are oriented along **a line that runs straight through the middle of home plate,** and his power (right) knee is only slightly bent. Excessive flexion of the power knee leads to the problems illustrated in Figure 2-5.

**Caveat. The pitcher does not start forward toward the hitter until he arrives at the balance point, his aiming knee lifts to its highest point, and a momentary pause occurs.**

In Figure 2-5 the pitcher correctly shows the hitter his left pocket and a part of the numbers on his back. Some pitchers even show both numbers (Hideo Nomo). However, the pitcher in Figure 2-5 has a problem!

Now study Figure 2-5. This is a side view of a right-handed pitcher – as seen by the hitter – at a point in his motion comparable to that of the pitcher in Figure 2-4. Notice the lubber line, and sum the body parts in

---

* "lubber line:" a borrowed concept. It means the fixed line on a vehicle's compass that is aligned with the vehicle's longitudinal axis. This comparison limps because the pictures are two-dimensional and the pitcher occupies three dimensions. But I am attempting to convey concepts, not mathematical exactitude. Man is not a machine.

**Lubber Line**

**Lubber Line**

K. VAN LOO

K. VAN LOO

**Figure 2-4**

**Figure 2-5**

front and back of this line. At this point the pitcher should fall neither backward or forward. He will not fall, but neither will he propel effectively, because the lubber line terminates at his heel, not at the ball of the power foot. This is the result of excessive flexion of the power knee. A frontal view would catch this pitcher leaning back on his power leg. Worst of all, notice that his left (aiming) leg is not beneath the knee; he has "kicked" this leg outward in an effort to balance on the power heel. He will waste kinetic energy to correct this imbalance – energy that he could have used in the throw.

The young pitcher may raise several questions here. 1) Why at this instant is balance along two axes so important? Answer: Once this stance is achieved, the pitcher has gathered together all those parts of his body

19

Lubber Line

**Figure 2-6**

*Shows correct anatomical alignment of body parts with the pitcher at the balance point.*

that, in another fraction of a second, will explode in a burst of kinetic energy. This energy **opens** the hands, **extends** the arms, **brings** the throwing arm forward **and drives the pitcher toward the plate**. If the pitcher is tipped left or right, backward or forward, some of the kinetic energy will be wasted correcting the off-balance.

2) Why must the pitcher **gather together his anatomy** before he throws? Why not just fling the ball with one or both legs and arms in various combinations of flexion and extension? Two reasons: The constraints imposed by **the rules** and **the conservation of energy**. During the 19th century, pitchers experimented with all sorts of mechanics and motions limited only by the ever changing pitching rules. Since 1893, **the rules** restrain the pitcher's use of kinetic energy by requiring the pivot foot to remain in contact with the rubber until the ball is released, and by limiting the movement forward to a single step. Up to the mid-1960s most pitchers brought their arms above the head in the windup sequence. Now this is less common. Raising the arms over the head steals small amounts of energy from the pitcher as he attempts to maintain balance when the elevated arms shift weight back and forth across the lubber lines. The raised arms added nothing to the pitcher's effectiveness and drew down his energy reserves.

With deliberate forethought I have discussed balance before explaining those motions shown in the remaining figures. Pitching a baseball is not unique in its requirement to achieve and maintain balance. Static balance (during a brief pause) and dynamic balance (while the body is in motion) are athletic skills required in most sports – everything from judo, to fencing, to tennis, to football. This balance skill goes beyond sports to numerous occupations. No one can come away from a ballet without marveling at the superb balance demonstrated by the well-conditioned, athletic dancers. Did you know that tightrope walkers balance on the ball of the foot? **Balance enables the pitcher to transform energy efficiently**. More plainly stated, a stumbling, teetering or wobbling pitcher consumes enormous amounts of energy to keep from falling on his face – or on his buttocks. To correct his ineptness, the unbalanced pitcher steals this energy away from his throw.

In some respects a pitcher is a cross between a catapult and a cannon. Catapults (a slingshot is a form of catapult) derive force from conversion of **potential energy** (the stretch of a spring or rubber band) into **kinetic energy** (the forward flight of the spring or rubber band and missile). Cannons use gun powder (potential energy) to explode and shove the shell (kinetic energy) toward a target. We will refer to these two comparisons as we take you through the pitching motion(s).

# Preparation

*Preparation consists of those stances, mannerisms and movements in the windup or the stretch which immediately precede the pitcher's arrival at the balance point (Figs. 2-7 through 2-10).*

Collage shows stylized approach to the first four elements in pitching motion.

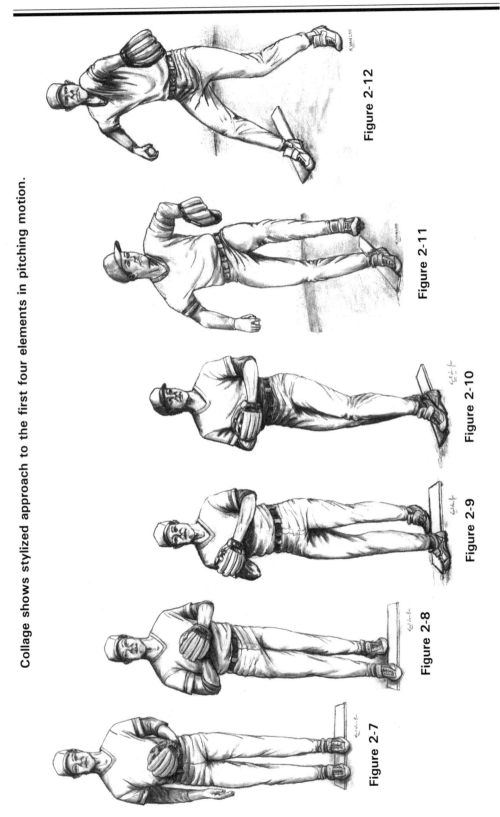

Figure 2-12

Figure 2-11

Figure 2-10

Figure 2-9

Figure 2-8

Figure 2-7

Consider Figure 2-7. Here the pitching dynamo, full of potential energy, stands atop his 12-inch hill. He is a right-hander and has taken his station on the right side of the rubber (left-handers use the left side). The stance on the right side of the rubber will eventually – later in his motion – enable him to hide the ball a fraction of a second longer because his pitching arm will come from behind the right side of the body. The knees

are bent slightly, and the toes of both feet protrude over the front of the plate. The right hand rests at his side. The ball is held in the glove with the seams turned ready for the appropriate grip. He could also conceal hand and ball inside the glove. **When pitching from the stretch**, and while taking the sign from the catcher, the pitcher holds the ball in his throwing hand. That hand rests against the thigh or hip until he draws his hands together and comes "set." Keeping the ball out of the glove until coming set, with runners on base, enables the pitcher to throw quickly to a baseman. Eyes are fixed on the target.

### Common problems:

1. Failure to concentrate on the catcher's target.

2. Disclosure of ball grip when the throwing hand is placed on thigh or hip.

   **NOTE**: I usually started in the center of the rubber, and then adjusted as I went along. If I was wild inside or outside, I shifted right or left on the rubber. See Figure 2-23.

**Figure 2-7**

In Figure 2-8, hands together in the glove, and glove held between belly button and rib cage, the pitcher takes a short step straight back with his left foot. The toes of that foot barely clear the plate. Too large a step back will result in an unnecessary expenditure of energy when the pitcher comes forward with the left foot. Weight is distributed evenly between right (power) and left (aiming) lower extremities. A gentle shove on the chest or back of this pitcher should not tumble him. Notice the elbows close to the chest. This pitcher is compact. Compactness aids balance. On a butcher's scale it is easier to weigh a stack of pork chops than a string of sausages.

**Common Problems:**

1. Leaning right or left.

2. Placing too much weight on the rear leg.

   **NOTE**: The position of my feet in Figure 2-24. Observe how I departed from the stylized approach shown here.

**Figure 2-8**

Still compact, in Figure 2-9 the pitcher firmly plants his right foot squarely in front of and touching the rubber. The rubber has two functions: 1) it marks the official distance (60 feet, 6 inches) from home plate to that point where the pitcher commences his throw; 2) it acts as an anchored block against which the pitcher pushes when he thrusts himself toward home plate. Think of it this way: If the pitcher tries to push a heavily loaded wagon uphill, his traction and pushing force are greatly enhanced if he pushes with his power foot against an anchored board.

**Common Problems:**

1. Placing power foot on top of rubber, or breaking contact with the rubber.

   **NOTE:** Study Figure 2-25. Notice that my right foot is not placed squarely in front of the plate. Instead the forefoot abuts the front of the plate while arch and heel span the leading edge of the plate.

**Figure 2-9**

Figure 2-10 shows the pitcher lifting his left knee. In a moment he will arrive at the balance point (Figure 2-4). The heel of his power foot has cleared the ground very slightly. Now he is adjusting his balance so that his weight rests on the ball of the power foot (right foot). In the rhythm of his entire motion, the steps taken to this point proceed at a slow cadence. When he arrives at the stance depicted in Figure 2-4 he pauses (almost imperceptibly) for a fraction of a second. See Figure 2-26.

**Common Problems:**

1. Balancing on heel of power foot (see Fig. 2-5).

2. Leaning or wobbling right/left and/or forward/backward.

3. Excessive flexion power knee.

4. Failure to keep head in a straight vertical line with belly button.

5. Failure to keep shoulders in a direct line with home plate.

6. Starting toward the plate before knee has arrived at its highest point in the lift.

7. Allowing hands to drift away from chest.

**Figure 2-10**

27

# Separation and Extension

*Separation refers to those movements which occur during and immediately after that instant when the ball is removed from the glove and the hands separate (Figs. 2-11 through 2-13a). Extension is that element during which the pitcher extends his extremities (Figs. 2-13b through 2-15).*

A problem develops in Figure 2-11. The pitcher has prematurely **separated** his hands and started toward the batter before his left knee reaches its highest lift – the static balance point at which a momentary pause occurs. This flaw is called "**rushing**." The throwing arm is **tense** and partly flexed at the elbow. This will result in a flaw called "**overthrowing**." He is "flat-footed", teetering backward and balanced on his power heel (see Fig. 2-5). He has "opened" the left shoulder and hip. "Opened" is an expression which means that the aiming shoulder and hip have turned to face the batter. This must not occur until the aiming foot has planted (see Figs. 2-17 and 2-18). In Figure 2-12 he extends his extremities, but wastes energy to correct the flaws seen in Figure 2-11. However, he plants his aiming foot pointed at third base – not at the target. His shoulders are not aligned with home plate. His left elbow has dropped below its shoulder. See Figures 2-13a and b for correct technique. "Rushing" and "overthrowing" cause wildness (see pages 54 and 58 and Fig. 2-31).

**Figure 2-11**                    **Figure 2-12**

K.VanLoo

**Figure 2-13a**

Figure 2-13a shows the pitcher's posture as he moves forward out of the balance point. In this illustration, the hands have separated and the throwing arm has dropped in a relaxed position – with elbow comfortably extended – behind the waist. His aiming elbow is elevated, flexed and pointed at home plate. The aiming knee is extending and descending as the leg and foot thrust toward home plate. The left hip and shoulder are "closed." "Closed" is an expression which means that front shoulder and hip are momentarily turned slightly away from the batter to conceal the ball. The pitcher in this situation shows the batter his left trouser pocket and the flexed aiming elbow. He is balanced on the ball of his power foot with power heel very slightly elevated.

31

**Lubber Line**
**Figure 2-13b**

Figure 2-13b shows a right-hander in correct **extension** a moment after the posture shown in 2-13a. This is a busy illustration, so we take it apart piece by piece. The extremities are drawn away from the trunk, but the pitcher is in dynamic balance. His head remains directly above his belly button. The shoulders are slightly, but evenly, elevated. Both elbows are level with shoulders. He has taken a long controlled stride forward with the left lower extremity which is flexed about 70 degrees at the hip joint and extended about 140 degrees at the knee. NOTE: The left foot plants flat, or on its toes, just as the throwing arm reaches full extension – not before. The left toes point straight toward the plate. The right foot is in front of, and pushing against, the anchored pitcher's plate. The trunk and lower extremities act like a catapult base. The throwing arm is nearly fully extended at shoulder and elbow – the catapult is fully cocked and ready to fire! The missile is hidden behind the back **under the hand.** Now the pitcher can start to "open" the aiming shoulder/hip and **rotate** the **torso** (see Figs. 2-17 and 2-18).

**The hand and wrist remain on top of the ball until the throwing arm starts forward, directed by the pitcher's guidance system.**

The **guidance system** consists of the left lower extremity and foot now aligned with home plate; the left upper extremity also points at home plate. The head and eyes are locked on the target with chin almost resting on the chest behind the left shoulder. **The eyes are level with the horizon.**

**Figure 2-14**

Figure 2-14 (upper body shot) shows the hitter's view. The ball is visible at this instant, but will disappear momentarily behind the pitcher's head and trunk as the throwing arm swings forward. Within that fraction of a second, when the ball disappears, the pitcher will quickly extend, flex or twist his glove hand and wrist. This movement distracts the hitter. The human eye is designed to scan objects and lock onto the closest moving part of that object – in this case the glove. When the ball reappears in front of the pitcher and approaches the hitter, the hitter's eye will pick up and lock onto the ball – after his eye discontinues its fascination with the moving glove. Most hitters do not realize that their eyes do these things. It is a natural reflex – an evolutionary survival mechanism. Objects moving toward the creature can hurt it. Hitters can train themselves to modulate or dampen the reflex, but only the great hitters can totally suppress it and ignore the pitcher's glove movement.

Figure 2-15 (full-length shot) of a left-hander an instant before his right foot strikes the ground. The points discussed pertinent to the right-hander are well-illustrated here. Note the position of the glove. This pitcher's wrist is sharply flexed. As he comes forward with his throwing arm this pitcher may extend his wrist, and that subtle movement becomes a distraction. His right elbow is shoulder high and pointed at the target.

**Common Problems:** Numerous enough at this critical moment to fill another volume. However,

K. VAN LOO

**Figure 2-15**

1. Bringing the throwing arm forward before the aiming foot is planted.
2. Failure to use body language to intimidate and distract.
3. Leaning forward or backward, left or right (wobbling).

---

### *Coaching Pearl*

Every pitcher does something different with the glove and many pitchers have no idea what their glove hand is doing. If we ran videos of 10 different pitchers at this point in their motion, we would find 10 different glove positions.

---

4. Failure to fully extend the throwing arm, called "short-arming."

5. Failure to keep the guidance system "locked on" (directed at) the target.

When you sum up all the activity occurring on the mound prior to production of the pitched ball, you must marvel at how a hitter ever comes to strike the ball squarely.

What are the other distractions to the hitter? There are at least three.

1. The pitcher's body movement toward the hitter prior to catapulting the ball: Examine the face and body language in Figures 2-13 and 2-14. These pictures do not show the pitcher extending a friendly social greeting. Like a boxer or judo player (or some say like a large wildcat) the pitcher is thrusting at the hitter. If his fists were closed and his arms long enough, he would punch the hitter in the nose. Some tall, heavily muscled pitchers exploit this concept. Their huge physique moving toward the hitter becomes a controlled, subtle intimidation.

2. The upward movement of the leading elbow until it hides part of the pitcher's face and points directly at the target. This body language – even though it is chiefly used to maintain alignment – subconsciously looks to the hitter like an intent to deceive. Persons who cover the face with part of the upper extremity frequently betray an intent to mask or blur a feeling or thought. Ask a good poker player; or watch the villain in a melodrama raise his arm and cape in front of the face to hide a dastardly sneer! Even though a hitter comes out day after day, and with malice of forethought, seeks to murder the ball, only the finely disciplined hitter can look past or ignore these distractions.

3. Finally, observe in Figure 2-14 that the pitcher's back is turned toward the hitter at an angle sufficient to show both numbers. With the back at this angle to the hitter, the "hidden zone" (zone in which the ball is not visible to the hitter) is widened. This delays the hitter's seeing the ball in flight.

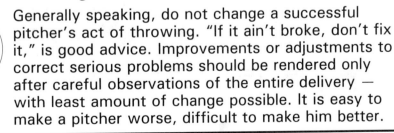

### Coaching Pearl

Generally speaking, do not change a successful pitcher's act of throwing. "If it ain't broke, don't fix it," is good advice. Improvements or adjustments to correct serious problems should be rendered only after careful observations of the entire delivery – with least amount of change possible. It is easy to make a pitcher worse, difficult to make him better.

The catapult comparison (see page 21) now needs discussion while you study Figure 2-13b. Also, look at our drawing of the catapult (Fig. 2-16). Granted, though, the catapult is an inanimate object, it functions very efficiently and reliably. There are features in the catapult common to all beings (human and otherwise) that hurl objects. Figure 2-16 has caught the catapult just before blastoff. The spring has been compressed fully and potential energy maximized. Had the "gunners" cranked the throwing arm down less than full way, the missile would travel less distance with less force. Hence, the importance of the pitcher fully extending his throwing arm in Figure 2-13b. Anything less than full extension, called "short-arming," results in less force.

The second important feature of the catapult is its stability just before blastoff. The catapult base is wide and long and rests firmly on broad feet. If the catapult did not possess these features it would vibrate or wobble excessively as the throwing arm came forward. Vibrations and wobbles in catapults, and in pitchers, steal kinetic energy and subtract from the force imparted to the missile. The pitcher in Figure 2-13b is stable (balanced) just before blastoff. His front foot is planted, power foot braced against the plate, weight distributed evenly on both sides of the lubber line.

Once the throwing arm starts forward, the pitcher enters a biomechanical phase known as the **acceleration phase**. Once the ball is released, the pitcher experiences a **deceleration phase**. The pitcher must not allow himself to enter the acceleration phase until he has fully, completely and dynamically balanced himself as shown in Figure 2-13b. All movement through the various phases and stances (Figs. 2-7 through 2-15) is virtually continuous and flows smoothly; there are no halts except for that brief pause shown in Figure 2-4 (static balance). The cadence now changes from a deliberate slowness to explosive quickness – **like the strike of a cobra**!

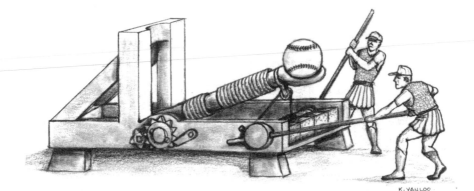

K. VANLOO

**Figure 2-16**

Collage shows pitchers in Figs. 2-13a and 2-13b
executing separation and extension correctly.

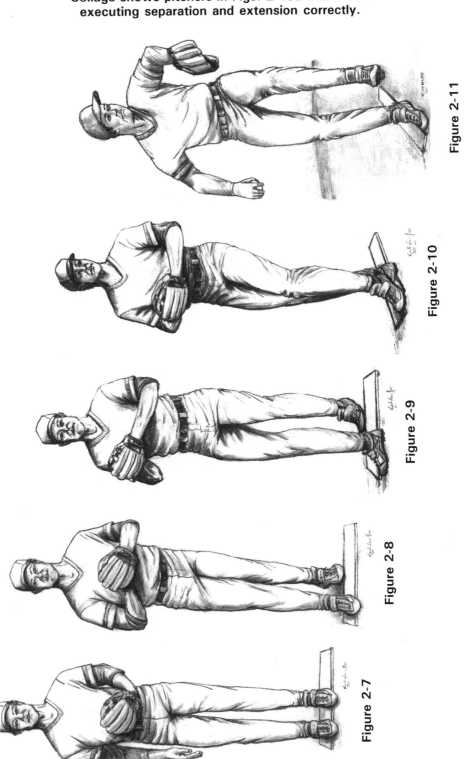

Figure 2-11

Figure 2-10

Figure 2-9

Figure 2-8

Figure 2-7

Figure 2-12

Figure 2-13a

Figure 2-13b

K.VanL

# Plant and Propel

*Plant and Propel occur as a consequence of the pitcher's act of extension. He first plants his forward foot, then rotates his torso as his throwing arm comes forward and his power foot pushes his body forward. The pitcher's body and arm synchronize in a harmony that allows neither arm nor body to "get ahead" or "trail behind" the other member of the duet (Figs. 2-17 through 2-19).*

In Figure 2-17, the catapult spring has been released and the throwing arm is arcing forward. The shoulders are still level. All the potential energy in the extended arm (Figs. 2-13, 2-14 and 2-15) has become kinetic energy. The head remains above the belly button. The glove and throwing arms are nearly equidistant from, and approaching, the trunk. The glove hand is retracting toward the left armpit from below and the throwing hand is passing the right armpit from above. If both arms and hands were not nearly equidistant from the trunk at this point, the pitcher's balance would deteriorate. Notice the power foot pushing against the rubber. Many pitching coaches correctly state that "the pitcher pitches with his legs and his arm." We shall study in a moment the importance of this pushing with the power foot. The aiming foot (left) is solidly planted and points straight at home plate. Note that the throwing elbow is shoulder high. Finally, look at his face. Note the **concentration** depicted in the facial expression and gaze of the eyes – level with the horizon. **The Front foot is planted, and now forward rotation of the torso begins as the throwing arm comes forward.**

**Figure 2-17**    K. VAN LOO

Figure 2-18 shows a left-hander nearly at the same station in his delivery as the right-hander in Figure 2-17. Note that his power leg is not as close to the ground as the right-hander's. The right-hander is a power pitcher and his push on the rubber is more forceful due to the decreased angle between the long axis of his leg and the surface. The left-hander is a breaking-ball pitcher and he is in the act of throwing a curve. This pitch generally requires less forward power. The kinetic energy in breaking pitches is partitioned between the ball's velocity and spin. The energy in a fastball remains principally with velocity. In Figures 2-17 and 2-18 the throwing hand is at the highest point in its arc enroute to releasing the ball. Note that the throwing elbow is shoulder high! The torso rotates forward.

**Common Problems:**
1. Failure to push with the power leg against the plate.

2. Failure to bring both hands equidistant from the trunk at this point in the motion.

3. Failure to keep the throwing elbow shoulder high.

4. Premature rotation of the torso before the aiming foot is planted.

**Figure 2-18**

K. VAN LOO

41

The ball explodes out of the throwing hand in Figure 2-19 (page 43). This is the moment in the motion that most closely resembles a cannon. The catapult spring brought the arm quickly forward, but kinetic energy born of the potential energy stored in the power leg, thigh, shoulder, arm, forearm – and the back – now shoots the ball away from the pitcher and toward the hitter, guided by the actions of the aiming side (guidance system, see page 32). A catapult is not an accurate weapon; it lacks a guidance system. The cannon is accurate because of its guidance system.

As shown in Figure 2-19 the right-handed **pitcher propels (implies a controlled movement)** his body toward the target. Some coaches refer to this movement as **"falling"** toward home plate. **Falling implies an uncontrolled movement.** Some pitchers actually do fall off the mound! Their control is a wonder to behold – terrible! I encourage pitchers to think "propel," not "fall."

With this propulsion the head and shoulders have now moved out ahead of the belly button and over the aiming knee. The weight of the head (in the human adult, about 15-20 pounds) adds to the total forces imparted to the pitch. The head and eyes point directly at the target and the eyes are level with the horizon. Tilting the head (head roll) creates aiming and balance problems (see page 59 and Fig. 2-32). The torso, legs and throwing arm follow the head during forward body movements. If the head tilts, the eyes leave the level horizontal plane, and the entire "catapult" destabilizes! The aiming foot is locked onto the target, and the power foot begins now (not earlier) to break from the rubber. The glove is tucked into the left armpit as the throwing arm passes in front of the body. The throwing arm, forearm and wrist are fully extended, and hand palm is down (pronated) – (see Chapter 3, **Movement**). The back is flexed at the pelvis. Note the shallow angle between the front of the power leg and the ground. This is a power pitcher. At this moment, **weight and shearing forces** are transferring to the **aiming leg** (see page 46).

Figure 2-19 also shows the palm turning to face the earth, because this power pitcher has just uncorked a fastball. Palm down positions at this point are used with fastballs, some change-ups, forkballs ("drops") and knucklers. Palm inward comes with curves and sliders; palm outward with screwballs (see Chapter 3, **Movement**). His eyes are level with the horizon. The head bears straight ahead and is not tilted right or left.

**Common Problems:** (most of which can inflict injuries on the pitcher)
1. Failure to anchor the aiming foot before the throwing arm starts forward.

2. Failure to maximize all forces forward just prior to ball release.

3. Failure to fully extend the throwing arm, forearm and wrist.

4. Failure to keep eyes level with horizon.

5. Tilting the head right or left.

**Figure 2-19**

# Follow-Through

*Follow-through (Figs. 2-20 through 2-22) commences the instant the ball leaves the pitcher's hand. Its sole purpose is to permit the arm and body to decelerate in a coordinated manner. The most serious pitching injuries commonly occur during flawed follow-through (Chapter 7, Injuries).*

Weight and **shearing force transfer** deserve further explanation. Weight is the force exerted by gravity – straight down to the earth. A shearing force runs horizontal to the earth, e.g., a shove.

Review Figures 2-4, 2-5 and 2-13b. In Figures 2-4 and 2-5 the pitcher's **entire weight** rests on the power leg. At this instant no shearing force is present. The pitcher in Figure 2-13b transferred about half his **weight** to the aiming leg as he brought it forward and planted the aiming foot. However, he exerted minimal **shearing force** because he simply stepped forward and planted. Shearing forces against the aiming foot appear when the throwing arm and body accelerate forward.

**Acceleration** is a change in velocity per unit of time. In Figure 2-13b the pitcher is preparing to accelerate his body and the ball; here both body and ball are at 0 mph. In Figure 2-19, the ball and body have reached maximum acceleration as the ball leaves the hand. **At this instant maximum shearing forces shove against the aiming foot and maximum weight transfers to the aiming leg.** Consequently, the aiming foot must be planted solidly.

When the throwing arm and body start forward, and while the power foot pushes, the weights of the various body parts – head, shoulders, arms, trunk – increasingly transfer onto the aiming leg. After the throwing arm passes the head and the hand releases the ball, **deceleration** of body and ball occurs while weight transfer and shearing forces diminish.

**Deceleration** is a decrease in velocity per unit of time. Human design is such that every act of acceleration is met with an equal act of deceleration. That's the good news, because without deceleration, extremities and trunk would rip and tear. The bad news is deceleration is that part of the pitching motion where most injuries occur to arm, shoulder and back (Chapter 7). More about deceleration later.

---

### Coaching Pearl

A pitcher who wears worn "spikes" or "turf cleats" is likely to experience skidding movements in his aiming foot as he accelerates forward. The skid destabilizes the catapult base and adversely affects control. A pitcher must be properly shod!

---

The power heel flies toward the sky in Figure 2-20 as the pitcher now decelerates his forward thrust. So forcefully has he pushed with his power foot that when it disengages from the plate it leaps skyward. The well-planted aiming foot still points to the target. Notice how this pitcher's throwing hand and forearm have swung in front of the aiming knee. The point at which the throwing hand/forearm come to swing by the aiming knee is the terminus of a power/deceleration arc described by the throwing arm which began behind the pitcher's back (Fig. 2-13), circled forward past his shoulder, and ended here. As depicted, the arc is distorted because we use a two-dimensional picture to present a three-dimensional concept. The glove has slid out of the armpit and migrated backward – not the best place to be! A line drive back at the mound might end up in his teeth. So complete is this pitcher's follow-through that his back nearly parallels the earth. His head is not tilted. Eyes are level.

## Common Problems:

1. Failure to follow through completely.

2. Failure to decelerate with the back nearly parallel with the earth.

3. Premature break of power foot from rubber (see page 54).

**Figure 2-20**

K. VAN LOO

### *Coaching Pearl*

Remember, many pitchers have no idea where their glove is going. They simply swing the glove arm in a way that feels natural; usually they are ready to field balls hit back to the mound.

A left-hander is shown in Figure 2-21. He has continued his deceleration arc beyond the aiming knee. His glove is adjacent to the right armpit ready to drop down should he need to field the ball. His power foot has flown off of the rubber and his spine parallels the ground. A superb follow-through. He allows that throwing arm to "hang." This pitcher has thrown a breaking pitch. Can you tell why? See Chapter 3, **Movement.** His head is untilted and eyes level with the horizon.

**Common Problems:**

1. Failure to follow through completely.

2. Failure to flex spine forward at pelvis.

3. Tilting head right or left.

4. Failure to keep eyes level with horizon.

K. VAN LOO

**Figure 2-21**

Both Figures 2-20 and 2-21 incorporate important notions about **deceleration**. The head, still fixed on the target, rests on a slightly extended neck. Extension of the neck toward the back is important, because this act puts the brakes on head movement which heretofore was completely forward and flexing. Were the head to continue forward in flexion, the pitcher at worst would fall on his face; at best he would lose sight of his target. The back is nearly parallel with the ground. The back arrived at this position while it decelerated after the moment of maximum acceleration seen in Figure 2-19.

What if the pitcher stopped his forward flexion at the moment of maximum acceleration (Fig. 2-19)? Whiplash! In a head-on car crash the occupants of both cars are at one moment in motion; the next moment stopped dead. Had both cars slowed and gently touched head-on: minimal damage. Pitchers who stop their forward motion with the back straight or only slightly bent often tear or strain back, shoulder and arm muscles. It takes time and distance to slow down on the road – and in the pitching motion.

Consequently, the throwing arm uses the deceleration arc to expend time and distance to slow down. Finally, the power leg, assisted by gravity, decelerates as it climbs skyward. It terminates all forward movement when it lands abeam the aiming foot as shown in Figure 2-22.

Ready to field the ball, balanced on both lower extremities, this left-hander has decelerated to a stop in Figure 2-22. He looks like an infielder ready to gobble up a ball; at this moment he is exactly that. His knees are slightly bent and he is up on the balls of both feet. His eyes, like radar, have followed the ball to its target. The response belongs to the hitter. We have dubbed in a smile

**Figure 2-22**   K VAN LOO

on the pitcher's face. His excellent mechanics have rewarded him with that wonderful word, bellowed out by the gentleman in blue: **"Stee-rike!"**

## Common Problems:

1. Failure to follow through completely. This failure results in decreased absorption of the forward forces. Injuries, especially to back and shoulder, occur at this point.

Figures 2-23, through 2-26 show how I executed those steps shown in Figures 2-7 through 2-10. My motive in presenting this material is to reinforce a coaching concept: "let success remain successful." With these mechanics I won 30 games for San Francisco (1946), 21 games in my rookie year with the Giants (1947) and 23 games the year the Giants went to the World Series (1951). From time to time I have wondered what would have occurred had someone changed (not corrected) these mechanics.

Figure 2-23 shows the start of my motion with right foot on the middle of the plate and left foot at the left edge. Starting in the middle of the plate allows me to adjust right or left as needed to correct right or left errant placement. The positioning of my feet also places me at a slight angle to the pitcher's plate. This is unlike the pitcher shown in Figure 2-7 whose

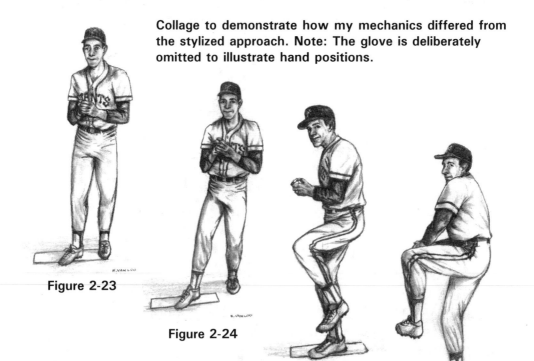

Collage to demonstrate how my mechanics differed from the stylized approach. Note: The glove is deliberately omitted to illustrate hand positions.

Figure 2-23

Figure 2-24

Figure 2-25

Figure 2-26

feet lie perpendicular to the plate. I preferred to start from the angle shown, because I was more comfortable rotating the left side of my body through a smaller arc to bring my shoulders in alignment with home plate: less movement, more stability.

The left foot and leg start back in Figure 2-24. The right forefoot rests in front of the plate, while the arch and heel lie atop the plate. I place my left foot off the side and to the rear of the pitcher's plate, and generally maintain the angle to the plate shown in Figure 2-23.

Figure 2-23                                    Figure 2-24

### Coaching Pearl

Everyone's dance style differs slightly, no matter what the tune. The smooth dancer is a comfortable dancer. Observe carefully how your protégés dance, and help them find the most comfortable steps.

As I start to pivot into a position where the left shoulder faces the batter in Figure 2-25, the right foot rolls slightly toward the instep instead of remaining flat in front of the plate as shown in Figure 2-9. My forefoot abuts the front of the plate, while arch and heel span the leading edge of the plate. When I push against the plate to propel myself toward the hitter, I push with the ball of my foot rather than shoving with the outside of the foot. My forte is control; my body is more stable and control more effective when I use this technique. This foot placement also enhances the power of my forward thrust (see Fig. 2-26).

The left leg lift is shown at its highest point in Figure 2-26. Notice my hand and glove hidden behind the lifted knee. The right toes and forefoot contact the front of the plate while the arch and heel span, and remain in contact with, the plate. This method enabled me to generate more power on my forward thrust, added several miles per hour to my fastball and slider, and stabilized my control.

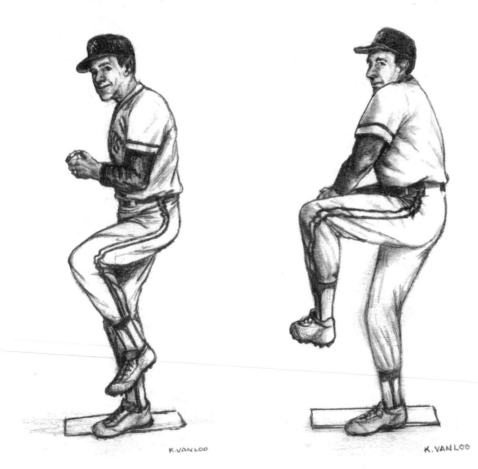

**Figure 2-25**          **Figure 2-26**

Take note of Figures 2-27 through 2-29. This is a high school pitcher who is an effective "control pitcher." The photos from which these sketches are drawn were taken as he pitched a three-hit shutout. In the first five innings he threw only 46 pitches: 30 strikes, 16 balls. Note that his delivery features a low three-quarter arm mechanic, yet he had no problems with horizontal control. Note several other small variances from the advice already presented in this chapter. Attempts to correct these variances produced no noticeable improvement in his pitching. His scholastic year-end ERA was 2.13, and his record showed nine wins and no losses.

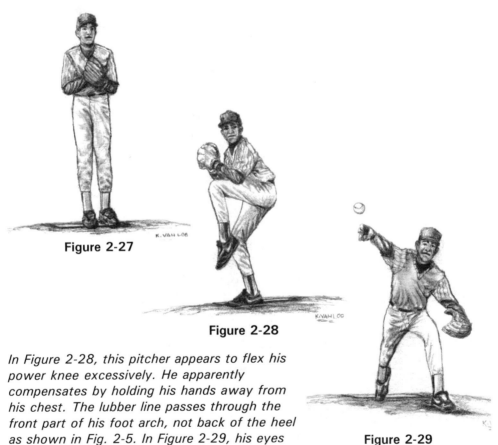

**Figure 2-27**

**Figure 2-28**

*In Figure 2-28, this pitcher appears to flex his power knee excessively. He apparently compensates by holding his hands away from his chest. The lubber line passes through the front part of his foot arch, not back of the heel as shown in Fig. 2-5. In Figure 2-29, his eyes are level with the horizon.*

**Figure 2-29**

# *Wildness: Mechanical Causes and Cures*

Wildness is more than imprecise control. It means that the pitch wanders far from the path and target intended by the pitcher. The miss is measured in feet, not inches.

1. Pitchers troubled with occasional wildness may be allowing the power side to upset the guidance system (aiming side). Observe such pitchers carefully to see if they pick up the power foot a split second too soon – before ball release. In these cases the pushing force suddenly terminates, and the upcoming power foot destabilizes the "catapult base." This creates a wobble in the aiming side or a stumbling movement in the power side as the power leg comes forward. Have such pitchers drag the power foot two to eight inches on the ground after ball release as shown in Figure 2-30. After this moment of drag, the power foot breaks contact with the ground and explodes toward the sky.

K.VANLOO

**Figure 2-30**

2. When a pitcher is habitually "wild high," or frequently has trouble getting the ball "down," shorten his stride **one-half to one inch**. The way I did this in spring training, or between games, was to take the pitcher out to the bullpen mound. I placed a stick in the ground at the point where the toe of his aiming foot naturally and usually planted. Then I moved the stick back a half to one inch, and instructed the pitcher to shorten his stride so that his aiming toe planted at the new spot with every pitch. Most pitchers want to overcorrect when you advise them to shorten their stride. The stick on the ground prevents overcorrection. **It takes very little correction to get a lower pitch**. Too short a stride produces low wildness. Both low and high wildness are forms of vertical wildness. See also page 59.

3. Another cause of high wildness is allowing the aiming foot to land heel first. It must land flat or toe first.

4. A third cause of vertical wildness is "overthrowing" (see pages 30 and 58).

5. When dealing with side-to-side (horizontal) wildness, note whether the pitcher is bringing his arm forward in a "three-quarter," or near-side-arm manner. If so, try moving the arm upward slightly toward the overhand position. This usually produces a straighter flight track in the side-to-side dimension. If the arm is brought up too far, the pitcher may fall into vertical wildness problems!

6. Another cause of horizontal wildness is failure to align shoulders, arms, legs and feet along a straight path from the pitcher's plate to home plate. See Figure 2-13b for correct technique.

7. Consult the control algorithm (Fig. 2-31). This algorithm presents a systematic approach to cures for wildness. Note that close observation of power foot movement and release points (bottom box in algorithm) may disclose the origins of the wildness.

8. Review Chapter 3, **Movement** for discussion of release points with various pitches. The release points depicted are located about 45 degrees in front of the pitcher, but vary with each individual. Release points too far forward induce low wildness, and those too far back lead to high wildness.

9. Do not attempt to fix errant mechanics during a game unless the fix is small and simple. If a young pitcher's mechanics are seriously flawed, it is better to "go to the bull pen" and summon a reliever. Work on the mechanics problem(s) between games.

I had two pitchers who suffered occasional episodes of wildness.

1. **Billy Pierce:** He told me (after he joined the Giants) that in tough games he had a tendency to work too fast, get careless, neglect his mechanics and lose his control. He was **rushing**! When I saw this, I would get his attention and motion him to slow down. This single remedy usually restored his mechanics and his control.

2. **Gaylord Perry:** Once in a great while he would lose his thinking and start to look at the ground while pitching. I would get his attention and point to my eyes. He knew what he had to do: Concentrate on the target. Frequently this restored his control.

In the case of both pitchers, simple suggestions during the game rendered the remedy. **Major mechanical flaws are not readily repaired during a game. When a pitcher falls out of the groove, invite him to take an early shower. Fix the mechanics in the morning.**

---

### Coaching Pearl

During the game the pitcher needs to concentrate on pitch selection, placement and tactics. His mechanics must flow naturally and not distract him. A pitcher who allows himself to be distracted by mechanical considerations easily loses mastery of the game.

---

# Coaching Axiom

When I became a major-league pitching coach and dealt with new pitchers just breaking into the "bigs," I knew that these athletes had ascended a ladder of excellence. They had come to major-league baseball because they were superb athletes. Consequently, I felt that if I contributed just a fraction of improvement to their skills, I had done my job.

The scenario is different for high school and college coaches who often need to make more adjustments in the pitching techniques of their players. However, my advice is to **observe, analyze and interfere as little as possible with the natural throwing styles of players at all levels**. Make small adjustments over a period of time. Many large changes in a short period of time can often hurt a pitcher.

Generally speaking, do not change a successful pitcher's act of throwing. "If it ain't broke, don't fix it," is good advice. Improvements or adjustments to correct serious problems should be rendered only after careful observations of the entire delivery. Introduce the pitcher to the least amount of change possible. **It is easy to make a pitcher worse, difficult to make him better.**

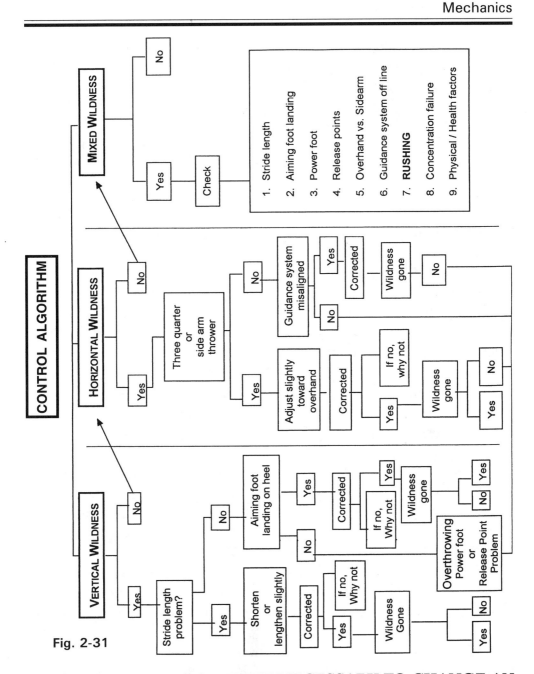

Fig. 2-31

## WHEN IS IT ABSOLUTELY NECESSARY TO CHANGE AN ELEMENT IN THE PITCHER'S MECHANICS?

There are three situations. (1) When a pitcher experiences **pain** or **increasing** soreness over several outings. Given the location of these symptoms, an observant coach can predict which element in the motion is the culprit (see Chapter 7, **Baseball Injuries**). Either symptom requires that a medical provider check for serious injury. After the provider has **coor-**

**dinated** with the coach, and released the pitcher to resume throwing, the coach addresses the flawed mechanic. (2) When the pitcher gives away the pitch by altering his mechanics, or displaying a special mannerism (see Chapter 5, p. 126) with certain pitches. Talented hitters will eventually spot these quirks – however small; launch time is here! In Chapter 3, **Movement**, I emphasize that all pitches (except the knuckler) are thrown with fastball arm speed. This helps to maintain consistent mechanics. Now, study Figures 2-17, 2-18 and 2-19. Note the difference in the angle between power leg and ground for the "power" and "breaking ball pitchers." Do these angle differences give the pitch away? No, because at this instant the hitter is trying to see the ball, not measuring angles. Mechanical changes that give the pitch away occur prior to that instant when the pitcher **starts forward** with the pitch. After a pitcher starts forward, the batter's attention is riveted on the ball. (3) When a hurler's pitches become ineffective (excessive walks/hits) over several outings. These three problems are not correctable within the confines of a game; two others: **rushing** and **overthrowing**, can be fixed during a game.

**Rushing** is failure to pause at the top of leg lift (Fig. 2-6 shows the moment of pause). Rushing usually appears during moments of "heavy stress" when a pitcher's emotions overrun his thinking, and he "rushes" to put his problems behind him. Rushing can ruin control, and it may also create an injury. A good catcher can pick up this problem and correct it!

**Note**: The "slip step" and "quick kick" (p. 136) are intentional forms of rushing used to reduce a pitcher's time to the plate with runners on first or second. The leg lift is decreased and there is no pause in these techniques. If control deteriorates, the pitcher may have to incorporate a pause at the top of the leg lift.

**Overthrowing** surfaces when a pitcher excessively tenses his arm muscles in an effort to "get more on the pitch." These pitches arrive in a spot higher than intended, because the tense muscles cause the pitcher to **release** the ball high.

When a coach finds a need to change a pitcher's mechanics, it is best he observe the pitcher's use of his body in a detailed head-to-toe or toe-to-head sequence. The simplest manner to accomplish this task is to focus on one part of the pitcher's anatomy at a time and observe exactly how that part moves during a sequence of throws with different pitches. The coach notes the flaws. After a thorough visual survey – supplemented, if need be with video tapes of the pitcher – the coach "steps back" and views the entirety of the motion. Generally, (and hopefully!), the flaw lies within only one or two of the **elements** discussed before.

# Mechanics Rehabilitation

The effective pitching coach is an excellent communicator. He punctuates his lessons with explanations and examples which are easy to grasp and translate into execution. **Example**: When the coach corrects high wildness with a minimally shortened stride, he directs the pitcher to **"show more pocket."** Reexamine Figure 2-26. Notice the hip facing the hitter. **"Showing more pocket"** brings more of the pitcher's back and buttocks into the hitter's view. Now, when the pitcher plants his aiming foot, the shoe print will fall short of the print made before the adjustment. The more pocket shown, the shorter the stride. This teaching trick prevents the pitcher's looking at the ground to shorten his stride. This posture also "closes" the throwing side to aid ball concealment and slows the pitcher who is **rushing**.

Study Figure 2-32. Notice how this pitcher's head has rolled backward and off to his left side. His eyes are not level with the horizon. This **head roll** has caused him to hyperextend (bend backward) his spine. Only an accident of nature will provide a properly placed pitch. The human adult head weighs 15 to 20 pounds – the weight of a **large bowling ball**. Place a 16-pound bowling ball off-center on a five-foot unanchored post. What happens? The post leans, wobbles and topples. Furthermore, this pitcher wastes kinetic energy to straighten his spine – energy subtracted from his pitch.

Study Figure 2-14. The left elbow is shoulder high, and, at this instant, pointed toward the target. A fraction of a second earlier, this elbow was sharply flexed into a point – shoulder high (Fig. 2-13a and 2-33). This point acts very much like a **gun sight** aimed at the target. As the elbow begins to extend (as shown in Fig. 2-14), it remains shoulder high. When fully extended (Fig. 2-13b) the elbow continues forward shoulder high, while the glove hand/wrist flexes or extends to distract the hitter. **Pitching a baseball is a high elbow event**.

Finally, examine Figure 2-34. Notice that this pitcher's aiming foot has not planted, yet he has come almost halfway forward with his throwing arm, and his torso has nearly completely rotated. The coach must counsel the pitcher to **"put the front foot down"** before he comes for-

---

### Coaching Pearl

Effective pitches come from a relaxed body working in an unhurried manner.

---

ward and initiates torso rotation. Failure to **"put the front foot down"** before coming forward and rotating destabilizes the entire catapult base.

**When the coach rehabs mechanics, he proceeds head to foot. First, the pitcher must think about what he will do, then perform; analysis of the outcome follows.**

Figure 2-32                    Figure 2-33

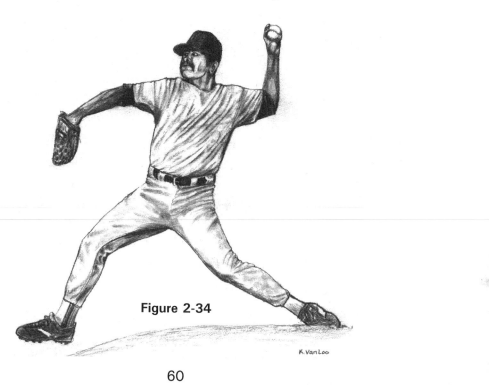

Figure 2-34

# 3

# Placement, Control and Movement

## In a Nutshell

1. Placement disarms the hitter
2. Control is the product of work, preparation, concentration and mechanics
3. Throw strikes on the corners
4. Keep the ball down
5. Change speeds
6. The game is a three-act play
7. Save something for the last act
8. Work fast
9. The pitches
10. Every good pitch has movement

*"Hitting is timing; pitching is upsetting timing."*
**Warren Spahn**

Every hitter (except Superman) has holes and **soft spots** in his swing. Throw a ball through the **hole** and the batter misses it; throw to a **soft spot** and he fails to strike the ball soundly; throw to a **selected soft spot**, and the batter delivers the ball to an area on the field chosen by the pitcher. A delusion? Not at all! The successful pitcher accomplishes his ends by **enticing** the hitter to hit selected pitches or by **deceiving** the hitter into missing the ball completely.

Not without care have I chosen the words **entice** and **deceive**. These words imply mental energy – knowledge, forethought, logic and assimilation of **visual input**. I discuss each of these cerebral activities in greater depth in Chapter 5: **Tactics**. For now it is important to know that in order to entice and deceive you must be able to **place** the ball in certain spots while using changes in speed, pitch selection and movement. **PLACEMENT DISARMS THE HITTER.**

If **placement** is the act of delivering the ball to certain **selected spots** adjacent to the hitter, what is control? **Control** comprises all the physical and mental activities used to **place** the ball in the selected spots. Fans, players and coaches often limit the word **control** to mean only absence of walks and wild pitches, or production of more strikes than balls. These meanings are correct but not properly inclusive. The effective pitcher may demonstrate superb control while placing the pitch outside the strike zone, e.g., to entice the hitter to swing at an unfavorable pitch. If the batter does not bite at this bait, the umpire calls a ball. Is that pitcher guilty of poor control? The answer is unequivocally no. Early Wynn (Hall of Fame 1972, 300 career wins, 290 complete games) often reached a full count as he **controlled** his **placements** around the strike zone to accomplish his ends. Jim Palmer (Hall of Fame 1990) reportedly stated that "...half of all third strikes are (placed) out of the strike zone." According to former catching great Tim McCarver, 90 percent of Steve Carlton's (Hall of Fame 1995) strikeouts came on balls, not strikes.

It is in this expanded context that we state: Control is the key to pitching. This is what Cy Young meant when he attributed his longevity in the big leagues to his control (22 years, 511 wins). During my own rookie year in the major leagues, I led the National League with the lowest average number of walks per game (2.07) as well as the best won/lost average (21-5, .808). The following year my average was 1.75 walks per game with a win/loss record of 18-12. **Up to 60 percent of all walks score!**

How does a pitcher develop control? How does a coach teach control? The answer contains at least four elements: 1) Physiological preparation; 2) Hard work; 3) Concentration; 4) Mechanics.

# *Preparation*

In Chapter 1 we studied the pitcher in spring training as he warmed up **every day** preparatory to throwing batting practice (or pitching in a game). What precedes the warm-up pitches? Answer: A group of activities that sufficiently raises heat energy within muscles, tendons and ligaments so that the pitcher "breaks a sweat." Because certain individuals can "break a sweat" without ever lifting a finger, e.g., at income tax time, other activities are required. (See also Chapter 8, **Pitching Physiology**)

Muscle physiologists have shown that muscles perform most efficiently, and are least likely to suffer injury, when warmed well above resting state temperature. The sources of this increased heat (from the chemical reactions of high energy phosphate compounds, etc.) is best left to a review of an appropriate textbook in human physiology. The list of theories and methods available to create this warming is endless and constantly changing. An acceptable regime follows: jog for five minutes; stretch in a progressive manner to involve every major muscle-tendon group, and finish with stooping, bending and twisting exercises. This regime should consume 10 to 15 minutes, and even longer in "cold" ballparks, such as the San Francisco water's edge stadium.

As the muscles warm, the temperature control center in the brain signals the blood vessels in the skin to dilate, and the sweat glands to excrete water (and salt). In man, cooling occurs when sweat evaporates. An example of nature's perversity! While the pitcher strives to generate heat, nature strives to diminish it. It is important, then, not to allow warmed muscles to cool. After initial exercises, commence warm-up throws at once. In the colder playing environments I encourage my pitchers to wear long-sleeve chokers to conserve heat. After the warm-up throws, or while your team is at bat on cold days, wear a jacket that covers the **entire torso and arms**. Placing only the throwing arm in a jacket sleeve really does no good, because other uncovered muscles are cooling, and cooling leads to stiffness and decreased muscle efficiency. Also, warm venous blood returning from the covered arm eventually mixes with cooler venous blood returning from the uncovered muscles, and, from sweat-covered, cooling skin. The exposed muscles and cooling skin act like a piece of ice placed in a hot cup of coffee. The net result is a cooler cup of coffee (the pitcher's arm). Caution: Beware of **overheating**, especially on hot, humid days. You might not want to wear a choker or jacket in that environment.

When preparing to enter the game as the starting pitcher, **throw at least 60 to 70 pitches to assure looseness**. On cooler days add 10 or 15 additional throws. After the first three or four tosses, blend in the entire arsenal of pitches including breaking balls. The importance of warming up sufficiently is best illustrated by considering the career of my team-mate, Sal Maglie, and that of Satchel Paige. Sal often encountered troubles in the first inning – poor placements arising out of imperfect control. Once he got past the first inning, he was one tough hombre to beat. My impressions were that he warmed up about 15 pitches shy of what he should have accomplished. Paige, in his younger years, frequently arrived at the ballpark late and had to hurry his warm-up procedures. He, like Maglie, was not throwing enough warm-up pitches; he also, like Maglie, often found himself in trouble in the first inning. **Many pitchers, coaches and fans are surprised to learn how many runs are actually scored in the first inning! This phenomenon is preventable**.

**Little-leaguers need to warm up less. Their bodies and arms are supple. Injuries to these youngsters come from excessive throwing; hence the limited number of innings a pitcher may throw in a week – as prescribed by Little League rules.**

**Baseball wisdom: If you are going to get beat, get beat in the eighth inning, not in the first inning because you failed to warm up properly.**

Start the warm-up at the full distance between home plate and the pitcher's plate (60 feet, 6 inches). Some pitchers start short of the full distance and work back toward the mound as the warm-up progresses. My observations have taught me that this technique, consciously or subconsciously, acts against the pitcher by creating a feeling that somehow it is more difficult to throw the regulation distance. If anything, commence the warm-up (soft throws) at a distance several feet greater than the regulation footage. After 10 or 15 throws move forward to the pitcher's plate.

# Hard Work

Precise placement is an art mastered through hard work. Many spectators, and even some practitioners of baseball, fail to appreciate that while, by custom, we refer to baseball as a "game," baseball is truly work. To perform well in baseball, even the "natural" athlete engages in repetitive, skill-building activities. Most baseball historians regard Satchel Paige as the paradigm of control and placement – after he warmed up sufficiently! What may not be common knowledge is how Satchel achieved his skill. Two of his mentors, Harry Salmon and Sam Streeter, allegedly had him practice throwing the ball over a book of matches until he mastered the technique at a 60-foot distance. Grover Cleveland Alexander (Hall of Fame, 1938), the legendary "finesse" pitcher, threw at soup can tops nailed to the side of a barn. Whether these two tales from baseball lore are factual is not known with certainty. These clubhouse stories are memorialized because they respect an axiom known to those who practice the profession of baseball: work, work, work; practice, practice, practice. This work habit begins early in life, and is an integral part of the personality of most successful persons. Work related to control development starts on the first day of spring training and continues throughout the season.

## *Concentration*

In Chapter 1, I touched briefly on the pitcher's need to concentrate on the catcher's glove during the entire throw. This technique begins with the first warm-up toss and continues through those pitches thrown with a teammate inserted beside the plate toward the end of the warm-up. Using a stand-in teammate enables the pitcher to see for himself how his offerings will travel to the hitters. These **visual techniques** bring the pitcher "into the groove" − a term meaning correct placement.

This concentration initiated in the pregame preparations cannot be dismissed and summoned capriciously within the framework of a game. The pitcher's "head must be in the game" even while his team is at bat. He consciously reviews what he has done, and what he plans to do as the game unfolds; he ponders the events as they present themselves. Proceeding in this manner, he is less likely to be surprised or outwitted. On those days when he is not involved in the game, it is his duty is to observe and search out the **weaknesses** and **tendencies** of the opposing hitters.

To illustrate the degree of concentration required, I draw from personal experience. When I pitched for the old San Francisco Seals, one day a boyhood friend came out to the park. He bought a seat just two rows back of the dugout. Throughout the game, at the top of his lungs, he hollered at me in repeated attempts to attract my attention. He called my first name, my boyhood nickname and perhaps a few unpublishable phrases. When the game was over, I started up the walkway to the locker room; he vaulted over the railing, and dashed in front of me. Even then I did not respond. Only after he wrapped his arms around me in a bear hug did I realize the presence of a dear old friend. So intently did I concentrate on the game that I was oblivious to any stimuli save my own thoughts and the game action. As long as I pitched in the minors and majors I was seldom aware of the fans, the public address announcements, or any activities not directly related to the game.

# Mechanics

Detailed discussion is presented in Chapter 2 - **Mechanics**. When a pitcher "falls out of the groove" the cause is often related to **loss of concentration** leading to a **change in mechanics.** This is due usually to fatigue or lack of self-discipline. In Chapter 1 I stated that certain character traits are imperatives for the successful pitcher. Among these qualities is restraint – anger control. Hitters (master psychologists that they are) will attempt to bait and distract the pitcher. Why? To disturb the pitcher's concentration and mechanics. The most effective bait is "audibles" intended to engender anger. Take the bait, and the pitcher will not stay out there long. Become distracted on too many occasions and the team may search for unpleasant remedies – removal from a starting role or a ticket to another venue (Saskatoon or Fairbanks and points north). Hitters successful at provoking a pitcher's anger are rewarded by favorable (for them) placements, suitable for rocket ball blastoffs.

# The Spots

To visualize placement concepts, study Figures 3-1 and 3-2. The **strike zone** as defined by the Official Playing Rules Committee in 1994 is depicted in Figure 3-1. Some major-league pitchers and coaches swear that the strike zone is really smaller than this figure shows, and even then, the zone may degenerate into what a particular umpire says it is. A ball passing through any part of the depicted zone without a response from the hitter should be **a called strike**.

In Figure 3-2, superimposed onto the strike zone, are nine spots with extensions to spots 3, 6 and 9. For simplicity, both right- and left-handed hitters are portrayed simultaneously. The hurler's duties include guidance of his pitches into these spots while deceiving and enticing the hitter – with a caveat that the ball should rarely enter the 5-spot or the Bermuda Triangle (left-handed hitters). The 5-spot is truly a "monied area" for all hitters. Spectacular ball launchings have originated in this spot and from the Bermuda Triangle area.

The 5-spot occupies the middle 12 inches of the 17-inch-wide plate. That leaves 2½ inches on the outside/inside corners. The pitcher must conduct his business within the confines of these narrow plate **edges**. Notice the vertical position of the 5-spot. It lies **up** in the **strike zone** – perfect placement for the disappearing ball trick. When a pitch arrives in the 5-spot, the sound that follows the crack of the bat is cowhide bouncing on tarmac – on the other side of the wall.

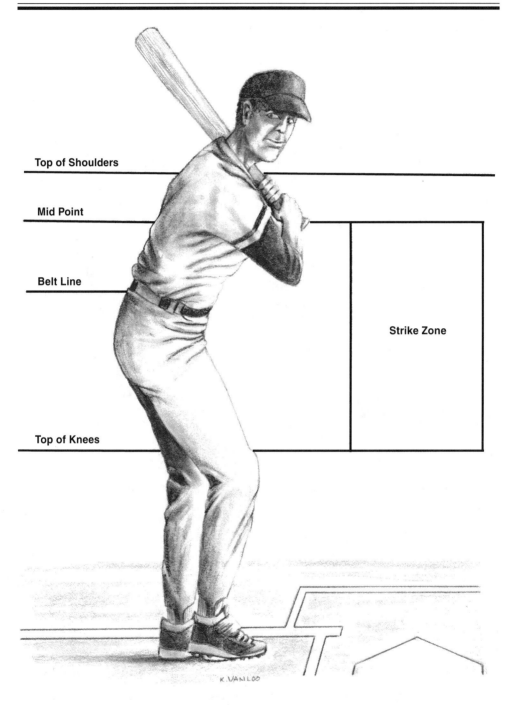

Top of Shoulders

Mid Point

Belt Line

Strike Zone

Top of Knees

K. VANLOO

**Figure 3-1**

*Depicts the strike zone as defined by the Official Playing Rules Committee, 1994. Note: The Committee in 1996 adopted a new lower level to "...the hollow below the kneecap."*

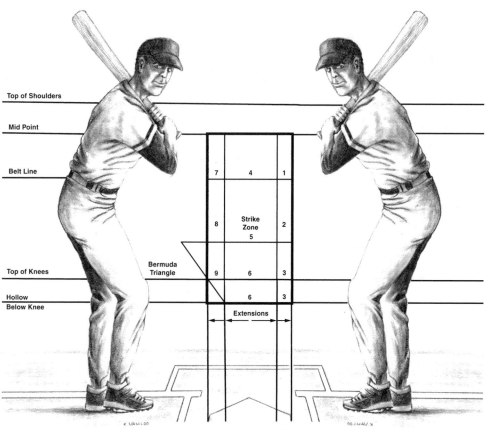

**Figure 3-2**

*This illustrates in bold outline the strike zone as currently defined by the Official Playing Rules Committee. Superimposed are an outline of the Bermuda Triangle ("sweet zone" for left-handed hitters), the nine spots described in the text and lower extensions to spots 3, 6 and 9. The "pitcher's corners" are spots 1, 2, 3, 7, 8, 9 and the extensions to spots 3 and 9.*

The "Bermuda Triangle" is a dream spot for most left-handed swingers and the source of nightmares for the pitcher. The mechanics of the left-handed hitter are such that balls sailing into this triangle have been known to vanish. There is no comparable area for most right-handed hitters.

The young pitcher should understand that many expert major-league pitchers cannot hit these spots precisely on a consistent basis. Reportedly, Tom Seaver (Hall of Fame, 1992) on his "good" days consistently threaded pitches within three or four inches of his target. We know Satchel Paige could do this, even at age 46! I have provided the somewhat elaborate schema of placement spots (Fig. 3-2) to show what the truly great pitchers could achieve and to serve as a reference during the discussion of **Tactics** in Chapter 5. However, a pitcher can succeed with pitches placed in spots with wider dimensions, e.g., "up-and-in," "down-and-in," "low-and-away."

The spots as diagramed (minus the hitter images) are useful for plotting pitch placement, velocity, motion and outcome during the collection of data on pitchers and hitters. For example, pitcher A delivers three pitches to hitter A (left-hander). The scout plots each pitch by number, type, spot and outcome, and velocity.

Examine Figure 3-3. First pitch: Curve low and away (spot 3). Called strike, 75 mph $\begin{smallmatrix}1\\C\\3\\CK\\75\end{smallmatrix}$ . Second pitch: Fastball down and in. Ball, 90 mph $\begin{smallmatrix}2\\F\\9\\B\\90\end{smallmatrix}$ . Third pitch: A change-up low and away, 80 mph. Grounder to third baseman $\begin{smallmatrix}3\\CH\\3\\65\\80\end{smallmatrix}$ .

The annotations in elipses are placed on the diagram itself and always listed in same order, e.g.,

4 .......................................... pitch number (fourth pitch)

F .......................................... type pitch (fastball)

3 .......................................... spot (three spot)

F7 ........................................ outcome: fly out to left fielder

87 ........................................ velocity (per radar)

Time at bat this game cue . (1)

Each scout will use his own shorthand. Whatever format is used it should be suitable for storage on computer discs – hence the spot is not only plotted, but enumerated. The same page can be used for any number of at bats for a given hitter in a game by adding a cue as shown. Some scouts may even use a lap-top computer for data collection.

**Pitchers must keep the ball down!** The reason: there are few competent low-ball hitters. Pitches arriving in spots 3, 6 and 9 (below the Bermuda Triangle) are likely to be hit on the ground – hopefully close to an infielder ready to gobble it up. Ground balls are generally less of a threat to do damage. Double plays and force-outs start with ground balls. Runners advance more frequently on fly balls, even those that are caught, e.g. the sacrifice fly. The 9 spot presents a problem with most left-handers, so use the 6 and 3 spots (with their extensions), and only the 9 spot extension for these hitters (unless you feel lucky).

**Pitcher:**
**Hitter:**
**Date:**
**Ballpark:**

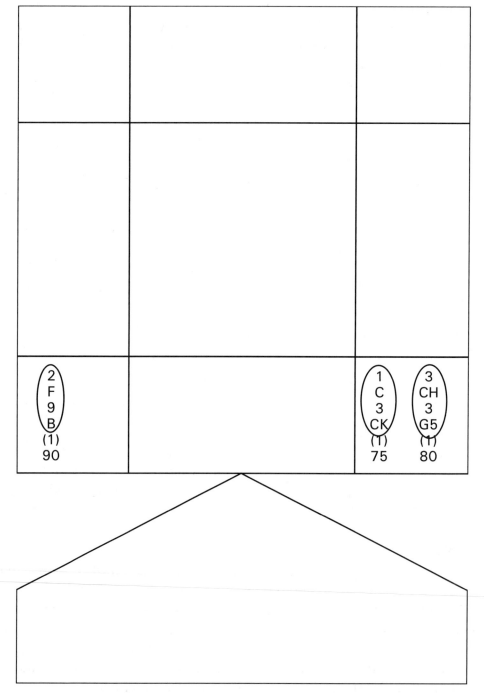

**Figure 3-3**
**Depicts the plots of three imaginary pitches**

The pitcher who keeps his pitches **down** understands the physics of hitting. He forces the hitter to use unfavorable motions. A batter swinging at a low ball is not swinging level. A level swing, or a very slightly upward angled swing (8 to 10 degrees), transmits the greatest force to the ball, because the bat strikes the ball squarely, even when the hitter's timing is slightly off. The best hitters strike the ball as it arrives at the front edge of the plate, and the human eye can best judge the instant of this arrival when the ball is **up** (belt high to just below the letters). Finally, the bat is a round stick, not flat, and to bring this round object forward to strike the ball squarely is easier when the pitch is **up**.

## Caveat: Pitching Too Fine

While the pitcher tries to conduct business on the edges of the plate – and down – he sometimes finds that his mental radar and body engines are just not in synch. He misses those plate edges, gets behind in the count and is forced to come in with pitches favorable to the hitter. What is the solution? Maintain concentration, keep the ball **down** and stop trying to do what, at that moment, you cannot do – catch the corner ("pitching too fine"). Jim Palmer observed that more walks (and hits!) are served up in close games by pitchers who try, but fail, to "pitch too fine." Bob Gibson advised that if a pitcher has to miss, miss outside. A mistake outside is a single; a miss inside is a home run.

## Velocity

A game is really a three-act play; each act is three innings. Like an excellent piece of drama, no two acts in baseball are the same. The pitching plot is simple: upset the hitters' timing with deception – different placements, movement and **speeds**. Skillful hitters are where they are because they are not easily deceived and because they learn fast! If the pitcher shows the same tendencies and routine in each act, the hitters will ambush him. If his first pitch is always a fastball up-and-in to a particular hitter, that hitter will plan to deal with the pitch. Should a pitcher truly vary his speeds, but the variances appear always in the same sequence, the hitter has three chances (strikes) in each at bat to "crack the code." The hitter is not alone in his attempt to decipher the pitcher's sequences. The hitter's coaches and teammates will lend the benefit of their observations. When hitters crack the code, the hook is next! In the vaudeville days, stage managers were known to remove substandard performers by using a padded hook secured to a long pole. This stunt invariably brought welcome relief to a weary audience. Want to avoid the hook? Keep the act **fresh** (change speeds), **moving** (work fast) and **full of punch** (throw strikes).

Some baseball pundits say, "A fastball is a fastball and a good hitter will learn to time the pitch before Act Three." How do you deal with this problem? There are several techniques.

The first has already been discussed – placement. **Place the ball in the hitter's hole or soft spot.** A second technique is to throw the fastball when it makes no sense to the hitter (deception). Third, keep the pitches down. Fourth, there are fastballs – and faster balls. Some are thrown at 80 to 90 percent power, others at 100 percent. Save the 100 percenters to get out of jams, or for late in the game. An example from my career will illustrate why you upshift or downshift your fastballs in tough situations.

In the 1950 Major League All-Star game at Comiskey Park, I came in to pitch for the National League in the seventh inning. We were behind 2-1. I felt sure Burt Shotton (National League All-Star manager) would lift me for a pinch hitter when I came to bat in the eighth. My objective then was to pitch one solid inning; I bore down with everything I had and struck out two hitters in the seventh. Surprise! Shotton let me hit for myself in the top of the eighth. So, I pitched to the American League in the bottom of that inning. Again, I bore down and struck out two hitters, because if we did not score in the ninth, the game was over. But Ralph Kiner hit a home run in the top of the ninth and tied the score. The ninth inning saw me still pitching and I struck out another two hitters. After I hit for myself in the eighth inning, I assumed that I would pitch three innings at most. But the All-Star rules at that time allowed a pitcher to continue beyond three innings if the score was tied and the game went into extra innings. I was not aware of that rule. After the ninth inning the score was still tied 2-2. I began to wonder how long I would have to pitch. Already I had shown the American Leaguers my fastball at 99 percent full power (of course, that was not my only pitch). As it turned out, I pitched a total of five innings, but struck out no one in the last two innings. In the 10th and 11th innings, I had to freshen my act with slower fastballs, change-ups and a variety of breaking pitches. The National League won 3-2. My pitching appearance covered nearly two "Acts." My change of velocities during the two acts came in reverse, but it worked!

So important is the fine art of changing speeds that without mastery of the subject the pitcher may soon find himself filling out an application for bus driver, or graduate school. Some coaches and pitchers believe that the hurler changes up only from a fastball. **NOT TRUE**. Learn how to change up off your breaking stuff. Careful, though. Do not let your arm speed give you away. The arm speed for all change-ups must appear to the hitter the same as the original pitch, be it a fastball or breaking pitch. The pitcher who has a fastball, curve, standard change-up and who can change up off his curve really has four pitches.

## Work Fast

Why? Five reasons:

1. A fusillade of missiles arriving at the plate stands a better chance of keeping the hitter off balance than a slow bombardment.
2. The fielders are continuously on their toes, ready to act, when a fast-working pitcher is on the mound.
3. A person working swiftly conveys an impression of competence.
4. The pitcher is a team's defensive leader. The fielders' eyes are upon him. How he behaves can elevate or depress their enthusiasm and energy.
5. A pitcher more easily "falls out of the groove" with his control, placement and cadence when he delays between pitches. More mistakes occur in this situation.

My teammate on the Giants, Jim Hearn, experienced middle- and late-inning problems early in his career. He took exceptionally long intervals between pitches. The catcher snapped the ball back to him. Jim walked around, kicked the dirt, brushed his hair back and displayed several other mannerisms before he set up to throw the next pitch. I wanted to help him, but I did not want to interfere with the relationship between himself and our pitching coach. One blistering hot day in St. Louis he commented: "Larry, how come you work so fast?" My answer: "The faster I work, the faster we all get back in the shade, outta that sun." I made my point (a practical team concept), and I did not offend.

## Movement

> *"Every major-league pitch moves some way or other.*
> *None go straight, not even the fastballs"*
> **Attributed to Ron Luciano,**
> **major-league umpire**

A pitch thrown without movement goes to heaven! The opposite can be said of a batter's attempts to hit balls thrown with **movement**, changed speeds and proper placement. The origins of pitch movement are found in the asymmetrical seam stitching, pitcher's grip, hand-wrist-forearm alignment at release, ball spin and wind resistance. Robert K. Adair in his treatise, *The Physics of Baseball* discusses at length the physical forces that bear upon the ball in flight. Adair points out that all thrown and batted balls spin – more or less.

**When there is nearly no spin, the ball flutters – like a butterfly.** A knuckleball acts in this manner, because the pitcher imparts minimal spin to the ball and allows uneven wind forces (resistance and drag) to play upon the ball. This fluttering pitch is disconcerting to hitter, pitcher and catcher. Hitters have likened hitting a knuckler to swatting an angry hornet with chopsticks. Pitchers seldom place the knuckleball in predictable spots, and leave the catcher to snatch awkwardly at the dancing sphere.

Bob Uecker reportedly commented that the best way to catch a knuckler is to wait until it stops rolling, then pick it up. Pitchers unable to locate the strike zone with their knuckler get behind in the count, are forced to come up with another pitch (often a fastball), then call on a local observatory to follow the trail of the ball leaving the planet!

## Terminology Related to Movement

Grip .......................... The arrangement of the hand and fingers around the ball.

Angle ........................ The direction that palm, wrist and forearm face at the release point.

Release Point ........... That point in the delivery where the hand releases the ball.

Pronate ..................... Turning of hand, wrist and forearm such that the palm faces inward, forward/down or outward (full pronation). **Pronation establishes the angle at pitch release.**

Supinate ................... Turning of hand, wrist and forearm such that the palm faces upward (catching raindrops).

Extension ................. Hand-wrist-forearm-elbow aligned straight ahead.

## *Points of Emphasis on Grips and Angles*

The **grip** is set inside the glove. The **pitcher begins to establish angle** of hand-wrist and forearm (palm forward, inward, outward) after the aiming foot strikes the ground – as the throwing arm starts forward. The angle is fully set just before the ball passes the head and is maintained throughout the delivery, to and including the release point. At the release point hand-wrist-forearm and elbow are **fully extended**. All these concepts are illustrated in Figures 3-4 to 3-51.

74

### Coaching Pearls

All pitches are thrown at fastball arm speed (except knucklers). The forces induced by fastball grip and angle of hand-wrist-forearm at release translate into maximum velocity. The forces induced by breaking ball grips and angles add to spin/veer and subtract from velocity.

1. The webbing between the thumb and index finger on a pitcher's glove should be closed (see figure 3-7) to conceal the pitcher's grip.

2. The pitcher should enter his glove to grip the ball in the same way for all pitches to prevent giving the pitch away (see p. 126).

3. As the throwing arm passes the head, the elbow should be at, or above, shoulder height.

4. **After receiving a new ball from the umpire, the pitcher should "rub the ball down" and inspect it. The higher the seams, the more suitable it is for all pitches except a knuckler. A knuckler flutters best when the seams are flat.**

# The Knuckleball

What is it that prevents a knuckler from spinning and produces flutter? The answers begin in the grip and physics of flight. Two knuckleball grips are shown in Figures 3-4 and 3-5. Notice in Figure 3-4 the knuckles of the index and middle fingers **do not touch the ball**. Instead the finger nails (trimmed square across) are imbedded in the seam. The "open viper mouth" grip (Fig 3-4) was used by a quartet of Washington Senator knuckleball pitchers in 1945. Figure 3-5 is one of the grips employed by 1990s knuckleballer Tim Wakefield. Notice how his thumb rides up on one side of the ball, while the ring finger encircles the opposite side – quite unlike the grips shown in Figures 3-4 and 3-6.

So, why the name, knuckler? Reason: from the hitter's view, the grip at release point (Fig. 3-6) appears as though the knuckles of two fingers are resting on top of the ball. When the ball is gripped as shown in Figures 3-4 and 3-5, the **largest smooth surface** of the ball (seams furthest apart) faces forward, while the **narrowest smooth surfaces** (seams close together) ride on the sides of the ball. Smooth side forward, increased stitch-

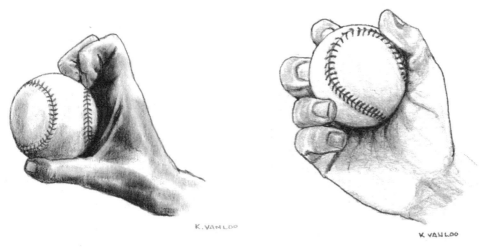

**Figure 3-4**

**Figure 3-5**

ing on the sides creates unequal wind resistance against, drag and turbulence around, the flying sphere. These unequal forces make the ball flutter. Consult also discussion of the breaking ball at the end of this chapter.

A knuckleball pitcher of the 1990s is shown in Figure 3-7 as he brings his pitch forward. Notice the relaxed stride – unique to throwing the knuckleball. There is a wide angle between this pitcher's power (right) leg and the ground. The knuckler is not thrown with a power motion (compare with Figures 2-17 and 2-19). Also note the arm and hand. He appears to be nearly "flipping" the ball. Figure 3-8 shows the knuckler as it passes the head of a 1950s knuckleballer.

**Figure 3-6**

Figure 3-9 shows the pronated hand at release point reaching toward home plate, palm forward. The pronated hand, wrist and forearm are fully extended at the elbow.

## Velocity

The knuckleball is thrown with a slower arm speed than the fastball. **All other pitches are thrown with fastball arm speed** in order to deceive the hitter. Since neither pitcher, catcher nor hitter can predict

Figure 3-7

Figure 3-8

the flight path of the knuckler, that of itself is sufficient to deceive all concerned; arm speed is irrelevant. The knuckler wends its weary way to the plate as an off-speed pitch. As discussed later under **curveball**, the slower speed assures greater movement.

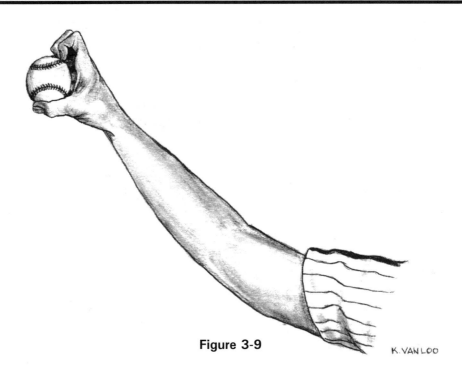

**Figure 3-9**

K. VAN LOO

## History

Past great knuckleballers include Hoyt Wilhelm, Phil Niekro, a quartet of Washington Senator pitchers who pitched on the same team in 1945: Roger Wolff, Johnny Niggeling, Mickey Haefner and Dutch Leonard. Present day masters include Tim Wakefield, Tom Candiotti and Charley Hough. Wilhelm, Niekro and Leonard continued to pitch in the major leagues into their 40s. Candiotti will turn 40 on August 31, 1997. Charlie Hough was still hurling and winning at age 46.

**Can a cause-and-effect relationship be established between career longevity and type of pitch most often thrown?** The answer remains (for now) an imponderable.

## *The Fastball*

The discussion of the unspun knuckleball serves as a prologue to the subject of spinning pitches, the most notorious example of which is the fastball.

Given their choice, hitters pick the fastball as the pitch they most like to hit. How do you deceive a hitter with a fastball? Placement, sequence, movement. **How does a pitcher induce movement on a fastball? Spin!**

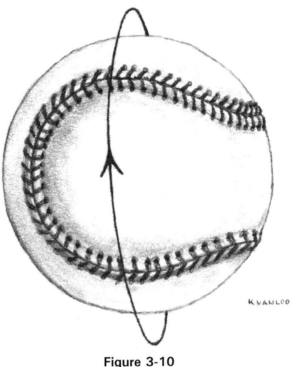

**Figure 3-10**
**Spin of a fastball as seen by the hitter.**

Many ballplayers do not realize that a fastball, properly gripped and thrown, spins backward toward the pitcher (Fig. 3-10). The pitcher's grip, the seam stitches and the alignment of hand, wrist, forearm and arm at release create the backward spin.

Figures 3-11 through 3-13 show three different fastball grips; four-seam grip (Fig. 3-11), two-seam grip (Fig 3-12) and along the seam (Fig. 3-13). The index and middle fingers lie **centered across**, or **along**, the seams on top of the ball; the thumb is **centered** beneath these fingers on the bottom of the ball. The distances from the outer sides of each finger to the sides of the ball are equal. The ball will move more when held as shown in Figure 3-13. I held mine as shown in Figure 3-14 – the truest way to throw a ball.

I gripped **all** my pitches as illustrated in Figure 3-14. To throw a slider or a curve I simply moved my index finger tight against the middle finger (Fig. 3-15) and relied on the angle of hand-wrist-forearm – along with the grip – to create the proper spin. This single grip method has an advantage: most high school, college and young professional pitchers put a fastball grip on the ball while taking the sign. If another pitch is needed, these pitchers often stir around inside the glove to change the grip. When

79

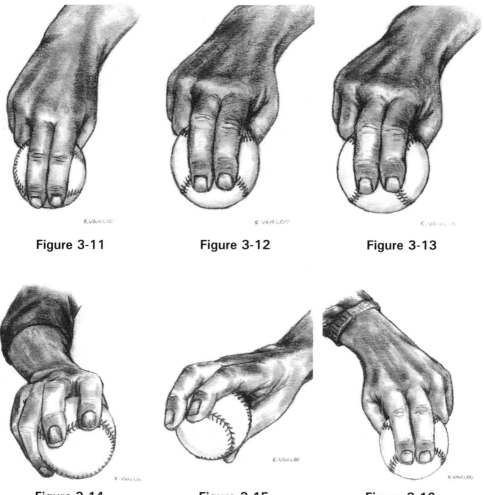

Figure 3-11　　　　Figure 3-12　　　　Figure 3-13

Figure 3-14　　　　Figure 3-15　　　　Figure 3-16

the batter or base coaches see this, the cat is out of the bag! Your astute opponents have "stolen the pitch." A left-hander's two-seam grip is shown in Figure 3-16.

Two additional fastball grips are illustrated in Figures 3-17 and 3-18. The four-seam grip in Figure 3-17 shows the index finger slightly back of the seam and the middle finger across the seam. This grip enables this pitcher to "cut" his fastball. This same pitcher shows a two seam fastball grip in Figure 3-18. His intent is not to "cut" the fastball.

When the fastball passes the head (Fig 3-19) the forearm, wrist and hand have pronated (palm forward). This angle of hand and wrist were set after the aiming foot hit the ground and the throwing arm started forward. Figure 3-20 shows a left-hander's fastball passing the head.

**Figure 3-17**

**Figure 3-18**

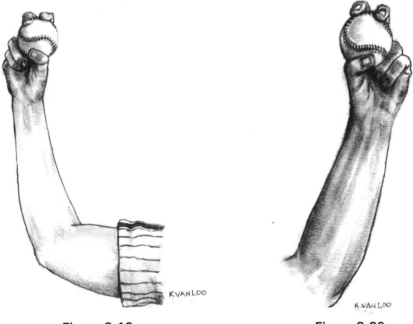

**Figure 3-19**                           **Figure 3-20**

Figure 3-21 shows the hand-wrist-forearm-elbow **firmly** extended at the fastball release point. At the instant of release the pitcher's hand – palm forward – looks like a quick "hello" wave. This configuration very much resembles the palmball release, **except** that the ball here is well out on the finger tips and not "stuffed" into the palm. Check Figure 3-51.

After the ball release, as deceleration occurs, the wrist flexes forward, and the hand – palm down – passes in front of the opposite knee (Fig. 3-22).

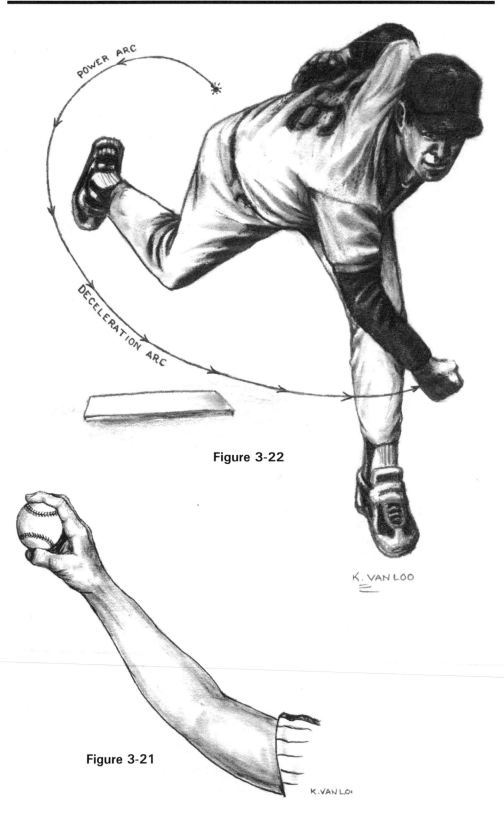

POWER ARC

DECELERATION ARC

**Figure 3-22**

K. VAN LOO

**Figure 3-21**

K. VAN LOO

82

---

> ### *Coaching Pearl*
>
> Review Figure 3-13. As the arm approaches the release point, the pitcher applies more pressure with the index finger than with the middle finger. This will impart a slight angular component to the backward rotation of the ball, and cause the ball to veer to the right and down when thrown by a right-hander, left and down for a left-hander.

Hand/wrist angle and cross-seam grip impart a brisk backspin to the ball. A well-thrown major-league fastball (90-95 mph) will rotate backward at about 1,200 rpm (about eight revolutions on its way to the plate) and will **appear** to "hop" three to four inches. Actually, the ball does not "hop;" instead, it momentarily levels out in its fall toward the ground. This level-out looks like a "hop" to the human eye. The four-seam fastball "hops" more than the two-seam because the four-seam has a higher-spin rpm. High-speed cameras show that the "hop" occurs about 15 feet in front of the plate. Understand that a 90 mph fastball arrives at the plate 0.4 seconds after release! (cf. Adair, 31-37)

**The hop on a fastball depends on the spin rpm.**

# Velocity

At all levels of play this is the pitcher's highest-speed pitch. Remember to save fastballs thrown at 100 percent power for tight situations (see my comments on the 1950 All-Star Game, page 72).

> ### *Coaching Pearl*
>
> All pitches, except the knuckler, are thrown with fastball arm speed.

# History

Using a ballistic pendulum, physicists in 1914 clocked Walter Johnson's fastball at 99.7 mph **crossing the plate**. In 1946, Bob Feller unleashed fastballs of 98.6 mph as measured by an "electric eye" spanning home plate. Since the ball decelerates about 1 mph for every seven feet of travel – total slowdown of nearly eight mph en route – Johnson's muzzle velocity* was about 108 mph and Feller's 107 mph (Adair, p. 31). The electronics of many radar guns held behind home plate measure the **average**

**speed** of the ball during flight. Other fastball masters and their radar-measured velocities are Goose Gossage: 99.4, 1980; Nolan Ryan: 100.4, 1974; J.R. Richard: 100, 1978.

**Given a 2.75-inch (diameter) bat and a three- to four-inch hop or dive on a fastball, it is a wonder that the hitter ever strikes the ball squarely.**

The **along-the-seams** grip (Fig. 3-13) imparts a slower backward rotation to the ball. When the pitcher applies more pressure with the index finger than the middle finger at the release point, this pitch, instead of hopping 15 feet in front of the plate, decelerates and dives several feet before the plate. The pitch becomes a "sinker" with an "inshoot tail." This "drop" is not as dramatic as that seen with the split-finger fastball (see below). The four-seam fastball is a power pitcher's weapon; the along-the-seam fastball is the weapon of a finesse pitcher. The two seam variety occupies a halfway niche. A four-seamer followed by an along-the-seam fastball creates a "change-up" sequence.

A fastball is an essential tool in the hand of the pitcher. (Note: not every pitcher in major-league ball can throw a fastball over 90 mph.) The fastball is often a "purpose pitch." Power and finesse pitchers alike use the fastball to set up other pitches, to change speeds, to adjust the hitter's stance (especially those who crowd the plate or "dig in"), to defend against the bunt and to surprise a hitter expecting something else.

---

### Coaching Pearl

A successful pitcher at any level must master at least three pitches; two of these must be the fastball and a change-up.

---

# The "Radar Cult" and Its Speed Trap

Occasionally, a coach or scout will be asked to evaluate a pitching prospect whose fastball exceeds 90 mph as measured on a radar gun. Be careful not to fall into the "speed trap!" A fastball is only as good as its placement and movement.

**There are three characteristics each pitch possesses: Placement, movement, velocity.**

---

\* *Muzzle Velocity means the speed of the ball at the instant it leaves the pitcher's hand.*

These characteristics are listed in the order of their overall value. Placement has the highest value. Reportedly a minor-league pitcher named Dalkowski had a fastball which exceeded 110 mph! Problem? Yes! Frequent lack of control. He never made it to the big leagues. Eddie Lopat threw a fastball which allegedly cruised at less than 86 mph. He was a great success, because he used his fastball as a **precisely placed "purpose pitch."**

## *The Curveball*

A curveball is a different creature. Its spin axis is opposite that of a fastball (Fig. 3-23), and its speed slower (about 15 mph slower). It is thrown with fastball arm speed. The curveball breaks down and out – in a direction opposite the pitcher's throwing arm.

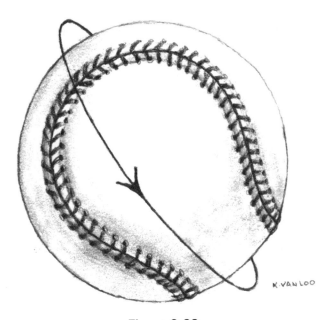

**Figure 3-23**
*Spin of a curveball as seen by the batter when thrown straight overhand or three-quarter arm by a right-handed pitcher.*

Figure 3-24 shows one kind of curveball grip. The index finger lies slightly off-center next to the middle finger. The middle finger is placed well off-center upon a **straight** seam at the edge of the ball. The thumb occupies the opposite pole of the ball. This offset grip will help set up the special curveball spin at the release point. My curveball grip is shown in Figure 3-25 and a left-hander's in 3-26.

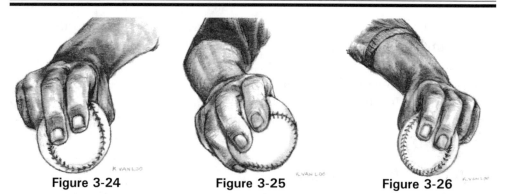

**Figure 3-24**          **Figure 3-25**          **Figure 3-26**

As the curveball passes the head (Fig. 3-27), the palm faces directly inward, (midway between pronation and supination). The offset middle finger pushes **downward** on its seam ready to start the spin which commences at the release point (Fig. 3-29).

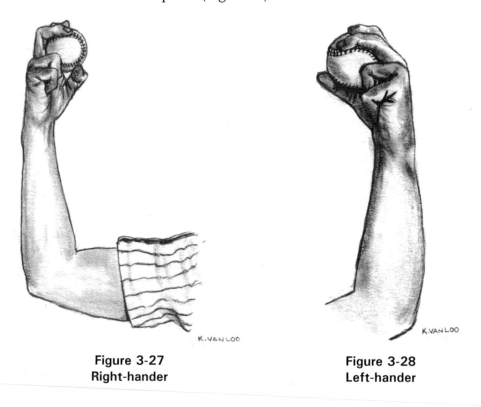

**Figure 3-27**
**Right-hander**

**Figure 3-28**
**Left-hander**

At the release point (Fig. 3-29) the palm continues to face inward. The hand-wrist-forearm-elbow have snapped into **firm** extension. This gives the appearance of a karate chop or handshake.

During deceleration the palm continues to face inward and slightly upward (Fig. 3-30) as it passes in front of the opposite knee.

Figure 3-29

Figure 3-30

## Velocity

The curveball travels with less velocity and more veer than a fastball for two reasons: ballistics and biomechanics.

Ballistics is the science that studies the motion of projectiles in flight. The en route velocity of a major-leaguer's curve ranges from 75 to 80 mph and it spins at 1,600 to 1,800 rpm (fastball – 1,200 rpm). The curveball arrives at the plate about 0.6 seconds after release (90 mph fastball – 0.4 seconds).

**Spin rpm** is determined by the biomechanical force (snap) imparted by the middle finger to its underlying seam at release. Hence, the importance of the grip. **The way a curve breaks** (down and out) is determined by the ball's rotation and position of hand-wrist-forearm at release. **Biomechanically, kinetic energy transferred to the curveball creates the rotation, adds to the spin and subtracts from velocity.** Arm speed remains identical to fastball arm speed.

The curveball also veers at differing rates with distance. For example, the curveball that breaks 17 inches, mound to plate, veers only about 4 inches at the halfway point. This means it veers 13 inches in the second half of its flight path. To pitcher and hitter alike, the ball appears to break near the plate.

The **amount of break** in a curveball depends on two other factors: **Flight time and spin**. The longer the flight time and higher the spin, the greater the break. Reason: The slower pitch has longer to act. Change spin or flight time and you change the break (cf. Adair: 13, 27-29).

### Coaching Pearl
A pitcher can change up off a curve!

## History

Candy Cummings probably threw the first curveballs around 1860, but he threw underhand! Most of the great pitchers had "good" curveballs. "Good" means the pitcher threw the pitch so it not only broke sharply, but arrived at spots chosen by the pitcher. The great pitchers knew how to vary flight time and spin to upset the hitter's timing. Master purveyors of the curveball who threw several different "benders," and who could change up off the curve were "Three-Fingered" Mordecai Brown (translated an anatomical deficiency into an astounding weapon), Hal Newhouser of the Detroit Tigers, Carl Erskine of the Brooklyn Dodgers, Sandy Koufax of the L.A. Dodgers and Satchel Paige.

# *The Slider*

A slider may provide the best (or worst?) of two worlds. A slider is often called a "nickel curve" because unlike a curveball, it breaks principally in a sideways direction without the "down-and-out" crispness seen in a well-thrown curve. If it were not for the hard slider, I would not have made it in baseball. During the 1940s and 1950s, I was one of the first pitchers to throw this pitch in the major leagues. To the hitters of that era this was a new pitch and caught them off guard because it looked like a fastball until it arrived near the plate and suddenly moved over. It is thrown with fastball arm speed. It travels at a higher velocity than a curveball, but slower than a fastball. In recent years the longest home runs have been hit off a slider. What does that tell you? It says that the pitcher supplied the energy with near fastball velocity and placed the ball poorly.

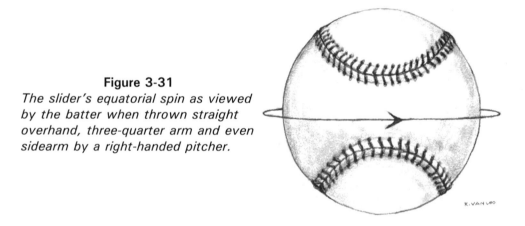

**Figure 3-31**
*The slider's equatorial spin as viewed by the batter when thrown straight overhand, three-quarter arm and even sidearm by a right-handed pitcher.*

One kind of slider grip is shown in Figure 3-32. This grip is nearly the same as that shown for a curveball, **except** the middle finger lies over a **loop** in the seam. The thumb lies on the opposite pole. A left-hander's grip is illustrated in Figure 3-33.

**Figure 3-32**                    **Figure 3-33**

89

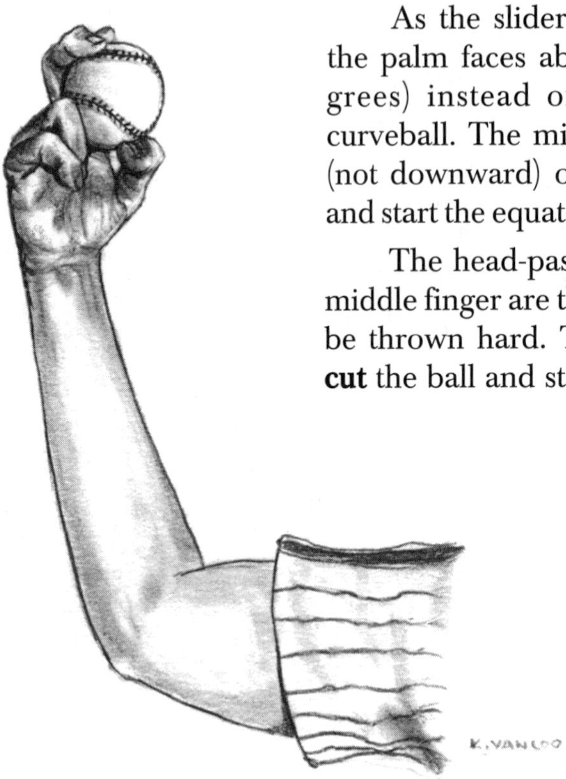

As the slider passes the head (Fig. 3-34) the palm faces about halfway inward (45 degrees) instead of directly inward like the curveball. The middle finger pushes **forward** (not downward) on its seam to "cut the ball" and start the equatorial spin at the release point.

The head-passing angle and action of the middle finger are the reasons why this pitch can be thrown hard. The angle and grip serve to **cut** the ball and start the equatorial spin.

**Figure 3-34**

Figure 3-35 shows my arm passing the head as I threw this pitch (hard slider) in my professional career. Notice that grip varies slightly from that in Figure 3-34. My index and middle fingers ride higher – toward the top of the ball.

**Figure 3-35**

At the release point (Fig. 3-36) the palm continues to face half inward (45 degrees). Recall that for the curveball the palm faces directly inward (Fig. 3-27) and with the fastball the palm is directly forward (Fig. 3-19). The hand-wrist-forearm-elbow have snapped into firm extension.

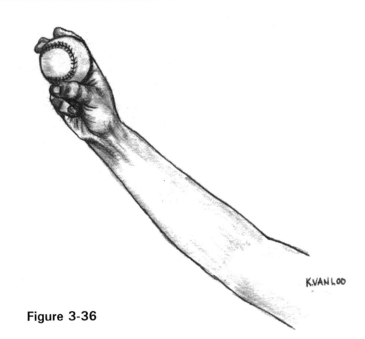

K.VANLOO

**Figure 3-36**

During deceleration the palm maintains its half inward turn.

Once mastered, the slider is an excellent pitch to upset a hitter's timing, given the appropriate game situation and pitch placement. The hitter "sitting on" a fastball or "moving up" on a curve is treated to this hybrid – much to his chagrin. The pitch moves over less than a curve and has less downward break than a curve, but its velocity – about 10 mph faster than a curve – compensates for its diminished movement.

## History

Cy Young called his slider a "nickel curve." He developed this pitch later in his career. However, this was not the slider we know today, but rather, just what old Cy called it – a curve – intended to break but a little. Mixed in with the rest of his arsenal, it was just another tool Cy used to tantalize hitters. Discovery of the slider thrown with near-fastball velocity is attributed by some to George Uhle when he played with Detroit around 1929. He referred to his new pitch as a "sailing fastball."

What happened to this pitch after Uhle's departure from baseball? Apparently it fell into disuse, because when I happened on the scene with the Giants in 1947 throwing a **hard slider**, National League hitters seemed surprised to see the pitch. Later pitchers like Steve Carlton (Hall of Fame, 1992) added something to this pitch which made it break with even greater and more devilish movement.

# *The Screwball*

This is an off-speed pitch that breaks in a direction opposite to the pitcher's curveball. When thrown by a right-hander, the screwball breaks to the pitcher's right and becomes an "inshoot" to a right-handed batter and an "outshoot" to a left-hander. Its spin is illustrated in Figure 3-37. It is thrown with fastball arm speed.

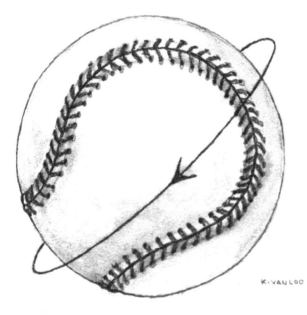

**Figure 3-37**
*The spin of a screwball as viewed by the hitter when thrown by a right-handed pitcher.*

One kind of screwball grip is seen in Figure 3-38. Unlike the curveball grip, it is the **index finger** that lies upon a straight seam at the ball's edge. The middle finger lies on the next seam and the thumb rests on the opposite pole.

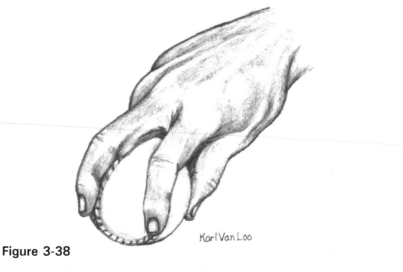

**Figure 3-38**

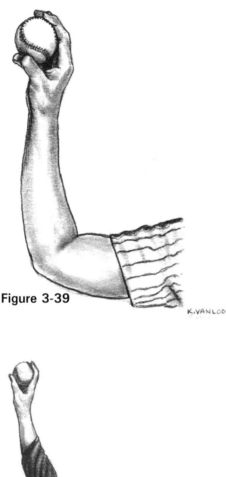

**Figure 3-39**

As the screwball passes the head (Fig. 3-39), the palm faces **outward** and wrist is straight. The elbow is at shoulder height. This relationship between elbow and shoulder induces considerable stress on the elbow during acceleration. Juan Marichal had the best screwball I ever saw; his technique is illustrated in Figures 3-40 and 41. Notice the extended elbow passing the head well above the shoulder! This maneuver dampens acceleration stresses on the elbow (consult Chapter 7, **Injuries**.)

**Figure 3-40**                **Figure 3-41**

The **index** finger pushes downward to initiate a spin at the release point (Fig. 3-42). At the release point the palm continues to face outward. The hand-wrist-forearm-elbow have snapped into a **firm** extension and **extreme** pronation. Notice that the thumb leads the way at the release point.

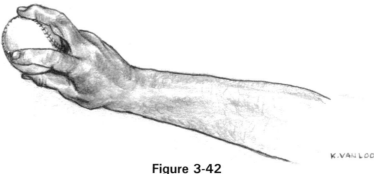

**Figure 3-42**

**Note:** During deceleration the palm will rotate to a palm down position, because this hand position is more natural. Maintaining a palm outward position after release is very uncomfortable.

# Velocity

The screwball travels no faster, and often slower than the curveball, but is thrown with fastball arm speed.

# History

The screwball is a difficult pitch to throw. Many pitchers never learn to throw it effectively. In addition to Marichal, there were, however, several grand masters of the screwball. These included Satchel Paige ("mystery pitch"), Christy Mathewson ("fade-away pitch") Carl Hubbel and Fernando Valenzuela. The screwball is a potent weapon because the hitter's logic leads him to believe that breaking pitches either hop, dive or veer in a direction opposite to the pitcher's throwing arm. The screwball veers toward the side of the pitcher's throwing arm.

Had I learned to throw this pitch correctly, I might have been around a lot longer. When I threw the screwball it bothered my elbow, because my elbow passed the head just above – instead of well above – the shoulder.

Christy Mathewson probably learned to throw this pitch from Rube Foster, an African-American who served unofficially as John McGraw's pitching coach. Mathewson apparently complained that the pitch bothered his arm, and he threw it only several times in a game, but this is hearsay.

Not given as hearsay was the fact that Carl Hubbel learned and refined the pitch as a minor-leaguer in the Detroit Tiger's farm system. Detroit is the point of origin of several pitch innovations: slider (Uhle, 1929), split-finger fastball (Roger Craig, 1984) and enhanced screwball (Hubbel, 1925). Hubbel added a wrist snap at the release point which left his hand fully pronated. At this **angle,** with the extra force applied by the index finger, Hubbel's screwball broke dramatically.

# The Split-Finger Fastball and the Forkball

Both these pitches are thrown with the same grip. Both spin like a fastball (backward, Fig. 3-10), but at less rpm. When well thrown, these pitches turn only two or three revolutions between mound and plate. Both are thrown with fastball arm speed; both pitches tend to dive near the plate. The difference is that the forkball is thrown with less force than the split-finger.

The grip for these pitches is shown in Figure 3-43. The index and middle fingers are spread and lie on the wide smooth areas at the east-west poles. The thumb rests on the south pole. Notice that a narrow smooth area between two curving seams leads the way. Some pitchers refer to this narrow area as a "fish-mouth." As these two seams revolve, they act like spoilers on an airplane wing, destroying the wing's lift, increasing drag and resistance to flight and dampening turbulence (**see The Bend (Veer) of the Breaking Ball** at the end of this chapter). When the spin and air speed slow below a critical number, the ball stalls and falls with gravity — "like a rock."

Though the forkball was around in 1940s and 1950s, I could not spread my fingers apart far enough to try this pitch. The split-finger fastball is a product of the 1980s.

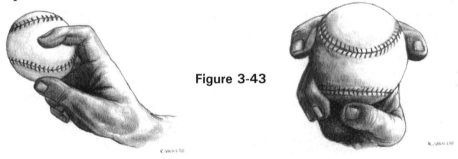

**Figure 3-43**

When the ball passes the head (Fig. 3-44), the palm faces forward (pronated), and at the release point (Fig. 3-45) it remains forward. At the release point the hand-wrist-forearm have snapped into full extension.

**These two pitches, when mastered, offer the pitcher the opportunity to change up using a "drop."** If only one is mastered, it still adds another breaking ball (down) to the arsenal.

With deceleration, the wrist flexes forward and the hand – palm down – passes in front of the opposite knee in the same manner as that shown in Figure 3-22.

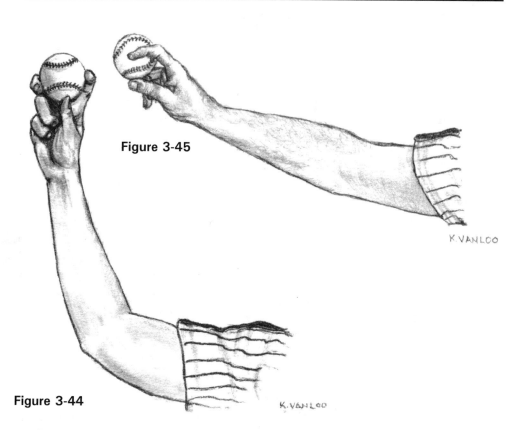

Figure 3-45

Figure 3-44

## Velocity

Both pitches travel at velocities slower than the fastball. The forkball is definitely an off-speed pitch; the split-finger is about 5-7 mph slower than the fastball (slider speed).

## History

**The Forkball** was first served up to major-league batters in 1942 by Ernie Bonham of the New York Yankees. That year, Bonham was 21-5. During the 1950s Roy Face rejuvenated the pitch. He attributed his mastery of the forkball to Joe Page (great Yankee reliever) when both pitchers played with New Orleans in the Southern League.

The forkball, and its progeny (split-fingered stuff), has a history that resembles the slider. Allegedly, the act of spreading the index and middle fingers until they lie along the sides of the ball has been around since at least 1908 when a pitcher with the Tacoma Tigers (Tigers again!) named Bert Hall started using it. It was a sensation on the West Coast for a brief time, then apparently exited the baseball world until recalled by Bonham. The pitch dropped out of sight again until Page and Face resuscitated it in 1955.

Roger Craig developed the **split-finger fastball** when he was pitching coach for the 1984 Detroit Tigers, the same year Detroit won the World Series.

The split-fingered offspring of the forkball became "the pitch of the 1980s" and early 1990s. Will it, too, submerge, only to surface later? Time will tell. Some of its outstanding practitioners include Jack Morris, Mike Scott, and lately, Hideo Nomo.

If we could all sit upon a high mountain peak and scan the history of baseball from its primitive origins until the present, I believe we would conclude that since the beginning of this century there have been no new pitches, just old ones returning with face-lift jobs.

## *Two Change-Ups*

**Conventional Wisdom: At all costs these pitches must be thrown at fastball arm speed: circle-change and the "stuffed ball" (sometimes referred to as a "palmball").** The circle change spins like a screwball (Fig. 3-37). The "palmball" spins very slowly, but like a fastball (Fig. 3-10). The circle-change breaks like a screwball, down and in. The grips for these pitches are shown in Figures 3-46 and 3-47.

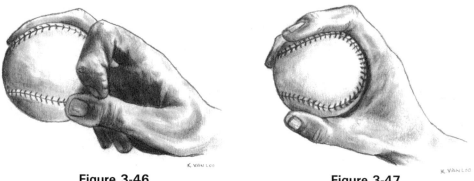

**Figure 3-46**          **Figure 3-47**

I used neither of these pitches. One way I threw my change was simply – at the last split second – to slow my arm speed. To throw a change in this manner required many hours of practice, because major-league hitters will quickly adjust to differences in arm speed. I changed up this way on both the fastball and curve. My technique seems to contradict the conventional wisdom spoken above. However, my slowed arm speed enabled me to impart a greater spin to both pitches.

My teammate, Sal Maglie, tried my method of change-up, but always gave it away. So, he put it away and depended on the palmball.

Pitchers who use the palmball and circle-change rely on grip to slow the ball. Those who use my technique are at risk of betraying their intent, but need not learn a new (at times difficult) technique. If you are a success with your present technique, continue. If you are failing, try the alternative. In any case, a pitcher without a change-up will probably not go far in baseball.

The grip for the circle-change is shown in Figure 3-46. Notice that the middle finger rides atop a straight seam and the index finger is curled down to touch the thumb which rests on the lower side. The grip for the "stuffer" is presented in Figure 3-47. The grip is like a cross seam, or along-the-seam, fastball, but the ball has been stuffed deep into the palm – hence the name "palmball."

### Coaching Pearl

Hold the palmball very loosely to facilitate its leaving the hand.

Figures 3-48 and 3-49 show the circle-change and stuffer passing the head. Note that with the circle-change the palm is turned outward (like the screwball) and forward for the palmball.

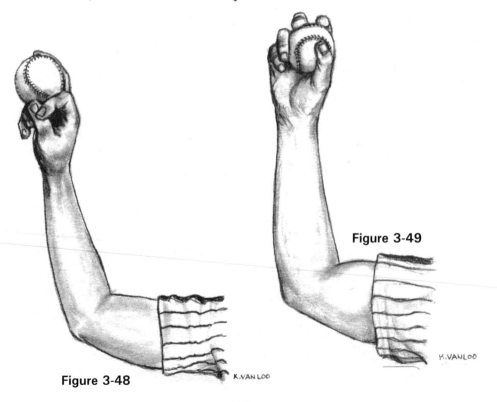

Figure 3-49

Figure 3-48

K.VAN LOO

K.VANLOO

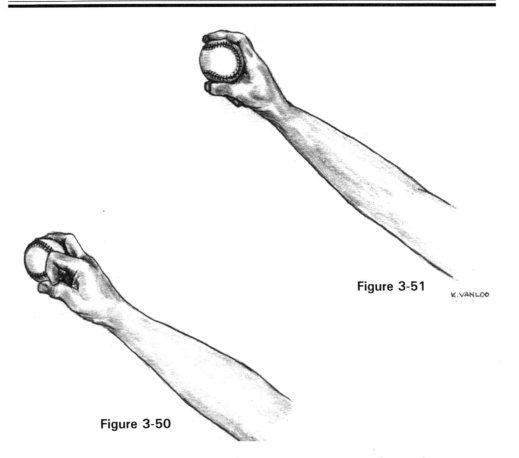

Figure 3-51

K. VANLOO

Figure 3-50

Figures 3-50 and 3-51 depict the two change-ups at their release points. Because the palm is turned outward, the "O" of the circle-change leads the way. The stuffer is released with the palm straight ahead. To release the palmball merely open the loosely held grip.

Not enough can be said about the importance of change-up pitches and techniques. Already discussed are changes off the fastball (four-seam versus two-seam), the curveball, the forkball, split-finger and now these. Call a professional baseball scout about a hot young prospect with a 90 mph fastball and off-the-table curve. His first question is (usually), "Does he have a change?"

Pitchers in high school, and occasionally in college, have gone the distance and won their games with only a fastball and change-up when nothing else was working. Needless to say, placement and control played a large part in their success.

In spite of its importance, the change-up frequently is given short shrift in the young player's curriculum. This is instructional disservice at best, negligence at worst.

# The Bend (Veer) of the Breaking Ball

What makes breaking balls bend (veer)? Answer: The pitcher's bio-mechanics and the laws of physics. Biomechanically, the pitcher's **grip** on the ball, and the **angle** of hand-wrist-forearm at the release point, begin the spin and start the flight path of the ball. From that point the laws of physics take over.

Examine the ball. The seams are asymmetrical and the stitches protrude above the surface. Important? Definitely, yes! The spinning motion allows the wind, created by the ball moving through air, to strike the protruding asymmetrical seams with more force on one side of the ball, and less force on the opposite side. Stated another way, **uneven drag and resistance** forces act on the ball and make it veer.

The curveball veers and descends in response to a spin opposite that of the fastball set up by the pitcher's grip and angle of hand-wrist-forearm at the release point. The fast backward spin on the cross-seam fastball allows the wind to support the ball in flight, or work against gravity – temporarily. With the split-finger fastball and forkball – which turn only three/four revolutions en route – the anti-gravity forces end abruptly when the **spin rpm and pitch velocity slow below a certain critical number.** At that point, the ball falls rapidly (dives).

What if there were no seams and stitches on the ball? Study a Ping-Pong ball – no seams or stitches. Regardless of how hit or thrown, the spin is low rpm and short-lived. Because of its reduced spin, this ball does not travel far, and as it slows, it flutters – like a knuckleball.

What would happen if a golf ball had no dimples? These dimples create a multitude of **symmetrical** seamlike elevations on the surface. It depends on how you look at it – dimples or elevations. These elevations cause the ball to spin. A golf ball without dimples flies only short distances, because it does not spin. The golf ball, like the fastball, spins backwards when thrown or hit (cf. Adair, 10).

Seams, stitches and dimples create **spin**. The pitcher determines the **kind of spin** (or lack of spin) on a baseball with his grip and hand-wrist-forearm angle at release. These factors play upon the seam/stitch asymmetry. The golf ball spin cannot be predetermined unless the dimples are impressed asymmetrically, and that has been done to correct hooks and slices!

The dimples and stitches also cause **turbulence** around the ball in flight. Turbulence works against air resistance (like a miniature propeller).

The greater the turbulence, the faster and farther the ball flies when propelled by a force (throw or hit). The stitches and smooth areas on the ball create uneven turbulence. Consequently, one side of the ball will tend to "fly faster" than the opposite side. This event contributes to veer.

In a nutshell, the asymmetrical baseball seams and stitches induce uneven wind resistance, drag and turbulence, causing the ball to veer. Wind resistance and drag also slow the ball (about 8 mph in 60 feet). Gravity forces the ball toward the ground.

Finally, spins are a mixed blessing to the pitcher, because when a hitter strikes the ball, he induces a backward spin. This spin greatly increases the distance that the ball flies — good for the golfer, bad for the pitcher.

The grips and hand-wrist-forearm angles discussed are merely starting points. **Every pitcher will have his own way of gripping the ball.** This all depends on hand size, comfort, experience and relationship of arm to trunk at release point (straight overhand, sidearm, etc.). **Man is not a robotic machine, and so much depends on the unique anatomy and physiology that each pitcher brings to the game.**

## *The Illegal Pitches*

**All these pitches require a change be made to the ball surface.** Either a foreign substance is added to the surface or the smooth surface between the seams is defaced. After just a casual review of this chapter, one does not have to be a Rhodes scholar to conjure up a host of ways to change the ball surface for the purpose of affecting the spin. These devices, like the pitches themselves, have been around for more than a century. Their names are memorialized in baseball language: "spitball," "greaseball," "mudball," "emeryball," "cutball," "shineball."

One has to be ambivalent about their presence in baseball: (1) the ingenuity enlisted to create the surface changes is a wonderment, versus (2) the intent to cheat. This is a difficult subject to discuss without appearing either sanctimonious or cynical.

"Let he who has not sinned throw the first stone."

For now, as long as these pitches remain illegal, it is best that coaches not pass them on to their young ballplayers to use. However, coaches and ballplayers should obviously learn how these pitches are thrown.

The **spitball** has been outlawed since 1921 (see Chapter 4, **The Rule Book**). With good reason has this pitch been banned. **It is hard to control**, and the chances for injury are greatly increased. The spitball depends on two factors to achieve its crazed flight: (1) reduced spin – it may turn only one or two revolutions en route to the plate; (2) it is hurled with fastball velocity. The result: a fluttering fastball! The pitcher who throws this pitch simply wets a small smooth area on the top of the ball. He grips the ball over the wet spot with his index and middle fingers and places his thumb firmly against the bottom of the ball. When the ball is released it squirts out of the hand like a wet sunflower seed. The **greaseball** is handled similarly.

The **mudball** requires that the pitcher add wet dirt to one side of the ball to create increased resistance on that surface. The **cutball** and **emeryball** are spheres whose cowhide surface has been subtly cut, gouged or roughened to alter air resistance. The **shineball** is a real piece of work! The pitcher in this case rubs one side of the ball against his uniform to polish or "shine" the ball. He thereby reduces the air resistance on that side, and by default, increases the resistance on the opposite side.

On that note, we proceed to address the Rule Book (Chapter 4).

# 4

# The Rule Book

## In a Nutshell

> *"The only certainties in life are death, taxes and rule changes unfavorable to pitchers."*
>
> ***Authors***

Cynics have been heard to state that "those who control the bottom line, write the rules." That is to say that, if the public wants to see more home runs: "juice" the ball, diminish the strike zone, hobble the pitcher. I am not a cynic. **Baseball, the American game, is really good to all that feed at its trough. Some are just better feeders than others.**

Since the dawn of written history, purposeful human activity has been guided by rules, regulations and statutes. Baseball is a purposeful activity – to provide amusement, entertainment and/or wealth. Socrates (an early baseball "color commentator," c. 350 B.C.) stated that all rules must possess at least five qualities:

1. Single sovereignty – the rules originate in a single source. The single source of Major League Baseball (MLB) rules is the Official Playing Rules Committee.

2. Universality – all persons have **basic** characteristics in common. Baseball players are competitive and want to win – at times, regardless of the cost.

3. Equity – fairness and balance. Baseball rules strive for a balance between offense and defense. The Committee is comprised of thoughtful, knowledgeable men who continuously search for a "sense of balance" in the game.

4. Codification – rules enumerated in a logical system. The *Official Baseball Rules* published by the Committee are the enumerated controlling code for MLB. The quoted rules are from this text (R. 7).

5. Circumstances alter cases and occasionally call for revision of existing rules. A landmark revision came after Ray Chapman, considered by many the best shortstop of his time, was struck in the head with a wet, muddy ball in 1920. The injury resulted in the only death attributed **directly** to a game in the major leagues. Chapman's death precipitated a rule change that called for immediate removal of discolored or "unfit" balls. (3.01(e)(2).

**Caution:** The rules discussed here are those in effect during the 1996 MLB season as promulgated by the Rules Committee. The rules are changed from time to time, and the reader is advised to consult the most current rules. Furthermore, each level of play has its own variations (however slight), and I do not attempt to separate high school, college and other amateur rules for discussion. Were I to comment on each rule as it changes, this book would require periodic updates. **My intent is to discuss the concepts generally held to underlie baseball rules over the last 150 years (1846-1996).** These concepts are firmly welded to the game and will likely undergo no substantive change. An understanding of the underlying concept invariably leads to an appreciation of the rule. Not every rule pertinent to pitchers is discussed – just those most often violated.

## Cartwright Rules

Alexander Cartwright is acknowledged as the first baseball lawgiver. In 1845 Alexander gathered, gleaned and codified what he considered the best rules of games played with sticks and balls. The first game played under the **Cartwright Rules** occurred on June 19, 1846, when Cartwright's team, the New York Knickerbockers, was defeated 23-1 in four innings by the New York Nine.

Four innings! What happened? Did darkness, disgust or despair set in? None of these. Cartwright's rules stated that the first team to score 21 runs (he called them "aces") was the winner. This rule persisted until 1857. Cartwright is not the first lawgiver nailed to the gibbet of his own rules.

## The Cartwright Legatees

The legacy of the Cartwright Code has endured considerable change and atrophy as circumstances altered cases. However, if today we walked on a Cartwright diamond we would find that then, as now, the distance between each base is 90 feet. The most galling change is the location of the "pitching station." Prior to 1881 the pitcher delivered the ball from a rectangular box after a running start which ended 45 feet from home plate. Pitchers ruled the game and the rule maker's sense of equity was offended. Fans wanted to witness well-balanced contests between offense and defense. Relying on the tenet of equity, the rule makers ordered the box back five feet in 1881. The running start was snuffed out in 1887.

Not equitable enough, the reasoning went in 1892. Pitchers were still overly dominant. Crank them back to 60 feet, 6 inches (pitcher's plate to the **back** of home plate) effective at season start in 1893. To assure maintenance of this distance, a plate was ordered **secured** to the ground and a new dictum decreed: The pitcher may take only one step back and one step forward before releasing the ball.

Pitchers are by nature thoughtful and adaptable. They saw to it that the plate would become more than a surveyor's stake or landscape ornament. Rule 1.07 directs that "...the plate shall be a ... slab of whitened rubber, 24 by 6 inches (one inch thick – authors) ...set in the ground...." **The pitcher adapted this dictum to his liking by using the plate as an immovable slab against which he pushes to propel his pitches.**

105

Not content to rest with the lemonade squeezed from the rinds of the "plate rule," pitchers busied themselves preparing arguments against other lingering inequities in the rules. Fair-minded men that they are, the pitchers pointed out that within a decade (1881 to 1892) they had been struck with two outrageous rules – without compromise: the "distance" and "one-step" rules. Compromise came in the form of altitude: The rule makers permitted the pitcher's station to rest (1893) atop a "mound." The height of this dirt heap was not prescribed until 1903 when its summit was **limited** to 15 inches (lowered to 10 inches in 1969 when the 1968 batting averages plummeted). The rule makers also declared in 1893 that bats flat on one side were no longer legal – another token of compromise. The lawgivers and pitchers had restored balance to the game.

# The Balk Rules

Baseball's "offense constituency" continued unabashed to nibble at pitching dominance after 1893. The offensive delegations had already gained a head start on the **balk** rules during Cartwright's era when pitchers had to deliver the ball underhand without a wrist snap. Pitches not thrown in this manner, with runners on base, drew a balk.

The balk rules find their roots in the concept that the pitcher must not **deceive** the runner in an effort to keep him close to his base – this after we clearly stated that it is the pitcher's explicit duty to deceive! The rule makers intended that only "legal" deceptions be permitted.

In 1950, the rules first unequivocally stated that following his stretch, the pitcher must come to a complete stop (one second) before throwing the ball. (8.01(b)). The concept prevents holding the runner close to his base with a surprise quick throw to the batter.

Are there other "illegal" deceptions with runners on base proscribed by the rules? There are six that the pitcher must heed.

1. When a pitcher in the set position throws to a base occupied by a runner, he "...shall **step ahead of the throw.** A snap throw **followed by** a step toward the base is a **balk** (8.01(c))." A step toward an occupied base immediately warns the runner that a throw is on the way. However, the "warning" may be delivered with lightning speed. That is what picking a runner off is all about.

2. As a corollary to (1), it is also a **balk** if "...the pitcher, while touching his plate, **feints a throw to first base and fails to complete the throw. (8.05(b))"**

3. A second corollary to (1) states that "...if a pitcher turns or spins off of his free foot (aiming foot, not the foot touching the rubber) without actually **stepping** (toward the base), or if he turns his body and throws before **stepping**, it is a **balk**." (8.05(c)). The concept is that the runner needs to be given notice, however brief, of incoming artillery.

4. The third corollary to (1) decrees that a pitcher "...**step** directly toward a base before throwing to that base, but does not require him to throw (except to first base only) because he steps." (8.05(c)) The concept here is that the pitcher may "fake" a throw to any base, except first base.

    **Note:** (1) through (4) are commonly referred to as the "stepping rules." The **failure to step** is the governing principle in declaring a violation.

5. Deceitful acts are condemned in the edict under 8.05(c): "...if, with runners on first and third, the pitcher while in contact with the rubber steps toward third, and then immediately...**in**...**the same motion** wheels and throws to first base, it is obviously an attempt to **deceive** (forgive us!) the runner at first base... (because) it is practically impossible to **step** directly toward first base before the throw.. such a move shall be called a **balk**. Of course, if the pitcher steps off the rubber and then makes such a move, it is not a balk." Why? Because when the pitcher steps off the rubber he becomes an "infielder" and can throw as he chooses.

6. Straddling the rubber without the ball and runner(s) on base "...is to be interpreted as intent to deceive and ruled a **balk**." (8.05(n)).

    **I did not balk often – just once in 20 years.**

# Illegal Pitches

    It is the 1990s: the epoch of fast foods, drive through-banking and urgent medical care. Why not an allowance for **quick pitches**? A quick pitch is one delivered before the batter is **"reasonably set"** in the batter's box. This is an umpire judgment call. The quick pitch is an illegal pitch, and, with runners on base, it is a balk; with no runners on, it is a ball. The reason for this rule: "The quick pitch is dangerous." (8.05(e)). The danger pertains to the hitter who, until he is "reasonably set," is preoccupied with adjusting his stance and is not directing his attention toward the ball.

## Other Illegal Pitches

    There are six of these demonic deliverances! (8.05(f) through (m))

1. "The pitcher delivers the ball to the batter while he is not facing the batter." (8.05(f)) A good trick, if you can do it – like a basketball hook shot.

2. "The pitcher makes any motion naturally associated with his pitch while not touching the pitcher's plate." (8.05(g)).

3. "Without having the ball, the pitcher stands on or astride his plate, or off the plate, and feints a pitch." (8.05(I)).

4. "The pitcher, after coming to a legal pitching position, removes one hand from the ball other than in an actual pitch, or in throwing to a base." (8.05(j)).

5. "The pitcher, while touching the plate, accidentally or intentionally drops the ball" **(with runner(s) on, this is a balk)**. (8.05(k)).

6. "The pitcher, while giving an intentional base on balls, pitches when the catcher is not in the catcher's box." (8.05(l)).

A short vignette (baseball story). Walter Johnson is said to have thrown so hard that numerous deposed hitters stated, "you can't hit what you can't see." His fastball was likened to a hissing watermelon seed as it darted by the hitter and exploded in the catcher's mitt. One day in Washington with two outs and his team well ahead in the top of the ninth, darkness began to set in (no night games in 1916). The hitter annoyed Johnson by fouling off everything he threw. Frustrated, Johnson slipped the ball into his back pocket, wound up and pretended to throw a pitch. His catcher simulated the hissing sound that Johnson's pitches were known to make and punched his mitt mightily. In the dim light of Washington's stadium, the hitter turned to the umpire for a call. Umpire: "It sounded like a strike. Yer out!" Illegal pitch? See (3) above.

## The Pitcher's Mouth

Unseemly utterances and wrongfully placed saliva can win a quick trip to the showers. When an argument arises between pitcher and umpire, there are certain words that the pitcher must not utter lest he be ejected. Common sense and respect for officials demand that certain words and actions be withheld. What words win early soap and water? Words you would not say to your mother.

There is another oral violation that "slips many a pitcher's mind" as he concentrates on his game. The pitcher shall not "...bring his pitching hand in contact with his mouth or lips while in the 18-foot circle surrounding the rubber." (8.02(a)(1)). Penalty for violation: "...Umpires shall immediately call a ball...." (a baseball misdemeanor). There is an exception! Happened in the early spring of 1996: "...provided it is agreed by both managers, the umpire, **prior to the start of a game played in cold weather,** may permit the pitcher to blow on his hand."

Baseball felony is to "expectorate" on the ball, **either** hand or the glove. Penalties: (1) Umpire shall call the pitch a ball; (2) warn the pitcher; (3) announce on the public address system the reason for the action (holy cow!); in the case of a second violation in the game, the umpire shall toss the pitcher out of the game (holy, holy cow!). 8.02(a) (2).

Why all this nervousness about expectoration! The "spitball" is a dangerous pitch even in the hands of the most expert purveyor. Second, it is considered a form of cheating because, through artificial means, the ball is given added movement in its flight to the plate (see Chapter 3, **Movement**). With this in mind the rule makers have long since decreed that the pitcher "...shall not apply a foreign substance of any kind to the ball... rub the ball on his glove, person or clothing (bet you didn't know this rule!) ... (or) deface the ball in any manner... (or) deliver what is called the "shineball," "spitball," "mudball" or "emeryball." (8.02(a)(2)(3)(4)(5)(6)). Knicks, scuffs, mud and cuts on the ball induce added movement during flight (see Chapter 3, **Movement**).

Pretty clear, isn't it? The penalties here are those enumerated above in the discussion of expectoration on the ball. Many famous cheats have flaunted these rules in an effort to retain their jobs. Well, baseball is a good job with (reasonable?) pay and sufficient stress to keep your mind and body nimble. But consider this: If you cheat, but your peers don't, what does that make you?

What **can** you put on your hands, or on the ball, except the sweaty palm of your hand? Answer: "...umpires shall carry with them one official rosin bag (don't ask me what constitutes **official** rosin) ...a pitcher may... (apply) rosin to his bare hand or hands... neither the pitcher, nor any other player shall **dust** the ball with the rosin bag... neither... the pitcher, nor any other player ...(shall) apply rosin from the bag **to his glove** or dust any part of his uniform..." 8.02(a) (7).

Rosin enables a pitcher to obtain a better grip on the ball especially for breaking pitches. **Caution:** Every time you plan a breaking pitch, don't pick up the bag! The hitters will know what is coming or, (see Liar's Dice in Chapter 5, **Tactics**) you can pick up the bag, then throw your fastball! **Common sense:** Rosin dust is not a benign substance. Splash it in the eyes: big-time irritation! Rosins are obtained by chemical means from oleoresin in the dead wood of pine trees. Not something you sprinkle on your breakfast cereal. If a pitcher dusts the ball with this stuff, and the ball is spinning (most balls do) what might happen as the ball approaches the hitter?

Now, even more serious stuff. "The pitcher shall not intentionally pitch (sic) at the batter..." 8.02(d) What is meant here is that you may not intentionally (in the umpire's judgment) **throw** to hit a batter. Pitching inside is a skill that must be mastered to survive as a professional pitcher (see Chapter 5, **Tactics**). However, it is an outrageous act to throw at a batter with an intent to hit him for two reasons: (1) you may seriously injure him: A heinous act; (2) you put a runner on base with status equal to that of a walk or a hit. Dumb!

It takes years to train an umpire to gain the skill and judgment needed in professional baseball. You might think you can fool these fellows by pleading **lack of intent** when you strike a batter. Forget it. The umpire's decision is final, irrevocable and without appeal. The court of appeals (league president, commissioner, etc.) will invariably back the umpire, and to make sure that you don't forget their censure, this same court may levy substantial fees, fines, penalties and interest.

**It is egregious (fancy word meaning "criminally bad") behavior to throw the ball at a non-player (a fan)!**

There are a few rules a pitcher should know because he is a pitcher.

1. At the start of an inning, or when appearing in relief, the pitcher "...shall be permitted to (throw) ...eight preparatory pitches **to his catcher**, during which play shall be suspended." (8.03). Why eight? Why not six or 10? Answer: Baseball tradition carved in stone.

2. "When the bases are unoccupied, the pitcher shall deliver the ball to the batter within 20 seconds **after he receives the ball**." (8.04) Actually, 20 seconds is a fair amount of time. Check it out next time you throw, because umpires do not (as a rule) carry stop-watches. Reasonable umpires officiating at amateur games often allow more than eight preparatory warm-up pitches, because the reliever often enters "cold" – with little or no warm-ups. Injuries occur when too little warm-up occurs (see Chapter 1, **Preparation** and Chapter 7, **Injuries**).

3. The sweatshirt worn under the uniform shirt must have sleeves that are not white, and not torn (or ragged) and not multicolored. 1.11 (a) (1) though (d). Concept: A white-sleeved or ragged, striped or multicolor sweatshirt distracts the hitter and unfairly delays the hitter's picking up the flight of the ball (rule of equity).

## Umpires

We could talk for hours (even days) about the rules of baseball. This is why one must have the highest respect for umpires at all levels. It is their duty to know, interpret and enforce the rules. They must possess judgment and common sense. These men are the unsung heroes of the game. Without their presence, chaos would reign. However, remember this: Even though umpires are "...dispassionate dispensers of pure justice, icy islands of emotionless calculation..." (George F. Will), they are, after all, only human. They will not change their decision just because you ask them to change. So why argue? When you argue you lose your concentration, maybe your game. And do not "show them up" with gestures, head shakes or other negative body language. "What goes around comes around." When you need a strike and the call is close... Well, I don't have to draw you a picture.

## *The Strike Zone*

An old song about aviators goes something like this:

> *"Those daring young men in their flying machines,*
>
> *they go up - idy up, up, up*
>
> *and they go*
>
> *down-idy, down, down, down..."*

The song could just as well have been written about the major-league **strike zone**.

1887 rule: Top of shoulders to **bottom** of knees – up, up-idy

1950 rule: Armpits to **top** of knees – down, down-idy

1963 rule: Back to the 1887 rule – up, up-idy

1968 rule: Back to the 1950 rule – down, down-idy

It is understandable why pitchers lament over the century past (1893 - present), and the pitching rules that have evolved. As my colleague has so aptly put it:

> *"The only certainties in life are death, taxes and rule*
> *changes unfavorable to pitchers."*

> *Al Jansen*

# 5

# Tactics

## In a Nutshell

1. Hitting is timing; upset the timing
2. Concentrate — first pitch, first strike
3. Exploit the hitter's greed; keep the ball down
4. Entice opposition to show its hand
5. Pitch selection depends on hitter and situation
6. Entire defense must read from same page
7. Be observant, analytical and logical
8. Know the hitter's history
9. Manage the base runner
10. Bunt and steal defenses

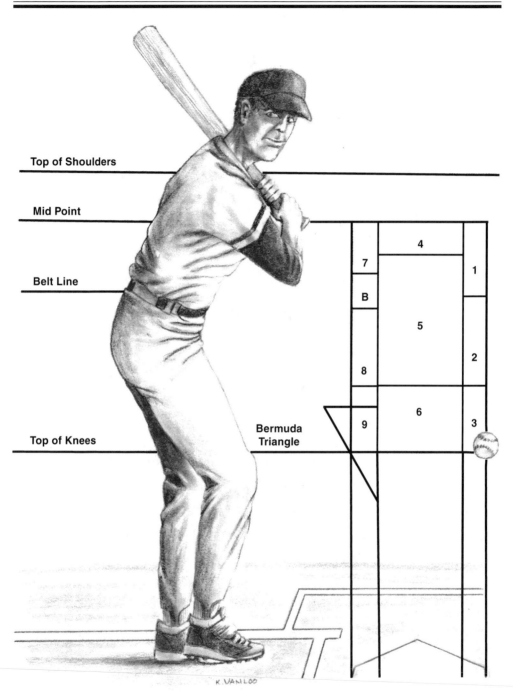

Top of Shoulders

Mid Point

Belt Line

Top of Knees

Bermuda
Triangle

4

7

1

B

5

2

8

6

9

3

K. VANLOO

**Figure 5-1**

*This figure shows the stance and position in the box of the second hitter. The ball is shown cutting the outer edge of spot three. If the hitter fails to act on this pitch, it is a called strike. See added note, Figure 3-1.*

The pitcher who employs correct mechanics and skillfully places his pitches will discover great joy using these talents to execute his pitching tactics. No two situations in a game are identical; nor does the same hitter present an identical problem to the pitcher with each at bat. However, baseball does lend itself to the creation of certain general tactical principles. These principles are not absolutes, and the experienced pitcher learns to adapt these principles as flexible guidelines. In this chapter, I present several **hitter-base runner situation problems** and discuss the options open to the pitcher. The purpose is to teach baseball logic. Baseball is a thinking person's game. Put on the head and hide of the pitcher and study these tactical problems.

The scenarios presented are common baseball problems for which there are a large number of solutions. In baseball, as in life, there are no absolutes. The solutions are presented in two contexts: professional (PB) and scholastic (SB) levels of play.

**The Hitter**: A left-hander has just stepped into the box (see Figure 5-1). He is the second hitter up this inning. Notice that this hitter shows a closed stance: right foot much closer to the plate than left foot. Observe also that this hitter's left foot nearly touches the back line of the batter's box. Finally the right heel is elevated, and the toes of that foot lightly touch the ground. Attention to every detail in the batter's stance (in the context of the game situation – see below) is the pitcher's and catcher's first task before selecting the spot, speed and movement of the pitch.

Given these facts about the hitter's stance, the pitcher can come to the following tentative conclusions: 1) the hitter expects a fastball; hence his position in the back of the box. This is a reasonable expectation given the situation described below. 2) The hitter has taken territorial control over the middle and outer portions of the plate with his closed stance. 3) He is not prepared to bunt, otherwise he would likely position himself toward the front of the box to assure that when he "drops the bunt" it lands in fair territory, and also to gain a step or two in his run to first base. This is particularly true for a right-handed hitter who wants to "bunt for a hit," because a right-handed batter needs to run an extra step or two to reach first base as compared to a left-hander – due to the geometry of batter's box and baselines.

The pitcher must be cunning! Perhaps this is all a deceptive charade. So much depends on the hitter's talent and tendencies. Perhaps this hitter can bunt from the back of the box. Babe Ruth habitually placed himself in the rear of the box, only to take two steps forward to greet a slower

115

breaking pitch. The Babe stayed put to pulverize a fastball. But Ruth was often able to predict the pitch from the pitcher's movements and ball grip before release, and he could see the spin on the ball as it left the pitcher's hand.

There is even more information to process. Mind you, this all takes place in seconds (see my comments on working fast in Chapter 3). Observe the hitter's practice swings, his facial expression, his body language. Consider the situation: How many outs? Runners on base? The score? Type hitter – power broker or a hacker? How fast afoot is this batter? What are the tendencies of the opposing manager in this situation (see below)?

If you have played this team before, many of these questions are answerable; contingency plans were (hopefully) discussed before the game (see Chapter 6, **Strategy**). If the situation is novel, you must rely on your instincts, intuition and – most of all – your intelligence.

It is important to realize that you choose placement of the first pitch in three contexts: 1) the hitter, 2) the situation, 3) the follow-on pitches. Planning ahead imparts a chesslike quality to baseball. Recall Spahn's words, "hitting is timing, and the pitcher's job is to upset that timing," – with an array of pitches featuring different speeds, movement and placement.

**The Situation**: Except where noted, the analysis and logic are PB/SB pertinent. Late in the season – first game of a doubleheader – bottom of the eighth inning – score 2 to 1, your favor. There are no outs and the first hitter reached first on an error. You are a right-handed pitcher whose control today is excellent; you have been hitting your spots. The pitch total is 97 which includes four hits and one walk. A rising fastball, smooth change-up and sharp slider are today's bill of fare. Your curve is not "falling off the table" as cleanly as you would like. The forkball (sinker) has been episodic. None of the last 16 hitters has gotten the ball out of the infield. Today you have been "in charge," but so also has the opponents' pitcher. The wind is calm after a thunderstorm the night before. The grass is damp. The field is located at more than 5,000 feet.

The left-handed hitter facing you hit a rocket line drive to the first baseman in his last at bat. He likes to pull "up-and-in" pitches, and you fed him a slider that arrived up and in. Your intent was a "brushback" unhittable pitch to move him off the plate (he showed a closed stance and crowded the plate just as he is doing now). However, you missed – a mistake! The hitter extended that lightly planted right foot not toward the plate, but straight at you as he "turned on the slider" and pulled the pitch into the first baseman's grasp. The "book" (PB: *Elias Analyst*; SB: *Advance Scouts*) on this individual shows that he is an excellent contact line-drive hitter and a skillful bunter. **Like most closed-stance hitters, he is vulnerable down and in.** He has hit only six home runs all season. Your dugout is quiet. The manager scans the opponents' roster with its yet unused pinch hitters as he prepares himself for a desperate thrust by that team in these late innings. Your pitching coach, arms folded, inflates a bubble gum sphere. Perturbation is absent. No one is up in the bullpen.

The opposing manager has several options. The runner on first is the leadoff hitter in the batting order and quick on the base paths – 22 steals in 24 attempts. Since the hitter is both a skillful bunter and contact hitter, a steal, sacrifice or hit-and-run are on the menu. How will you pitch this batter?

Because the hitter is left-handed, the catcher's view of the runner on first is partially obscured, especially when the catcher handles inside pitches. **THE FIRST PITCH MUST BE A STRIKE.** But where? With what velocity and movement? **Pitching is not a profession for the slow-witted.** Concentration is an imperative. You need to hold the runner close to give your catcher that extra fraction of a second on a throw to second, **but do not allow the runner to distract you.** His worst harm comes with a steal. It is the hitter who can really hurt you. Allow the first baseman and catcher to watch the runner for you. These teammates know that you have to concentrate on the hitter, and they will alert you if the runner leans, breaks or fakes.

The hitter and his manager also know the first pitch will be a strike, thrown hard with a quick kick or "slide step" to reduce flight time to the plate. But where? A diagnostic maneuver here may help before pitch and placement selection. After you "come set," step back abruptly with your right foot and break contact with the pitcher's plate. Snap a look at first while catching a glimpse of the hitter out of the corner (peripheral vision) of the right eye. You just might catch the runner "leaning," or the hitter starting to "square" for a bunt.

So you do just that. "All's quiet on the Western Front." Runner isn't leaning; batter not squaring. The bunt may still be on, but hitter and runner are clever at baseball poker. Your manager makes a decision. He has seen something, or maybe he is acting on intuition. He brings your third baseman in on the grass to field a bunt. Your catcher calls for a low, away fastball – a strike in the 3-spot. That pitch placement will prevent the hitter from putting the ball in the hole between first and second (hopefully). The velocity from your four-seam fastball will result in a hard bunt that travels to an infielder (including yourself) faster, cleaner and assures – at least – a putout at first.

Another alternative is to "waste" a pitch – too wide to bunt or pull – definitely not a strike. Reason: While runner and hitter did not tip off the plan when you stepped back off the rubber, maybe a waste pitch will draw them out. You decide not to waste a pitch.

A glance at the runner, followed by a "lock on" the catcher's mitt with your visual radar, a quick kick, and the pitch is on the way. Batter executes a "pivot bunt" (does not square) and drops the ball down the third-base line. It's a hard bunt, but has lots of backspin. The third baseman is on it, "like a wolf on a meatball." Then inexplicably, the third baseman, ball in hand, slips on grass still moist from a rainfall the night before, cannot "find the handle" and has to "eat the ball." Runners safe on first and second; no one out.

**This situation could get serious!** The next hitter up is a burly right-hander, the first of three power hitters. Although he can crush the ball, he is slow afoot. His teammates refer to him as "the three-toed sloth." He will be followed by the cleanup hitter, and by the fifth member of the batting order. All of this trio are among the league leaders in slugging average and runs batted in. **Your team captain is at shortstop, and now calls timeout.** The umpire acknowledges the timeout. Pitcher, catcher and infielders confer. Still no one is up in the bullpen.

**The conference**: You, the catcher, pitching coach, infielders, outfielders and manager had gone over all the hitters before the game, as well as situations like this. "The book" on this hitter states he "pulls" most pitches. He peppers the third-base foul line with rocket drives (many of these are hits) on pitches down and in. Throw pitches up and in anywhere around the 5-spot and it's airliner time. However, he is an impatient hitter with a conventional stance* and will lunge at soft stuff down and out, up and out. The *Elias Analyst* (PB) shows that 20 percent of these lunges end up a weak hit to short-right field or right-center (a .200 hitter when he lunges). Pitch him hard stuff, low and away: He hits it sharply on the ground between first and second; occasionally he launches a drive through the box. He likes to swing at first pitches. When he **lunges** at hard stuff low and away on the first pitch, his batting average drops to .142. He is also greedy, and has announced his intent to win the "RBI crown." He now has an opportunity to "bring a runner around" to score.

Way to get him out: Make him lunge at hard stuff low and away to produce a ground ball on the right side for a double play. He is not a skillful bunter, but he has surprised the defense twice this season with sacrifice bunts in similar situations. The **advance scouts** have confirmed all this information. High school and college teams often do not have "book" or "analyst" materials at their disposal, and must necessarily rely on advance scouts to provide timely, accurate information.

**This Hitter – This Game:** First time up he rifled a line drive straight to the third baseman "on the line." That pitch was a mistake, down and in (3-spot) – a four-seam fastball that got away. You wanted that pitch to be down and away. Second at bat you threw a hard slider on the first pitch "in tight" (2-spot). You had planned a sequence of pitches to "set him up" for hard stuff low and away. The first pitch was supposed to be a ball well **inside** to move him back off the plate and give you the outside corner. Instead, that pitch caught the inside corner of the plate at the belt line. He turned on it and pulled it down the line. This sent the left fielder chasing ricochets around the inside of the left-field corner. By the time the fielder had surrounded the elusive sphere, this burly guy was standing on third base, breathless. As the "book" states, he is not exactly a thunderbolt on the base paths. He trundled in to score minutes later on a sacrifice fly by the cleanup hitter. So far, that is the only run scored against you. Last time up, you took over the outside corner and fanned him on five pitches with a mix of hard and soft stuff away. However, this is a smart hitter; he learns fast.

**What does this leave you?** (The conference begins).

"How're you goin' to pitch this hitter, Larry?" The shortstop captain asks.

"Hard stuff, low and away, Al. I want him to lunge to take away his power. We need to have him put something on the ground to the right side."

"He's ready to kill anything inside," Wes, the catcher adds. "We want no mistakes inside, Larry."

"OK. Let's hope the book's right and he lunges," Hank, the third baseman observes. "That'll give the right side of the infield something to handle for a double play."

---

*Conventional Stance: both feet equal distance from inside boundary of batter's box. **Open Stance:** front foot farther from inside boundary than back foot. **Closed Stance:** reverse of open stance.*

You comment: "Whitey (first baseman), in on the grass to handle a sacrifice bunt. If he doesn't bunt and lunges at hard stuff low and away it's coming to the right side. Be ready, Eddy (second baseman)."

"Yeah, and I'll hold the runner close at second," Eddy adds. "That'll increase our chance to get a force at third on a bunt to you, Larry, or to start a double play on a hard grounder. I'll break toward the hole (between first and second) with the pitch so I don't give it (the pitch) away."

"The way we're goin' to pitch 'im, the worst case scenarios are a solo force at second, or a hit on the ground between first and second," Wes comments. "Eddy, be sure you break early enough."

"All right, let's break it up men," the umpire wheezes. "Leave the board meetings for the owners," he scowls.

"Protect the line, just in case, Hank (third baseman). I'll close the hole between third and short," Al (shortstop captain) directs as the meeting disbands.

**So, what is the point of all the dialogue?** Have baseball coaches become playwrights? No! This trite imaginary scene illustrates several important concepts that deserve emphasis.

# Points Learned From the Dialogue (PB and SB)

1. The pitcher is in charge. He tells the captain how he will pitch to this dangerous hitter. Catcher concurs.

2. The captain wants everyone reading from the same sheet. That goal prompted him to call timeout. The infield must understand exactly how the pitcher will pitch to the hitter in order to deploy correctly.

3. The entire plan could have been transmitted by the manager from the dugout, using hand and arm signals.

4. The captain has already signaled the plan to the manager as the conference breaks up. The manager concurs.

5. Do not create a large hole between third and short or leave the line at third unprotected on this hitter. A mistake inside on any pitch can reward Burly with a hit through the hole – or down the line for extra bases. The placement has to be correct to obtain the desired result: a ball hit sharply on the ground to the right side. The pitcher cannot afford to make a mistake with a pitch inside now.

6. No percentage in having the first baseman hold his runner on. That runner has nowhere to go with a man on second. Deployment of the third baseman is critical. The choices are (1) to play him **"in for the**

bunt," (2) **"even with the bag"** for a quick start on a double play, or (3) back of third to **"guard the line"** and take away an extra-base hit down the line. The team chooses the third alternative. A bunt down the third base line belongs to the pitcher, but such a bunt is difficult, if not impossible, when the placement (low and away) is correct.

7. The manager trusts his captain and battery. Neither he nor the pitching coach has strolled to the mound.

8. **A pitcher's memory has to be active and accurate. He has to recall not only what each hitter has done today, but also what each hitter has done in previous games, and what each hitter's career tendencies have been, as described in "the book" (PB) or as observed by the advance scouts (SB).**

**The Opposing Manager ("Red"):** He knows what the conference was about and has a plan to foil the defense.

"Red" will watch the first pitch to see if his hunch is correct: "Larry will probably throw hard stuff away. He will likely fire up his 100 percent fastball, saved up for a jam like this. Larry will be careful this time to stay away from inside stuff. I'll give Burly the "take" sign to see what Larry does on the first pitch. The manager flashes a "take" sign to the third base coach. This hitter is greedy. He does not like "take signs" with runners on. You catch his brief facial reaction to the sign. So does your catcher. You throw a hard slider low and away (bottom of 9 spot). It catches the corner. Strike one. The hitter appears puzzled. Burly fails to catch up with your next pitch – a fastball up a notch from the slider and away (top of 9 spot). The count is 0 and 2.

"Red" reasons: "Larry's way ahead in the count. He's got room to work on Burly. Larry will stay out of the strike zone with a breaking ball to tempt Burly. That slow slop won't give the catcher a good chance to throw. **Put on the double steal!** If we get third, and nailed at second, I have at least one out to get a sacrifice fly. Risk? If Burly's out on strikes and the runner's nailed at second – double play!

What prompts "Red" to consider risking a steal with Burly at bat, followed by the fourth and fifth hitters? You have "rung up" all these hitters each at bat. Except for Burly's triple earlier, none of these batters has gotten the ball out of the infield. You are not tiring: you are still in control. "Red's" tendency in this situation – with heavy artillery coming up – is to sit back and let things happen. He also knows that your team relies on this tendency, and very likely does not expect a steal. Today he will play his hand differently. He has an excellent runner at second (22

121

steals/24 attempts). Third base is the easiest base to steal (see below). The runner going into second is slower, but "Red" forecasts a low velocity breaking pitch well out of the strike zone – not a good pitch for the catcher's throw to second or third.

**Third base is the easiest base to steal! (PB and SB)** Why? The pitcher's back is to the runner at second. The pickoff throw to second is the hardest pickoff throw to make. With a right-handed hitter up, the catcher's view of third base is partially obscured, and the catcher has to throw past the batter to nail the runner at third. Because neither right- or left-handed pitcher can see movement at second when looking toward home, the runner at second can take a longer lead than a runner at first or third.

**The Catcher's Plan:** should the double steal occur, the catcher will throw to second to nail the runner. He chooses this tactic, because third base is the easiest base to steal (see above). The runner on second is an extremely competent "bag thief," and the man on first is slower afoot. If the catcher throws to third and fails to nail the runner, he ends up with the **go-ahead run on second and no one out!** With a throwout at second, "Red" has only one chance at a sacrifice fly. The catcher ponders (ever so briefly) the odds: "Those guys think we're gong to waste a breaking ball out of the strike zone. We'll fix that notion now. There, Larry! Your best heater low and away." Larry nods assent at the sign flashed by Wes.

**The Steal:** "Red's" intuition is not correct, and Burly misses (or ignores) the sign. You throw a "high gas" fastball low and away. Burly cannot resist the temptation to get a piece of that pitch. He is also behind in the count and must act to defend the plate. He swings, makes contact and drives the ball hard toward the hole between second and first. Eddy breaks with the pitch, and, going fast to his left, snares the white pill on its second bounce. Because the runners were on the move with the pitch, Eddy has only one play: to first for a single out.

**The Pitcher's Nightmare:** Now there are runners on second and third and only one out. The next move is up to your manager. His tactic is predictable: intentionally pass the cleanup hitter to load the bases and set up the double play for the fifth batter. Your manager flashes the sign to the catcher. The catcher stands and relays the "I.P." sign to you. Four balls correctly thrown away from the hitter – shoulder high – loads the bases. Time! Leo (your manager) strolls to the mound. Right- and left-handers are now up in the bullpen and throwing.

**The Fifth Hitter:** Why play the fifth batter (a left-hander) to hit into a double play? Why not bring the infield in and plan a force at the plate? Part of the pregame meeting was devoted to a discussion of this hitter's credentials, tendencies and recent history. Lately, with runners in scoring position, this batter (usually a pull hitter) has been going after hard stuff low and away. This impatience has catapulted him into a league-leading spot among those crashing into double plays. His rocket shots to the left side of the infield are grist for your team's competent double play mill.

Manager spits, then starts: "How do you want to handle this guy, Larry? Wes, Al, Eddy and Hank join the discussion. "I'll set him up for the low-and-away double-play pitch." "Make it look like you are missing up and in with two sliders, Larry, then a heater low and away for the put-away," Wes adds. "Well, if you guys think you can pull it off, go with it," Leo concludes.

**Awakening From the Nightmare:** The first pitch is a hard slider up and in, real tight – singes the hitter's nasal hairs. Instinctively he backs off the plate a few inches as he resumes his stance for pitch two. Another slider up and in – vibrates the adam's apple. Hitter mumbles an unprintable epithet. Wes calls for the fastball on the third pitch, and, **at the last instant** edges to the outside corner to receive Larry's heater. The hitter's delight over a fastball that threatens no grave bodily harm is short-lived. He catches up to the pitch late with the end of the bat, and cracks a one bounce liner to Al who starts the double play. You are out of the inning! Leo ejects his plug and sighs with relief.

# Why This Menu of Pitches?

*"Don't try tricky stuff, if it means the game."*
### *Leo Durocher*

There was nothing tricky here. You knew what you had to do based on your knowledge of the hitter and the situation. You used your mind to direct your **best pitches.** Fortunate for you, the pitches arrived at the plate, placed as you and Wes had planned. You **adjusted** the hitter's stance in order to give yourself the outside corner. Had the hitter failed to swing at the third pitch, it would have been a called strike. He did swing, but instead of striking the ball with the "sweet zone" of the bat, he managed only to make a late connection with the end of the bat. You saved up your best heater (100 percent power) for this jam, and pulled yourself out of a problem.

**Pitchers do not react to problems; they solve them!**

# Situation No. 2

Leo calls you in as the "closer" to pitch in the bottom of the ninth inning. Score remains 2-1. You, a right-hander, will pitch to the sixth and seventh hitters (both right-handed batters). Perhaps "Red" will use a left-handed pinch hitter for No. 8. Your best pitches are a 92-96 mph fastball, a palmball change-up and a wicked forkball. Your delivery and arsenal of pitches vary substantially from Larry's. Many hitters around the league (PB) are in the habit of taking your first pitch to check its velocity (4 mph spread). You began as a closer at the beginning of this season. Much to the chagrin of the pitching coach, you seldom get a strike across with your first two pitches to the first hitter. The coach has worked with you, talked to the manager and visited the parish priest – all to no avail.

Hitter "six" is a shortstop batting .272. He is a hacker, not a power hitter. Two fastballs at 93 and 94 mph miss inside. The second pitch sends "six" tumbling backward into the dirt. Wes calls for a forkball, down the middle. The change in speed and centered location are too good to resist. "Six" hacks at it; the ball comes back to you on two bounces – an easy out.

"Seven" is next. He is a catcher who bats left (throws right, of course). He has been having a terrible season at the plate – batting average .226. In years past, he has hit with power. He led the league in doubles twice, and was among the top 10 home run hitters four times. He is now in the autumn of his career, but he can never be "taken for granted." Wes calls for a fastball up and in (8 spot - on the corner). The pitch looks good at first, but then descends into the "Bermuda Triangle." The ball hits the wall in right-center on three bounces, and "seven" goes into second standing. One out and a runner in scoring position. "Red" replaces "seven" with a younger, faster pinch runner.

"Red," as predicted, chooses to pinch hit a left-handed batter for the weak-hitting, right-handed eighth batter. "Pinch" has just come off the disabled list. He made the "D.L." with a back strain which is now mended. "Pinch" is a power broker who ordinarily plays first base. The "book" on "Pinch" states he is very susceptible to speed changes – inside/outside, not up/down. Wes calls for a fastball away. At 96 mph you miss away (2 spot). Ball one. Next pitch is a palmball change inside (8 spot). "Pinch" looks like a whirling dervish going after this change-up. Count 1 and 1. On the third pitch, the seams of your fastball catch the inside corner for a called strike. "Pinch" voices his disagreement with the call in concise, well-chosen phrases.

"Pinch" has a character flaw: he frustrates easily, perhaps because he ruminates over his mistakes. Presently, he reasons that you are on to his weakness: inability to handle inside/outside changes in speed. He figures you will go back outside with your change-up. You anticipate his logic; so does Wes. Wes calls for a forkball, down! To a frustrated "Pinch" the incoming forkball looks like a change down the middle, belt high. Alas, poor "Pinch" fans the air as the forkball drops below his lumber. Two outs.

"Red" dredges up another left-handed pinch hitter whose credentials pale next to those of "Pinch." "Pale" is a nervous rookie, anxious to establish his worth. He may be too anxious. Wes calls for a forkball (6 spot). A nervous swing follows and "Pale" grounds out, Eddy to Whitey. Runner on second is stranded, the game belongs to your team.

**What are the lessons for the "closer?"** Eighty percent of all walks start with a count of 1 and 0! Sixty percent of walks score! With his tendency to miss on the first two pitches to the first hitter, he is at high risk to give up a run in his inning. In close games, this is unacceptable.

**Analyze, for a moment, the closer's role. In effect he is a starter pitching the first inning.** Recall our earlier comments about the first inning — a "time bite" when too many runs occur. The first inning nearly became the undoing of my teammate, Sal Maglie, and the legendary Satchel Paige, because of their failure to warm up correctly. Review our advice on the details surrounding **the warm-up:** (1) throw enough warm-up pitches; (2) crank up the breaking balls early; (3) uncork at least half of the throws from the stretch; (4) use a teammate (helmet on!) to simulate a right- and left-handed hitter. A disciplined, detailed warm-up is worth the effort. If you succeed as a closer, your appearances should last only one inning.

Fortunate for the closer in the problem above, a veteran catcher managed his efforts. What the closer lacked in control, Wes balanced with psychology. The closer lost a pitch in the 'Bermuda triangle" at the worst possible time. Lucky for him the ball was not pulled and sent soaring out of the park.

The solutions given here are but a few of the many alternatives that could have been chosen. Present these situations to 10 pitchers or 10 managers and you will hear 12 answers! The purpose here is to teach you to think. Notice the pitcher never once allowed his emotions to interfere with his logic. He was too busy thinking to be scared or angry.

**Pitchers do not react to problems; they solve them!**

A collection of problem management techniques now deserves attention and comment before our chapter-ending discussion of base runners.

**Mannerisms that give away the pitch**. The list is endless. The offense is in a constant state of alert to catch the pitcher doing something special before certain pitches. If the pitcher sees that the hitters always seem to be ready for a breaking ball, change-up or fast pitch – even when well-placed with good movement – he needs to enlist everyone's help to detect the problem. In my case, I entered the glove to grip the ball one way for a fastball, another way for a curve. During a game against the Pirates in 1947, the third-base coach whistled to the hitter each time he saw me enter the glove with my palm turned to the left (to grip the ball for a curve). It finally dawned on me what the coach was seeing, so on the very next pitch I shook off several signs from my catcher, Walker Cooper, until he gave me a fastball. I entered the glove as if to grip a curveball. Sure enough, there was the whistle! The batter was a right-hander, so I rifled that fastball down the slot, and high. The hitter leaned over the plate as he strode toward a pitch that was supposed to be a curve. Fortunately, the hitter was quick on his feet, and he ducked under the fastball that blew his hat off. The hitter: Hank Greenberg in his last year.

Hank grounded out on a curveball with the next pitch. On my way to the dugout I trotted by the third-base coach. "Somebody's going to get hurt, coach, if you continue to signal my pitches." Aghast, he replied, "What? Me signal?" The coach's lack of subtly – his whistle – provided me an educational experience.

**Caveat: Never throw at a hitter!** My use of the fastball in this case was intended to upset the hitter's timing.

**The specific mannerism that gives a pitch away ordinarily occurs before the pitcher starts forward!** Once the pitcher starts forward, most hitters direct their vision toward finding the ball. The search for the giveaway mannerism starts with the top of the head and ends with the feet. Tradition holds that Babe Ruth protruded his tongue ever so slightly **before** he came forward with his curveball. Ear wiggling, eyelid closures, hand position, glove entrances, knee knocking, footsteps are all giveaways. Many scholastic pitchers initially grip the ball for a fastball, then stir around in the glove to regrip for breaking balls – a sure betrayal of intent.

# *Pinch, Bunch, Shift and Setup Speed Changes*

Every pitcher handles the excellent hitters differently and all ballclubs play these hitters in their own special way. When the Cincinnati Reds called me up from Seattle in 1956 as a player-coach, they knew that I had always pitched very well against the Braves (formerly a Boston club). When I went to Cincinnati, the Braves were roosting in Milwaukee. Consequently, the Reds scheduled my first appearance to be the opening game of a series at Milwaukee.

Eddie Matthews (Hall of Fame, 1978) had been a thorn in the side of the Reds' pitchers for years. They were unable to put him down consistently. At the pregame meeting the Reds asked me how I would pitch Matthews because they knew I had years of success squelching his power and bruising his batting average when I was with the Giants. I said that I would set him up to swing at a change-up that he would surely pull to the right side. I suggested that the shortstop **pinch** toward second (play close to the bag), and the outfield **bunch** right–center fielder shift to right center and the left fielder move to center field.

The Reds chorused: "It won't work, Larry. We've tried all that, and Matthews still hammers us." My response: "He'll sit down today. If you don't mind, try it my way and we'll see."

I did set Matthews up by stimulating his anxiety to hit with a couple of pitches he did not like: both called strikes. Then I changed up off my curve, and sure enough, he went for it and pulled it to the right side for an infield out. We repeated the scenario three more times that day with different pitch sequences, each ending with a change-up, each with the same results.

Cincinnati was pleased and awed, because their pitchers had repeatedly tried these sequences with Matthews, to no avail. When the change failed, these pitchers tried blowing fastballs by him. No one could get a fastball by Matthews. He was too quick. The hottest fastball often ended up somewhere in left field while the left fielder was eating lunch in center.

Mentally and physically Matthews was a brilliant hitter. He understood what I was doing to him. The question in his mind was **how** and **when** the change-up would appear. Invariably he "got out in front of" the change-up, and pulled the pitch. To hit the change-up effectively, Matthews had to supply nearly all the power. Rarely did he hit my change-up out of the infield.

127

# *Liar's Dice*

The mental duel between pitcher and batter resembles a game of "liar's dice." Liar's dice is an ancient game usually played by two participants. It is a game of bluff and pretense. Skill at this pastime depends on comprehension of the laws of probability. The outcome depends on the situation, recall of what the opponent has done during the present "hand" and an understanding of the opponent's tendencies. Sound familiar?

Both players start with five or six dice and an opaque can. The rollers place the dice in the cans, shake and invert with care to keep the dice hidden beneath. Each peeks at his/her dice and creates a plan. The previous roll winner makes a statement about the total number of ones, twos, threes, fours, fives or sixes standing upright under both cans. The statement may bear no element of truth and must relate to only one species of numbers (ones, twos, etc.). The second roller counters the first roller's statement with one of three options: (1) a higher number of the same species, or (2) higher number of another species, or a call to "show."

Once a "show" call is made, both players must uncover the dice. The first player, if not called to "show," can exercise any of the three options above. The counterbidding continues until a show is commanded, or the last bid amounts to the total number of dice held by both players. When a "show" is commanded, the last player's statement is proven to be correct or incorrect. If correct he/she wins. If incorrect the last player's statement is called a "lie" and that player must set aside one dice. The game continues until one player loses all his/her dice.

The dynamic duel between pitcher and batter is a replica of the contest in "liar's dice." The outcome depends on how pitcher and batter analyze the situation. They must recall what each has done on this day and in games past, the tendencies of each in the situation at hand, and the understanding each has regarding the laws of probability.

Competent pitchers exercise their wits multitudinous times during a game. The pitcher repeatedly asks himself:

1. "What does this hitter think I will throw now?"

2. "What does he want me to throw?"

3. "Does the hitter think I know what he wants and therefore I will throw something different?"

# The Used-Car Salesman

The possibilities here are endless. Employ the used-car salesman's approach. Once you know what the customer wants, give it to him, almost. If a hitter uses a closed stance, you and he both know he is vulnerable down and in. So maybe he thinks you will attack his weakness instead of giving him what he wants – fastball, middle to outside corner of the plate, belt high. So give him what he wants, almost. The pitch zooms in and appears ready to nip the outside corner. Perfect! He swings and misses for one of two reasons: (1) Your entree was almost what he wanted, but it **surprises him** that you did not attack his weakness. (2) It was a fastball, belt high, outside corner, but at the last instant it dove off the table. Reason: Split-finger fastball. Who is the winner? The liar?

# Baseball Defense is Like Military Defense!

Military men tell us that the successful attacker erodes the defensive bulwark. Hitters erode the defense by putting runners on the base paths. Prevent that and the fort remains secure. Bats are siege guns; base runners are broachers; the pitcher is the defensive catapult. The pitcher's mission is to silence the siege guns and hold broachers at bay. In other words, keep hitters off the base paths.

**To keep runners off the base paths: (1) throw strikes; (2) walk no one; (3) put the ball in play to a fielder for an out.**

**Put the ball in play.** Seven fielders wait anxiously to come to your assistance. Perhaps you want a "six-pitch inning", but you have a penchant for strikeouts. Best case scenario: you strike out one hitter with three pitches. That leaves only three pitches to finish the job. Not realistic. Put the ball in play – preferably to an infielder. Note: six-pitch innings are a rarity even in the best of hands, and I discuss the subject only to make a point. The point: conservation of energy. An effective starter should be able to complete nine innings with pitch counts of 130 or less. Throw more than 135-140 pitches and the "catapult" starts to wobble and wear. When the "catapult" wears and wobbles, fewer strikes are thrown, walks occur, hits appear and "big innings" happen.

**Strikeouts are exciting, but wearing.** Pitchers who accumulate enormous strikeout totals are a thrill to behold – definite crowd pleasers. Generally such maestros wield a fastball to carry out their deed. During a game, about 55 to 60 percent of an average major-leaguer's pitches are fastballs. Only 20 to 25 percent of my pitches were fastballs. In the hands of a competent hurler the fastball is used to (1) set up other pitches, (2) to get a called strike on a 3-and-0 count, (3) to change speeds, (4) to adjust the hitter's stance (those who crowd the plate or "dig in"), (5) to defend against the bunt, (6) to surprise a hitter expecting something else and (7) to terminate a hitter's dwell time at the plate. However, the fastball is just one tool in a pitcher's kit.

Strikeouts are not mandatory, and are often costly. Fanning the hitter is seldom done with three pitches. More often it takes four or five – occasionally six – throws. **Pitch counts soar when strikeout gunners take the hill.**

**Occasionally strikeouts are the best option, e.g., runner on third with less than two outs and no chance for a double play.**

Carl Hubbell (Hall of Fame 1947, ERA 2.97 in a 16-year career) led the league in strikeouts only one season – 159 whiffs in 1937. Those who played against him commented with admiration on his array of pitches. Billy Herman once said that it was not uncommon for an opposing team to stand on the top step of the dugout to watch Hubbell weave his tapestry of pitches: curveball, screwball, slider, two or three changes-ups and a fastball. Cy Young (Hall of Fame 1937, 511 career victories) led the league in strikeouts only twice in a 22-year career! Orel Hershiser (1983-1992 ERA 2.87) never once won the strikeout crown. I rest my case.

**Leadoff hitters on base.** When any of the first six hitters in the batting order is the leadoff man in an inning, and reaches any base, he scores 70 to 80 percent of the time – high school through major-league baseball. Unacceptable. The best way to prevent this occurrence: **first hitter, first pitch, first strike!** Getting the first pitch in for a strike – swing and miss, foul ball, called strike or ball put into play – is extremely important. This technique reduces pitch counts, puts the hitter in a hole and pleases your fielders. **A pitcher throwing first-pitch strikes portrays competence**. Throughout my pitching career I usually wanted the batter to swing at my first pitch. For some of the methods I used, see **where and how to throw the first pitch.**

**First pitch: Where and how**. This depends on at least five pieces of evidence gathered by catcher and pitcher. Where to **place the pitch** is in part dependent on the hitter's intent.

1. **Observe the hitter's stance:** closed (front foot closer to the plate than back foot); open (the opposite feet positions); conventional (feet aligned so neither foot is closer to the plate). In the **closed stance** the hitter generally wants to control the outside corner and middle of the plate. This hitter can lunge or dive across the plate to catch the outside

corner and beyond. He is vulnerable low and in. What do you do about it? (a) Go inside and brush him back, or (b) let him have the outside and fool him with speed changes.

The **open stance** hitter has opened his stance to handle pitches inside. Or he will swing that front foot in, so he ends up in a non-open stance, i.e., conventional stance or closed, based on his estimate of where you will throw the ball. He is vulnerable away, and has given you the outside corner. This hitter can usually kill anything inside – near the inside corner of the plate. The open stance batter who swings that front foot has a weakness. He is making rapid changes in his balance and center of gravity as he rotates on his back foot and advances his front foot to address the ball. His tendency is often to angle his swing up slightly. Attack him low and away.

The **conventional stance** is difficult to manipulate. Babe Ruth, Ty Cobb, Joe Dimaggio, Ted Williams and Mike Piazza bear witness to that.

2. **Note the hitter's position in the box.** If he has moved up, he is looking for breaking stuff, knucklers or wants to bunt. If he is deep in the box he is probably "sitting on" a fastball.

3. **Watch the check-swing.** Where his bat went tells you where he wanted the pitch. He was fooled, but quick enough to withhold a full swing for a strike.

4. **If you are not sure** what the hitter expects after observing these clues, go low and away and see what his feet do. If he steps toward the pitch and swings, or checks his swing, he has told you he wanted (or expects) a pitch low and away. If he pulls away he anticipated an inside pitch. A straight-ahead stride gives you no clue.

5. **Pitch placement also depends on the situation.** Review the hitters and situations presented above. Perhaps we are getting too fine here. Just remember, the best hitters have a hard time hitting .330: three or four hits in every 10 at bats. Just don't walk them! Try hard to stay ahead of the hitters. Maglie and I threw 80 or 90 percent breaking balls and the hitters knew this, but they still had to hit it where a fielder couldn't catch it. I always taught my pitchers: the game is good, if you don't walk batters.

**Radar furnishes information for both defense and offense.** Fans who are observant notice the restless prowl of men behind the screen at home plate armed with radar guns (gunners). Offensively radar furnishes critical information to hitters on pitch speeds: velocity of fastballs and breaking pitches. As the game wears on a small drop in fastball velocity can mean a pitcher is tiring.

The pitcher can use radar information to identify problems. Fresh into the game a pitcher may wonder why his "breaking stuff" is sailing straight with just a ripple for a break. The "gunner" can tell him that he is throwing his breaking pitches five or six mph higher than usual. Recall that the widest curveball hooks come with high spin, **low velocity**.

**Radar is a useful weapon for deceit.** Take a few knots off the fastball in the late innings and let the offensive "gunner" pass the word to the hitters. Remember we showed you how to save a little heat for late innings. After the pitcher thinks he has given "misinformation" to the offense "gunner," uncork a surprise! Bring on the 100 percenter. The look of bewilderment and frustration in the hitter's face is reward enough, and sends a message: "Don't try to fool with an old fooler."

**Game Postmortem:** What I did with pitchers the day after they pitched. I sat with them and went over the lineup. I asked each pitcher to recall what every batter hit, what the count was and where the ball was hit. The "gun chart" discussed in Chapter 3 is a useful tool for these sessions.

**Always ask "why."** Why was each pitch used? Why did the result occur? I think this is the best way to learn how to pitch. In the big leagues you'll see the same hitters year in and year out. So you will invariably recall how to pitch to each hitter. Remember though, hitters are constantly adjusting their techniques and you have to change your approach.

For instance, when I faced Stan Musial in a one-run game on his last at bat and no one on base, I knew he had three swings to hit a home run. I did not want to make a mistake inside, because I knew he would pull the pitch over the right-field fence. The first time I faced Musial he hit my curveball change-up. So when I faced him during the remainder of the season (1947), I put that pitch away and used other stuff – successfully. Next season I tried that change-up again against Musial, and he hit it poorly. So, I continued to use it as needed from that point forward, most of the time with good results. Why did Stan have trouble with that pitch from me? I don't know, and I didn't ask him, because I knew he wouldn't tell. Furthermore, the question might awaken his awareness, and prompt him to adjust his approach.

In scholastic ball, the pitcher has fewer opportunities to address a given hitter. The college and high school pitcher needs to observe everything about the hitter: his stance, checked swings, practice swings, foot movements. When these observations are blended into the situation at hand, the thinking pitcher will reach reasonable conclusions. Though the conclusion may be correct, it remains for the pitcher's talent to successfully execute the plan.

**Pregame meeting:** (See also Chapter 6, **Strategy**) In the clubhouse (PB), or gym, meeting room, behind the dugout (SB) – wherever – the team must meet. The purpose of the meeting – discuss the opposition: hitters, pitchers, manager, coaches. Review plans to meet various situations.

What do the meeting participants draw on to make plans? Depends on the level of play. Remember this: all repetitive human behavior develops patterns. The larger the number of repetitions, the more fixed – and predictable – the pattern. In major-league baseball the number of repetitions is enormous during a season. Team statisticians daily gather the numbers, and the *Elias Baseball Analyst* harvests huge amounts of data for statistical analysis. In addition, managers and coaches impart wisdom born of prolonged observations and experience.

**A word of caution about statistics:** statistics can provide only an appreciation of the odds that something will occur, based on past occurrences. Statistics cannot predict precisely the outcome of a specific situation or the exact fate of an individual. We all know of persons in their 80s who have drunk alcohol to excess and smoked since teenage years. **Statistically** such persons should have long ago met their demise, but they live on. However, statistics cannot account for individual differences, unique situations, and human enthusiasm and will power. George E. Will has pointed out that: "Baseball analysts... often have a... misplaced confidence in their ability to reduce reality to numerical expression... Statistics must be read with an eye out for the human factors that skew numbers."

**Carelessness**. An occasional baseball pundit will state that pitchers of yore (Mathewson, Johnson, Young, Coveleski, Gibson and others) "coasted" when given big leads. "Coasting" is meant to imply that placements became less precise, speed changes less frequent and time between pitches elongated. Those old-timers got away with coasting, say the pundits, because the strike zone was larger (shoulder top to knee bottom), the ball was "dead" and "dirty"; "dead" because of looser yarn winding, and "dirty" because stained and bruised balls were left in the game. (In 1925 the National League changed all that and more than doubled the total balls used in a season: 22,000 in 1924, 54,000 in 1925). Sounds like an attractive theory, but it is false. Pitchers then, as now, were concerned with mileage. Fewer pitches equates to greater arm mileage – you can take that to the bank. If you don't believe that, remember what Cy Young (511 wins in 22 years of pitching or an average of 23 wins per season) said about his longevity in baseball. His long career rested on his control, precise  placement and speed changes.

To ease up when you are ahead is dangerous. You spend too much time cleaning up the clutter you create. Got a good bullpen? Sure! They can come in to extinguish your trash bin fires. That's called "reliever job security." But why should the bullpen clean up your careless mess?

Instead of easing up when you have a big lead, use the opportunity to work with new pitches you have developed. You will surprise the hitters with a fresh bill of fare in the late innings. To correctly work with a new pitch requires judgment. Make sure that you are ahead in the count before you throw the pitch. Remember, the hitter's analysis of your approaches is based on what you have shown to that moment. Your new pitch is not a part of the hitter's equation.

---

### Coaching Pearl

Never use a new pitch unless you are sure you can control it.

---

**The Pitchout**. This pitch is used once or twice in a game. The pitchout is a pitch that the pitcher throws away from the hitter, usually chest high, and always a fastball.

Three reasons to call a pitchout: (1) A fast runner is perched on first. The presiding pitcher is habitually slow delivering the ball to the plate (see **Managing the Base Runner**, next page). The manager, or the catcher, sees something that tells him the runner may go on the next pitch. So the pitchout is called. The pitcher needs to "quick kick" or "slide step" (p. 136), so the catcher has more time to make his throw. You just have to hope the runner goes, otherwise the pitchout becomes a wasted pitch. (2) Fast runner on first with a good hit-and-run batter at the plate. The pitcher gets behind in the count. Good time to hit and run because the pitcher, behind in the count, will try to come in with a sure strike – just what the hit-and-run batter needs to carry out his nefarious deed! If the catcher or manager sees the hit-and-run coming, call the pitchout and nail the runner (he is going on the pitch). (3) Runner takes a long lead on the pitcher. Could be any base, but usually first base. The catcher thinks he can pick him off. Fire a pitchout and let the **catcher** throw down for the pickoff. If the runner has started for second or third, the catcher nails him there. If the long lead is off third, catcher rifles a throw there for the pickoff. The "back pick" has to be executed with lightning speed, because an alert runner will scramble back the instant he sees the catcher rise to receive the pitchout.

---

### Coaching Pearl

The catcher must not give away the pitchout. Although he sets up on the outside corner, he has to make it look like he is set for an ordinary pitch. If the catcher rises too soon to receive the pitchout, a good runner will not break.

---

When the defense is stealing the offensive signals and detects a hit-and-run or steal sign, the defense may not want to let on that they have purloined the semaphore. Reason: If the offense believes that their signals have been compromised, they will change the code. Not good! When signals are stolen, the defense can elect to throw an "almost pitchout." This is a hot pitch, easy for the catcher to handle and throw, but not a "hot and high" fastball – an obvious pitchout. Try a fastball, well outside, just above the belt. This looks like a miss, not a pitchout.

**Watch the opponents' batting practice.** Observe carefully each hitter to see whether he is doing something different when thrown breaking pitches, or whether he has modified his stance or swing. This is especially important with struggling hitters. These hitters may be incorporating new techniques to pull out of a slump or improve their average.

**Bunting.** There is no excuse for a pitcher's failure to bunt. Pitchers have a deserved notorious reputation for poor hitting. The least a pitcher can do to help his own cause is to be a masterful bunter, and move base runners along. Select a hitting coach or another player to assist your mastery of this skill. Learn to place the bunt where the tactical situation dictates. Master the "square around" and "pivot" techniques. Learn also to "show bunt" then swing away – the so called "butcher boy" routine. This is your opportunity to participate in offensive play (offensive to the opponents – not to your teammates.)

## Managing the Base Runner

**Prohibition.** The most effective management is prohibition – prevent the runner's occupying a base, courtesy your lack of skill. Skill implies throwing the first pitch for a strike and staying ahead in the count.

Once the runner is on, there are several techniques to keep him in place, or to nail him. I will discuss eight.

(1) **Time to home plate** ("release time"). Maximum time from the start of the motion (the stretch, always) to "pop" in the catcher's glove should be no greater than 1.5 seconds – high school to the major leagues. Superb release time is 1.2 seconds. A high school pitcher whose best fastball may be 75-80 mph will consume 0.6 seconds of "air time" (time from release to arrival in catcher's mitt). That leaves 0.9 seconds to get the pitch off. An elaborate, high leg lift burns up time. Young pitchers need to learn the "slide step" or the "quick kick." In the "slide step,' the knee is raised minimally to attain the balance point. This act keeps the aiming foot close

K. Van Loo

**Figure 5-2**
*Shows the pitcher in the "set" position. Note that the power foot toe is aligned with the middle of the aiming foot arch. This foot positioning helps maintain both feet along the pitcher plate-home plate line when the pitcher steps forward. Placement of the aiming foot forward or back of this point adds to "release time" (see above), because this foot then has to "swing" into proper alignment as it steps forward. The swinging movement consumes time. This stance is balanced and permits the pitcher to turn quickly for a throw to any base.*

136

to the ground throughout its forward movement to the plate. The "quick kick" is executed much the same way, except the knee is elevated higher than in the "slide step" technique, but not to the height attained in the windup. After quickly reaching the balance point, the aiming leg darts forward **without a pause** to plant its foot. Some pitchers need a slightly higher knee lift to maintain power when pitching from the stretch. Nolan Ryan's extremely high leg lift actually shortened the flight time on his fastball by 0.2 seconds! But remember, Ryan's fastball was traveling at nearly 100 mph (slightly less than 0.4 second flight time). Some pitchers never get their release time below 1.5 seconds, and consequently give up excessive numbers of stolen bases.

(2) **Rhythm of Set-and-Throw.** Effective base stealers rely on two factors to snatch a base: leadoff and "jump." "Jump" is jargon for the timing of the runner's pivot and start toward the intended base. The earlier the jump, the higher the odds for a successful steal. The runner starts his "jump" when he is convinced the pitcher has started his motion toward home plate.

The pitcher needs to confuse the runner with unpredictability about the moment of movement – toward home plate or toward the base. The pitcher creates this deceit by varying his launch times and "lookovers" after coming set. On the first pitch he may pause two seconds before delivering the ball; on the second pitch one second (minimum time allowed by the rules); on the third pitch, three seconds, and so forth. He also varies the number of "lookovers." Creating unpredictability tempers the runner's jump, and reduces his efficiency. Good runners have timed pitcher's "set-to-throw" and release times for a century.

(3) **Moving the Runner Back.** Throwovers, stepping off the rubber, fake throws (except to first) are time-honored methods. **Caveat:** one of the runner's jobs is to entice the pitcher to lose his concentration. Runners "lean," fake steals, take steals – all calculated to distract the pitcher. Allow the catcher, manager, and basemen to watch the runner and call the throwover. **Well-executed throwovers are really pitches, but are rarely included in pitch counts.**

(4) **Concentrate on the Hitter.** This is a corollary to (3) above. The hitter is the person who can hurt a pitcher – bad. Deal with him first and foremost. This is not to say that the pitcher totally ignores the runner; it is to say that the runner is usually second priority on the threat list. If a three-toed sloth is perched on first – no threat to steal – why throw over there? Is someone hoping the hitter will get a phone call? With some

pitchers, throws to first are a knee-jerk reflex: "Oh, I've got a runner on first! Now, I'll have to throw over there a couple of times." Ridiculous.

(5) **The Catcher and Base Runner.** "Pop to pop time": baseball jargon that denotes the time consumed from the time the ball pops into the catcher's mitt to the time the pop is heard in the baseman's glove. Professional catchers average less than two seconds. The better catchers are around 1.80 seconds. That's quick! Time your catcher by tossing some pitches to him while a coach, holding a stopwatch, times the interval. Surprised?

The easiest pitch for a catcher to throw on is a fastball pitchout; the worst is a knuckleball or sloppy curve. Remember that with a left-handed batter at the plate, a catcher's view of first is partially obscured. Third base is obscured by a right-handed hitter.

(6) **Forkballs, Split-Finger Fastballs, Sinkers with Runner on Third.** These pitches, in the best of hands, occasionally crash into the dirt around home plate. In a one-run game with a runner on third, less than two outs, and less than two strikes on the hitter – got a catcher who knows how to block an errant dirt ball? The battery is dealing with high risk, and the pitch must be right.

(7) **Proficient Base Stealer on Base and a Power Hitter up.** Throw soft stuff low and away, the runner may steal. Come in with heaters, and the power broker may take the hurler downtown. This is a pitcher dilemma. By now we know that pitchers are problem solvers.

**If you get a lemon situation, make lemonade.**

The pitcher can keep the ball down and fast and use the power hitter's strength to produce a hard-hit ground ball for a double play. If the hitter fails to hit the ball and the runner breaks, a pitch "with heat" helps the catcher nail a stealer.

While the pitcher solves his problem, the offense is continuously conniving to beat him out of a double play. With a runner on first, or runners on first and second, the offense may unleash a steal or a hit-and-run or dump a sacrifice bunt to unhorse the pitcher's plans.

(8) **Left-Handed Pitchers with Runners on First and Third.** The "southpaw's" back is to the runner on third, and he faces the runner on first. Should the offense try a double steal, it will usually occur with less than two outs in a close game. In this situation, the runner on first starts toward second before the pitch. If the pitcher "steps" and throws on him, that runner is a dead duck, but the runner on third will score. Prevention

of this outcome is a matter of common sense. Why would the runner at first deliberately insert himself into a situation nearly guaranteed to produce an out? He wants to draw a throw, so the runner on third can streak for home. The solution: step off the rubber toward second base. Fake a throw to second, turn and throw home immediately. Worst case scenario: it was all a charade to buy the runner on first a free ride to second, while the runner on third stayed put after faking a dash for the plate.

**Caveats:** (1) The step and fake to second have to be convincing enough to fool the runner at third into believing that the pitcher is distracted, confused or rattled by the movement at first and has forgotten about the runner at third. (2) If the runner on third is a bolt of lightning, a fake to the second baseman may allow the runner to score. In this situation, step off the rubber, look toward second, and then immediately throw home without the fake. (3) If the runner at third breaks for home without stopping when the runner at first takes off for second, third baseman and catcher need to scream for the pitcher to throw home. Remember, the left-handed pitcher's back is toward third base.

**The second baseman's charge.** This is a defensive tactic used often at the high school and junior college level of play. The offense starts a double steal before the pitch with runners on first and third. In response the pitcher "steps off," looks the runner back to third, then throws to the second baseman who is "streaking in toward the grass." The second baseman either tags the runner going to second or throws to the shortstop at second, or throws home if the runner on third "breaks." This defense is complicated and risky, because the pitcher gives up the ball to an infielder who must choose between the three alternatives given above. Best **KISS**, as the saying goes: "keep it simple, stupid!" Nothing is more amusing than to see a second baseman running helter-skelter, holding the ball aloft, dealing with two runners, one of whom threatens to score. Best the pitcher retain possession of the ball, and decide where to throw.

The first-and-third double steal is a sinister offensive plot that counts on the pitcher's **doing something stupid**, e.g., committing a balk, throwing to a poorly positioned infielder on the "right side," or experiencing a sudden case of indecisive paralysis. The defense logic must be **to prevent the runner on third from scoring**, even at the cost of a runner making it to second without a tag.

Ordinarily the offense undertakes this tactic only when the runner at third is extremely fast, although Babe Ruth stole home 10 times, and Lou Gehrig 15 times, using schemes similar to those described above. Mo

Vaughan stole home on August 20, 1996, while participating in a first-and-third double steal!

The level at which the participants play is a factor in "defending" the first-and-third double steal. Professional teams play together for months – years, even. Their middle infielders and first basemen are fast and have strong arms. Professional players work hard to perfect defenses against this steal. High school and college teams are often less proficient. Many runs score as a consequence.

**There are at least four additional defenses against a first-and-third double steal**. The first of these is used when the runners "break" before the pitch. The pitcher steps off the rubber, "looks the runner back" at third, then quickly throws to the first baseman. The first baseman, ball held head high, sprints toward the runner going to second. (This runner wants to get involved in a "rundown" to distract the infield, and allow the runner on third to score.) As soon as the runner going to second turns his back on the first baseman and speeds toward second, the shortstop starts toward the runner at full speed, takes the throw from the first baseman, quickly tags the runner and whirls–ready to throw home if the runner on third "breaks." **This defensive tactic is the one preferred by many minor- and major-league teams,** because one – sometimes two – runners are tagged out.

This maneuver is more effective than the simple fake to second and throw home. Its success depends on the speed and accuracy of the pitcher's throw to the first baseman, the sprinting talent of the first baseman and the timeliness of his throw to the shortstop. Of course, if the runner on third has "broken" for home when the pitcher turns to "look him back" to third, the pitcher throws home. If the runner on third "breaks" while the first baseman sprints toward his runner, the catcher calls for a throw to the plate. The catcher's judgment has to be impeccable.

**The second defense is pure pitching. No outs. Infield is playing "in."** After the pitcher comes set, the runner on first breaks for second; runner on third "breaks" or fakes. Pitcher places a fast pitch to get a hard hit ground ball on the **left** side of the infield in case the hitter swings. If the hitter fails to make contact, or "holds up" on his swing, the runner coming from third is tagged out, or returns to his base. If the batter makes contact and hits the ball hard on the ground to the left side, the infielder's throw nails the runner coming from third. Risks: runner going to second gets a "free steal." Batter gets a hit with runners "on the go." Advantages: the offense expects the pitcher to throw to a baseman. The pitch to the plate destroys the steal home and often befuddles the hitter whose response is less than perfect.

**The third defense is a fastball away!** If it works, you get two-for-one on this play: an out at third, and no one scores! This defense presupposes that the runner on third either fakes a steal with a long lead, or stops short when he sees the pitch going home (see second defense above). The fastball must be a pitch that the batter does not hit and the catcher handles easily, because as soon as he receives the ball, the catcher comes up throwing and nails the "bold one" at third. This ploy works best with a left-handed batter because a right-handed batter partially obscures third base for the catcher, and the catcher must throw **past** the batter to third. Consequently, many mangers will try a first-and-third double steal only with a right-handed batter at the plate.

**The fourth defense** is executed by the middle infielder charged with covering second on the steal. It is used when the runners break with the pitch. In this case the catcher comes up throwing **toward** second. The middle infielder cuts in front of second base, receives the catcher's throw on the run and rifles it back to home to meet the flight arriving from "third city."

Each of these defenses has to be rehearsed in practice. For the second defense, pitcher and catcher need to have already "set the hitter up" with pitches likely to produce a hard-hit ground ball to a left-side infielder.

On the third defense, the catcher is "firing on a target of opportunity." That means that both catcher and third baseman simultaneously see the faked steal/long lead at third. The third baseman has to anticipate the throw from the catcher! With the fourth defense, both infielder and catcher need to communicate with a prearranged signal prior to the pitcher "taking his sign;" or this defense may be planned during the pregame meeting (Chapter 6).

# Bunt Defense with Runner on Second

These defenses work with a runner at second only, or runners at first and second. **The defensive logic is to force, or tag, the runner going to third**. The first element is pitch placement: a high, hot, slightly away (outside corner) pitch is the pitch most likely to result in either a pop foul, or infield pop-up (hopefully, both catchable), or a **hard-hit bunt**. Such a bunt is easier to field and throw to third. Of course, the master bunter often overcomes all obstacles. If the third baseman charges the bunt, the shortstop must "rotate" to third **ahead of the runner**. The risk: batter fakes a bunt, then strokes a hit through the hole left by the shortstop, or the runner(s) steal (see below under "Classics").

A second plan features a pickoff at second. After the pitcher comes set, the third baseman **starts to charge, the shortstop begins a rotation** toward third, the second baseman **slips up behind the runner** at second whose attention is focused on the left-side infielders' ballet. Pitcher whirls toward second, throws: **Gotch-ya! Sit down!** Absolute requirement: timing! This all has to happen in the blink of an eye.

# Other Classics

Practiced for more than 100 years are several offensive intrigues which continue to tantalize the defense. (1) Runners on first and second in a bunt situation with a right-handed hitter at the plate. Hitter **squares** to bunt (not a pivot bunt); runners go, but hitter only fakes the bunt. Catcher struggles to throw to third around the hitter still lingering in a bunt pose. Throw comes late, wide or both at third. Solution: Throw should have gone to second. Note: if hitter (in umpire's judgment) intentionally obstructs the catcher, interference will be called. (2) Runners on any two bases. Pitcher legally fakes (to second or third only!) and/or throws to a baseman. The offensive bench screams, **"Balk!"** Hearing this false accusation, and believing it to be true, the defense suddenly drops its guard. A runner executes a delayed steal while the infield snoozes. Another variation: the "balk" scream shreds the air as the pitcher comes set. The rattled pitcher then actually balks. Terrible!

A misdirected action brought on by a deceptive shout occurred to me when I pitched for the San Francisco Seals. It was the eighth inning of a scoreless tie. With a runner on second and no outs, the hitter dropped a bunt down the third-base line. I got to the ball quickly, and, as I snatched up the ball, a shout crackled out: **"third, third!"** The third baseman had come in to field the bunt, but the shortstop had not rotated to third. The reason: the runner stopped about 30 feet from second base and waited for me to "commit." These were incorrect actions on the part of both shortstop and runner. Both should have been in a foot race to third base. I responded to the shouts and threw hard to an unattended third base! The ball skipped deep into left field. The runner came around third to score, and I lost the game 1 to 0.

Afterwards, Lefty O'Doul, manager of the Seals commented, "Larry, you learned something today. Know the voices of your players. The shout to throw to third came from the **third base coach**!"

**Tenets Worth Noting.** A pitcher oblivious to the perils that surround him may soon feel the long hook reaching out to separate him from his miseries. There are at least five "60 percent" peril-related tenets:

1. Over the last 50 years, or so, the team scoring the first run won 60 percent of its games!

2. Competent pitchers throw 60 percent of their breaking balls for strikes.

3. Efficient pitchers throw 60 percent of their first pitches for strikes.

4. A walk to a leadoff batter results in a run 60 percent of the time.

5. Sixty percent of all walks start with a count of 1 and 0!

# Brushing Off the Sign

Instead of shaking off the catcher's signs when there is a runner on second capable of stealing those signs, try the brush-off method. It works like this: If the catcher gives you two fingers and you want one, brush your leg once (nonchalantly!); if you want three, brush your shirt once. The formula: to lower the number, brush below the belt; to raise the number, brush above the belt. The battery can create an array of subtle signs to deceive sign snatchers.

# Summation

We could fill volumes on baseball tactics. This is but a start, albeit an exciting start. The objective here is to prompt the reader's thinking, planning and coordination of defensive logic. Tactics, and strategy, make baseball provocative – to mind and body. Athletes of other nations have discovered the pleasure of baseball's heart-stopping intrigues and surprises. With breathless eagerness they have assimilated the "American Game" into their own cultures.

# 6

# Strategy

## In a Nutshell

1.  Pregame meeting
2.  The "Book"
3.  Elias Sports Analyst
4.  Advance scouts
5.  The stadium, playing surface, weather
6.  Umpires and fans
7.  The bullpen
8.  Starter vulnerabilities
9.  Managing base runners
10. The offense

> *"Luck is the residue of design."*
>
> **Branch Rickey,**
> **attorney and baseball executive**

Another way to state Mr. Rickey's terse metaphor is: "We make our own luck by careful planning." The word **strategy**, as used in this book, means the game plan created before the team takes the field. It is a **general overview** of how the game will be conducted. **Tactics are specific decisions and actions executed on the field** (Chapter 5, **Tactics**).

The team conceives and assembles its strategy during the **team meeting** before the game. Each club has its own approach to this meeting. During my eight years as a pitcher, and 11 years as a pitching coach with the Giants, the starting pitcher ran the defense portion of the pregame meeting. The starter discussed how he would pitch to each batter. Coaches, players and manager reacted to, and commented on, the pitcher's plans. For example, if a right-handed pitcher planned to entice ("set up") a right-handed leadoff hitter to swing at hard stuff low and away, the fielders commented on the ways they would deploy themselves. Fielder deployment is an art and depends on several variables: (1) Whether pitcher and batter are right- or left-handed; (2) the "tendencies" of the hitter when he is ahead or behind in the count, and when he has runners on; (3) the "tendencies" of the opposing manager in various situations; (4) the pitches and placement the pitcher will use to "set up" the hitter (so-called "purpose pitches"); (5) the pitch and placement for the **"sit-down" pitch**.

Discussions about fielder deployment are filled with traditional baseball terminology. Such talk flows in concise, specific Anglo-Saxon phraseology – beautifully suited to describing the intricacies of this game. The conversations include terms like "shift" in which the outfielders or infielders, or both, move to the right or left side of the field to deal with pull hitters. Infielders speak of **"pinching the middle"** where the second baseman and shortstop simultaneously deploy themselves closer than usual toward second base. Outfielders use the term, **"bunch"** to describe deployment of the center fielder toward right or left field; the opposite fielder drifts over toward the "bunched" pair.

The "book" on each batter is reviewed, supplemented by comments from the "battery" which faced the batter last. The *Elias Baseball Analyst* is consulted. (PB) This and other documents from the Elias Sports Bureau supply **cold numbers** and **situational statistics** on each team, manager and player in the major leagues (not a help to college and high school coaches who have to rely on memory or **advance scouts**). The *Analyst* shows, for example, that player A has stolen second base 20 times in 22 attempts (cold numbers). Seventy-four percent of his steals come when the count is 0-and-2 (situational stat).

These numbers portray **a tendency in player** A, driven by a logic that is clear to all: when many pitchers are 0-and-2, they stay outside the strike zone and entice the hitter to swing at an unfavorable third pitch. These pitches frequently make it more difficult for the catcher to nail the runner perpetrating a steal. Conversely, player A may learn from Elias that 92 percent of the pitches thrown by today's pitcher, when he is ahead in the count with runners on, is hard stuff close to, or within, the strike zone. This fact may dampen his theft lust.

Be cautious about statistics, though. Remember that a "stat" represents the result of several, or many, events (depends on the sample size). It is not a guarantee of performance or outcome; **it reflects only what has happened,** not what **will happen**. Statistics are numbers which can seldom stand alone. They must be applied thoughtfully to be useful.

> *"Stats are tough. After all, 99 percent of men with hemorrhoids use toilet paper."*
>
> ### *The Authors*

This quote provides a fact, but what use can we make of this fact?

Supplementing "the book" and Elias' documents is intelligence gathered by the **advance scouts** who have attended the opponent's games immediately before the present series. Reports brought or sent to the team can be critical to the strategy, e.g., a new quirk in a batter's swing, an unexpected variation in an opposing manager's tactics, or a nuance in a hurler's pitch selection.

Other data studied in the pregame strategy meeting are:

1. **The style of ball the opponents prefer**, e.g., "small ball" or "big ball."

2. **The stadium.** A fly ball carries five to six percent farther on a hot, dry, calm-wind day in Denver's rarefied air as compared to the commonly chilly, wet air of sea-level San Francisco. Dry, hot air at 5,000 feet is thinner and offers less resistance to buffet the ball than the thicker, heavier, cold air at sea level.

Ball and player performance differences created by altitude, temperature and humidity are pertinent to high school and college teams, especially during regional tournaments and playoffs. Teams from Long Beach, California (a seaside city with frequent fog), or Sacramento, California (an inland city, dry, hot, 120 feet above sea level), would find the environs of Reno, Nevada (inland mountain/desert city, 5,046 feet above sea level), strikingly different. Less obvious, a team from Tucson, Arizona (desert town 2,641 feet above sea level), would discover definite ball and player performance differences in Albuquerque, New Mexico (desert town 5,352 feet above sea level). Players acclimatized to sea level barometric pressures and atmospheric oxygen often experience a mild discomfort at the higher altitudes. Athletes arriving at sea level from mountain cities occasionally note a minimal feeling of exhilaration, if anything, but certainly no discomfort.

3. **The condition of the grounds**, e.g., natural grass or artificial turf. When **identical** circumstances prevail, a sharply hit ground ball travels faster across artificial turf than across closely cropped natural grass. Given this, the double play should be easier to execute on an artificial surface. On the other hand, hard-hit ground balls on an artificial surface are more likely to "shoot" through the holes between infielders; line drives to the outfield may skip and ricochet violently. Furthermore, the height of natural grass can be varied easily, depending on the whim of the groundskeeper, the strategic needs of the home team or the aesthetic taste of the stadium administrator. Artificial turf is relatively unfavorable to bunters because the bunted ball's ground speed is faster – all other factors being equal. Consequently, an infielder's throw on a bunted ball is more likely to force a runner or produce an out at first.

Several universities have created either an artificial turf infield (University of Texas) or an entire field covered with this type of surface (University of Hawaii). High school and college teams inexperienced in playing on artificial turf should prearrange extra practices on the host field prior to competition.

Infield soil composition and firmness also affect the ball's bounce and travel time. The wetness or dryness of the field affect foot traction for base runners and fielders alike. A wet field generally dampens a "running team's" effectiveness.

4. **The weather.** At Wrigley Field, if the wind is "blowing in," the distance traveled by fly balls to right center is shortened. When the wind "blows out," the balls fly out. A knuckleballer is more effective in calm air than in gusty conditions. Crosswinds can seriously hamper a pitcher's control on any pitch.

5. **The umpire crew**. Home plate umpires (umpires rotate field stations with each game) have **tendencies** also, and thereby self impose eponyms like "low-ball umpire." An umpire with this "moniker" calls

strikes at and slightly below the knees if the pitcher shows him that he can consistently hit the spot.

6. Finally, the expected **behavior (or misbehavior) of the fans**, e.g., excessive booing, stomping, hurling objects onto the field. I mention only six, but there are countless details to review before the game.

> *"A battle is won or lost by – among other things – the care taken in the planning. Overlook the least detail and your reward is defeat."*
>
> ### Napoleon

Of great importance during the strategy session are plans for the bullpen. "A manager is only as smart as his bullpen!" Whitey Herzog reportedly uttered this terse observation. Among the "smart" managers who have used their bullpens brilliantly are Sparky Anderson, Tony LaRussa, Leo Durocher and Earl Weaver. In 1901 starting pitchers hurled complete games 87 percent of the time. By 1990 the percentage had plummeted to around 11 percent. The rising presence and effective use of relief pitchers has to be counted a factor in this change.

During the present epoch, a "quality start" is a phrase awarded to starting pitchers who survive six innings, and are still ahead when they either continue to pitch or pass the ball to a reliever. Relievers are a useful anomaly on the body of baseball: professional subspecialists. They come with curious titles and credentials. There are "long relievers," "setup men," "closers." There are even sub-subspecialists brought in only to deal with certain types of hitters! The number of specialists on the roster, as well as the timing and frequency of their employment are important considerations for the manager. Scan the sports page of your newspaper. You may be surprised to learn that the total number of pitchers used in a major-league nine-inning game is six, seven, even eight pitchers. It is not unusual for one manager to summon the talents of five, even six hurlers during a game.

Ordinarily, an effective starter will endure six or seven innings and give way to a "setup man" who will go one or two innings. The "closer" brings down the final curtain. The effective manager frequently reviews with his relievers and starters the role each plays in the grand scheme of the team. This builds rapport between manager and pitcher and improves morale, because all parties know what to expect, with the understanding that the game situation may, and often does, change without notice.

Watchful to avoid overuse of any reliever, the manager fits his relief to the situation at hand. Mindful that there is yet a season to finish filled with games in the weeks to come, the manager continually stirs, blends, folds, mixes and matches his bullpen personnel. Since 1960, more than one pennant has been lost through misuse, overuse or abuse of the bullpen. Whatever the game situation and bullpen status, **the most important principle in deploying the relief pitcher is to deploy him in time.** When relief is needed, a tardy summons to the bullpen can leave the reliever with a huge pile of dung to shovel away.

**Starters are vulnerable** – and, consequently, may need relief – in at least four situations: (1) the first inning, (2) the fourth/fifth inning, (3) the eighth inning (4) and when rhythm or concentration breaks down. The **first-inning problems** usually arise from improper warm-up techniques (see Chapter 1), and are nearly always avoidable. By the **fourth/ fifth inning**, the hitters have "scoped" out the pitcher's offerings. They have calibrated their **timing** clocks. Launch time is at hand, **unless**, as Roger Angell said of Catfish Hunter, the pitcher continues to "...weave a tapestry of deceit...experience...efficiency." Angell meant that, while the pitcher pursues his seduction of the hitter with deceitful pitches, the devices used to achieve this end are not a carbon copy of an encounter earlier in the game.

By the **eighth inning**, the pitch count has risen, especially if the starter is given to producing strikeouts. A well-pitched complete game, with a modicum of walks and strikeouts, exacts a tax of 130 to 140 pitches. Tony LaRussa has allegedly stated that a pitcher becomes vulnerable after 120 pitches. This is probably too conservative. On the other hand, some have nursed the accusation (but never convincingly assembled the proof) that Billy Martin wore out his 1980 Oakland Athletics starter staff with overwork. That staff garnered 94 complete games, nearly twice the number of any other team in 1980. It is curious that no one has computed the average number of pitches per game for each of these starters.

The opposing bench often seats a number of master psychologists who cleverly fathom the exact moment to call a timeout or to regurgitate a demeaning epithet for the purpose of interrupting the pitcher's **rhythm or concentration**. Pitchers can also be their own worst enemy by allowing **carelessness** to creep into their work when handed a comfortable lead, **or after two outs in an inning**. Carelessness rapidly and irreversibly infects rhythm and concentration.

It becomes a delicate balance for manager and pitching coach to know precisely when to warm up a reliever, when to insert him and how long to keep him out there. It all depends on the game situation, the batter(s) coming up, the progress of the starter or prior reliever. None of this can be known during the pregame meeting (crystal balls are in short supply in the baseball world). "Baseball people" understand the odds: Teams ahead in the eighth inning win 90 percent of the time, due in some measure to effective bullpens.

## *Knee-Jerk Relief*

Knee-jerk relief is an ailment in which the manager, driven by habit, tendency or routine, brings in a relief pitcher even though the starter (or reliever) is performing well. Examples abound! Three will suffice. (1) The manager who has to use a closer in the ninth inning. (2) The manager who harbors a preconceived notion about the maximum number of pitches a hurler should throw in a game. (3) The manager who feels he must "swap out" relievers based on the pitcher's or batter's right- or left-handedness.

The logic that prompts use of a reliever should be simple: The pitcher now on the mound is "not getting the job done," because he is tuckered out, and/or he is losing his control, his "stuff" or his thinking.

Ordinarily, relief is not based **SOLELY** on a statistical fact. Remember: statistics cannot predict with certainty what **will** happen. Statistics can provide only an appreciation of the odds that something will occur based on past occurrences.

**TAKE HEED: The pitcher who is performing well now is a known quantity. His relief is yet untried in this game.**

Food for thought: Scan the newspaper pitching line scores. How often do you see six, seven, eight innings of well-pitched ball ruined by a reliever? Ask yourself why this reliever was used.

**Defenses against base runners.** The management of opposing base runners is a prime topic during the strategy meeting. Some managers totally control the defense against runners by calling the pitchouts and throwovers. Other managers allow catcher and basemen to make these calls. "Tendencies" play a large role in discussions about base runners: tendencies of opposing runners and managers. When the manager directs the base running defense, it is because he wants pitcher and catcher to concentrate on the pitches.

In 1948 during a game against Brooklyn, I was concentrating on my pitches while allowing Jackie Robinson to dance around with a large lead off first. Whitey Lockman, our first baseman, called time and trotted over to the mound. "Larry," he said "you're not keeping an eye on the runner!" "That's your job," I replied. At that time, manager-catcher-first baseman colluded to signal pitchers' throws to first base. When the catcher flashed the "throwover" sign to me, I turned and threw. When I was not receiving that sign, I was concentrating on placement and pitch selection. What Lockman meant was that after coming "set," I kept my focus solely on the catcher without turning my head five to 10 degrees over the left shoulder – the characteristic pose of a right-hander with a runner on first. Whitey and I became close friends. He came to know that I could get the ball over to him quickly when needed. With time he appreciated that my first duty was to concentrate on the pitch.

The overall approach to the day's **offensive plan** comes under the purview of the manager and rarely involves the starting pitcher, because the pitcher is usually a deficient provider of offense, able only to dump the occasional sacrifice bunt. However, all information is useful to the pitcher's total involvement in the game.

The authors of game strategy construct the plot for the play in the pregame meeting. The performance of "stage business and dialogue" then passes to the cast of players.

## A Windy Vignette

Chicago's Wrigley Field winds can complement or confound a pitcher's efforts. Winds "blowing out" favor the hitter; winds "blowing in" benefit the pitcher. On a day when the winds were blowing in, I was scheduled to pitch. Leo Durocher piped up during my briefing in the pregame meeting, "Wind's blowin' in this afternoon. That oughta banish any home run thoughts the Cubbies have today, Larry."

The winds blew "in" during the entire game. In spite of that, Hank Sauer cracked two of my pitches out of the park – home runs against the wind!

# 7
# Baseball Injuries

George A. Jansen, M.D.

## In a Nutshell

1. Pain gets worse with exercise; soreness gets better
2. Accidents
3. Shoulder injuries
4. Elbow injuries
5. Wrist and hand "sprains"
6. Back "aches"
7. Hamstring "pulls"
8. Knee injuries
9. "Gastroc pulls" and Achilles tendon rupture
10. Ankle, foot "sprains"

---

**Patient:** *"Doctor, when I go like this, it hoits!"*
**Doctor:** *"So don't go like that."*
                                        ***Henny Youngman***

---

Simple common sense, briefly stated. Coach, trainer, physician and pitcher work together to discern **precisely** what "hoits," what caused the "hoit" and how to fix it.

**This is not a medical text; this is a book about pitching. The comments in this chapter are offered as general guidelines to assist player and coach. Treatment protocols are best left in the hands of the medical provider and his/her consultants. For detailed descriptions and discussions of musculoskeletal anatomy, physiology and biomechanics, the reader should consult textbooks appropriate to these subjects. Our aim is twofold: (1) To present information suitable for non-medical persons; (2) to raise the awareness of players and coaches regarding the significance, care and prevention of common baseball injuries.**

"Ask two doctors for an opinion and you get three opinions." Another Henny Youngman quip.

The guidelines that follow are conservative, perhaps too conservative for some. However, Hippocrates once admonished: "First do no harm!"

## *Pain and Soreness*

There is a difference between **pain** and **soreness**. A pitcher who returns to throwing after the winter break, or on the fourth day after a "start," or after any other interval of nonthrowing, may well experience **soreness** and **stiffness** in various parts of his body. These symptoms should resolve as he warms up (see Chapter 1). If the soreness and stiffness steadily **increase** over a period of time (length of time depends on circumstances) this is not soreness. This is **pain**. Pain is nature's way of telling you that significant injury is present.

What about the "circumstances." A professional pitcher in spring training experiences soreness and stiffness which increase during the first three or four days, then slowly resolve, so at the end of a week he feels fine. On the other hand, a little-leaguer who is stiff and sore more than 36 to 48 hours needs to be rested. If his/her symptoms continue, this may be pain; see your doctor. **Special caution**: If a little-leaguer experiences **back pain** that lasts more than several days, stop play and consult the physician.

As a general rule apply ice to sore, stiff or painful parts for the first 24 hours. Ice reduces swelling and inflammation, and mollifies pain. Do not use heat until directed by a trainer or other qualified health provider. If a part or joint **swells**, elevate it, apply ice and consult a health provider.

When severe pain appears as a result of acute trauma (a sudden injury, like a collision or fall), this may indicate that significant damage has occurred. If there is any doubt, remove the player from the game for evaluation by the trainer or other health care provider.

After he was struck in the foot by a line drive during the 1937 All-Star Game in Washington, Dizzy Dean insisted on continuing to pitch in spite of excruciating pain in his (unbeknown to him) fractured large toe. That injury, not promptly attended to, may have ruined the remainder of Dizzy's career.

**First aid for nearly every acute extremity injury is encapsulated in the word, RICE:**

R – **Rest**

I – **Ice**

C – **Compression (splint or Ace wrap)**

E – **Elevation**

## *Accidents*

In 1947 a radio announcer broadcasts a spring training game between the Giants and Indians in Tucson, Arizona.

"Bob Feller steps in to face the Giant rookie, Larry Jansen. Jansen starts him with a curve low and away. Swing and a miss. Strike one. Feller shakes his head. Looks like he was impressed with Jansen's curve which just fell off the table. Jansen has the sign. Cranks it up. Feller swings and lines one back at the box. Good grief! The ball struck Jansen in the face!... He went down!... He appears to be all right, but that had to hurt! Mel Ott, the Giants' manager has come out to the mound; the infielders are gathered around Jansen... Ott is removing Jansen from the game."

That was the very first time I pitched for the Giants against another team. What happened? At that time the stands behind home plate were filled with fans, many of who wore white shirts. I simply lost sight of the ball against the white background. Facial surgery was required because my cheek bone and upper jaw were fractured.

Although the doctors allowed me back to practice in two weeks, I was restricted from strenuous exercise. After the season opened in April, I made two brief relief appearances, but did not start a game until mid-May. I beat the Braves 2-1 in that start (see Chapter 11, **A Pitching Career**). To wait so long for a start was really an opportunity. I had a chance to study the hitters around the National League. I ended the season with a 21-5 record (.808), best in the league.

**Coaching Significance**: Do not allow white-shirted persons to loiter behind the backstop!

On May 8, 1957, Herb Score of the Indians pitched against the Yankees. Gil McDougald hit a line drive back at Score which smashed into his face (nose, right cheek and around the right eye). Reportedly the blow affected Score's vision in the right eye. I can certainly sympathize with his plight.

Facial injuries are dramatic and usually game-ending for the pitcher. Pitchers (maybe it's fortunate the mound is back at 60 feet, 6 inches) are the closest players to the batter, except for the catcher – catcher's injuries are in a league of their own and discussions about them would fill volumes. Batted balls repeatedly bombard the "pitcher's station." The pitcher has to be a lightning-quick infielder not only to prevent injury, but also to field his position and make putouts!

**Trivia question: Who holds the record for the most Gold Glove awards in a career? Jim Kaat (pitcher!) and Brooks Robinson, third baseman: Each had 16. The injuries to Herb Score and to me were not preventable – not Kaat, not Robinson, not Pie Traynor for that matter – would have stopped the cannon shots that felled Score and me. Nevertheless, a pitcher must drill and discipline himself to field his position.**

---

### *Coaching Pearl*

An excellent prescription to sharpen a pitcher's infielder skills proceeds like this: Line up two or three pitchers against a backstop. A coach, heavy bat in hand, stands 50 feet away and slams the ball in different ways at the pitchers. This is done on a daily basis until the pitchers master the art of fielding these hits. Repeat the treatment as needed. For youngsters, use a firm rubber ball (not a baseball, but same size as a baseball) **to prevent injuries.**

---

Over a season the percentage of batted balls put into play at the "pitcher's station" is six to seven percent; at third base and shortstop, 12 to 14 percent. The pitcher, therefore, is responsible for handling a significant number of batted balls – just about half what the left side of the infield handles – but traveling at substantially faster or slower (bunts) speeds.

# *Terminology*

Acute (sudden) and chronic (long-standing) injuries begin with a **mechanism of injury (MOI)**. The **MOI** is the exact movement(s) that produces the injury. A skillful clinician can often say, "Tell me where you hurt, and I'll tell you what you were doing when you hurt yourself." In pitching, the culprit **MOI** is invariably a **necessary, but improperly executed,** part of the pitching motion.

# *Repetitive Use Injuries*

Each phase in the pitching motion provides an opportunity for repetitive use injuries. These are really recurring subtle injuries that arise from movements that are performed over and over again.

With each passing decade, new technology allows us to examine in greater detail the **MOI**. High-speed photography, telemetrics coupled to computers capable of rapidly generating line figures, high-speed electromyography are but a few of the analytic tools available.

Once the injury produces symptoms, a precise diagnosis can be reached by careful history, physical exam, X-rays if indicated, CT (computed tomography) and/or MRI (magnetic resonance imaging), and when absolutely necessary, arthrogram (X-ray taken after a special dye is placed in the joint). Of all these diagnostic steps, the most important are the first two: history and physical exam.

---

### *Coaching Pearl*

It is important for the coach to inquire about the **MOI**, because improper conditioning and warm-up, or faulty mechanics lie within his scope of expertise for correction.

---

As we discuss each injury, we frequently refer to illustrations in Chapter 2, **Mechanics**, because **injury is** often **the result of flawed mechanics**. The mechanics shown in these illustrations are correctly executed (except for Figures 2-11 and 2-12). They serve as departure points from which to begin discussions about flawed mechanics that ultimately lead to injuries.

# *Week-Ender or Spring Disease*

Nearly every Monday, and for several weeks in spring, we see at our clinic a significant number of patients who have violated the dictum: "Begin all new activities gradually and moderately."

Office workers unable to pursue yard chores, home repairs and hobbies during the week dash into weekend work frenzies to catch up. Inhabitants of the northern states, housebound all winter, emerge in spring to unroll a series of activities performed at fever pitch.

"Doc, I didn't feel any pain while I was trimming my hedge (or digging post holes or lifting motor parts or cutting back the weeds or moving furniture or – the list is endless)."

It's all part of nature's perversity. Nature does not warn you in these circumstances when enough is enough. Next day you hurt, and need help. What happened? Unconditioned and untrained body parts suffered injury during the work frenzy. Muscle strains and joint abuse follow. Had the office worker, or northern shut-in, warmed up before working, and set a limit on the amount of work or reduced the number of specific repetitions, the total damage would have been much less.

How do we know when enough is enough? The ground rule in sports is: when it starts to hurt **STOP**! From our comments above, you know that if you wait until it hurts, you have already gone too far. So, we rely on experience. The discussions in Chapter 1 on spring training are the result of 150 years of baseball experience. Fifty throws a day for batting practice – after an adequate warm-up – is reasonable. Even at that, it is expected – and normal – to feel some stiffness and soreness the next several days. Each day the soreness should improve as the warm-up commences.

After a day of pitching in a starting rotation, when should you throw again? Depends. Everyone is different. Assume a five-day starting rotation. Rest the arm for 48 hours. First day, ride a stationary bike 15 minutes. Second day, stair climb 15 minutes. Third day, play a game of pepper 15 minutes. Fourth day, ride the stationary bike 10 minutes and loosen up with 15 to 20 throws. Fifth day, you are the starter!

A different recipe needs be assembled for little-leaguers: much less throwing than high school age – and older – pitchers.

**Caution**: Do not warm up little-league pitchers during practice, then direct them to perform other chores, followed by pitching. Once the little-leaguer is warmed up, "pitch him." Our experience is that interrupting a session of throwing with other practice activities, followed by a return to throwing activities on the same day, creates unnecessary soreness and injuries in these very young players.

## *Shoulder Injuries — Overview*

Most pitching injures are the result of repetitive, but subtle, wear and tear over an extended period of time. These injuries occur during the acceleration and deceleration phases of the pitching motion. By far, the most serious injuries occur during the deceleration phase, because deceleration forces are nearly twice as great as the acceleration forces. Also, deceleration forces act for a shorter period of time on muscles whose size and strength is significantly less than the muscles of acceleration.

The shoulder is a ball-and-socket joint. The ball is located on the top of the arm bone (humerus), and the socket (glenoid) is formed from the union of several bony elements within the shoulder. Because this joint is a ball-and-socket arrangement surrounded by muscles and ligaments, the arm bone can travel forward, backward, sideways, **and most importantly, upward**. The muscles surrounding and attached to the shoulder rotate and swing it through its multiple planes of motion. It is precisely these muscles and ligaments that are at risk for injury. Exercise physiologists refer to these muscles as "dynamic stabilizers." Their job, in addition to moving the shoulder, is to make sure the ball remains in its socket. Also, vulnerable to injury are various "static" (immovable) stabilizers associated with the joint. Among these stabilizers are several ligaments, the capsule around the joint and the socket itself.

## *Shoulder Injuries During "Cocking"*

Study Figures 2-13 through 2-15. These figures show the pitcher with arms correctly extended at the shoulders. The elbows are also extended and elevated to shoulder height. The catapult is fully "cocked." Some sports medicine experts include parts of the forward arm motion in the "cocking" phases. However, when a pistol is "cocked" the hammer is pulled fully to the rear, and not coming forward! Looks innocent enough, but at this moment certain muscles may have sustained small strains. The pitcher strains muscles in this phase of the pitching motion by failure to attain full extension **in a relaxed manner**. Too rapid, or too violent an extension damages those muscles that carry the arm up and away from the trunk (deltoid and supraspinatus muscles), and those that rotate the arm backward (rotator cuff muscles). A too hasty, abrupt movement into this extended pose can also strain the long tendon of the biceps muscle, stretch the joint capsule and unduly bang the ball (humeral head) against the side of its socket.

Other underlying factors which contribute to injury at this phase are failure to fully extend the elbow ("short arming"), improper warm-up, throwing too many pitches after a layoff of more than several weeks ("spring disease") and/or improper conditioning (see Chapter 8).

**Pain** from muscles and static stabilizers injured during this phase is felt in the **front of the shoulder**.

# Shoulder Injuries During Acceleration

Now examine Figures 2-17 and 2-18. These illustrations show the pitcher's arm coming forward while the elbow bends out-ward (valgus) during the **acceleration phase** of the pitching motion. Here the arm bone (humerus) begins to rotate inward. The muscles that bring the arm forward and rotate it inward are now subject to stress and strain. During this phase, muscular damage occurs when the pitcher **fails to correctly align** his extremities and trunk along the pitcher plate–home plate line. This malalignment occurs in two forms: an **incomplete**, or a **"past-point"** pivot on the power foot. The **incomplete pivot** leaves the right-hander's aiming foot aligned to the right and the left-hander's to the left of the true line. The pitcher unconsciously attempts to correct this shortcoming by **overrotating** his arm inward. He thereby disrupts deceleration of the throwing arm and shoulder.

During the "past-point" pivot, the right-hander's **aiming foot** ends up to the left and the left-hander's to the right of the true line. Some refer to this as the pitcher's "falling off" to the left or right. When the pitcher "falls off" to the right or left, he unconsciously attempts to correct the overswing by **underrotating** his arm inward, and thereby frustrates a smooth deceleration. There are several excellent major-league pitchers who "fall off" on nearly every pitch. One must wonder what this throwing quirk does to the longevity of their arms. Study Figures 2-13 and 2-19 to understand the correct relationship of power (pivot) and aiming feet.

Repetitive use injuries arising out of this phase cause **pain inside the shoulder** (rotator cuff, socket) and along the upper, outer portion of the arm. In addition to malalignments, improper warm-up, faulty physical conditioning and "spring disease" predispose the pitcher to these injuries.

# Shoulder Injuries During Deceleration

Finally, review Figure 2-19. Here the shoulder has come fully forward and the elbow is fully extended as the upper extremity passes the point of maximum acceleration and enters into deceleration. The muscles of deceleration (rotators) located in the back of the shoulder "take the heat" here, because they are slowing down the inward turning of the arm and are keeping the ball in its socket. Injuries also occur within the socket itself if the rotator muscles are improperly conditioned.

The most flagrant mechanical flaw creating this deceleration injury is **incomplete follow-through**. Study Figures 2-20 through 2-22. Notice how these pitchers correctly flex the spine forward on the pelvis, and how the throwing arm swings through its arc as proper deceleration occurs.

**Pain from this repetitive injury appears in back of and inside the shoulder**. Ordinarily, this is a deeper and more intense pain than that appearing in the front of the shoulder, because it is symptomatic of a more severe injury.

---

### Coaching Pearls

Pain in the front of the shoulder is due to improper "cocking." Pain inside the shoulder and along the upper outer portion of the arm arises from imperfect acceleration. Pain in the back of the shoulder arises from flawed deceleration. Muscular injuries occurring in deceleration are more serious than injuries sustained during other phases of the pitching motion.

---

# Shoulder Impingement Syndrome and Rotator Cuff Injuries

This condition is one of the most common causes of chronic shoulder pain in pitchers. The cardinal (not the St. Louis type) symptom is a nearly constant aching **pain deep within the shoulder**, often accompanied by a throbbing **pain along the outside (lateral) area of the upper arm**. Early in the disease, pain appears during the "cocking" and acceleration phases of the throwing motion. In advanced forms of this injury, even passive rotation of the arm bone causes pain.

The term "impingement" is a medical term, popularized in 1972 by an orthopedic surgeon named C.S. Neer, M.D. The term means that certain shoulder muscles (especially the rotators), tendons and bursa rub against bony and/or ligamentous structures when the arm is moved overhead. The most notorious bony culprit is thought to be the archlike acromion process and coraco-acromional ligament inside the shoulder.

161

The acromion is a bony beaklike projection extending from the shoulder blade (scapula) into the shoulder. Beneath this arch passes the tendon of the supraspinatus muscle – an important rotator cuff muscle-tendon responsible for lifting the arm overhead, and away from the trunk while drawing the head of the arm bone into its socket. When the arm is lifted overhead, the supraspinatus tendon is vulnerable to rubbing and fraying against the overlying acromial arch. This tendon has a poor blood supply, and consequently, is slow to heal.

Some experts in sports medicine hold that the term "impingement" does **not** suggest there is **insufficient room** for the rotator muscles and tendons to move under the acromion. The term more correctly refers to inadequate **dynamic** (rotator muscle), or **static** (ligament, capsule) shoulder stabilizers. These stabilizers are "designed" to assure that the head of the arm bone (humerus) moves properly within its socket to prevent impingement of the rotator cuff muscles. The pitcher who experiences shoulder impingement problems has either improperly conditioned his shoulder muscles or has damaged his stabilizers through repetitive misuse – **flawed mechanics**. Occasionally, the damage follows acute trauma (see shoulder dislocations below).

Rotator cuff muscles, as the name suggests, cause the arm bone (humerus) to pivot and rotate within its socket. Most non-medical persons are surprised to learn that the rotators originate on the shoulder blade (scapula) and insert on the upper portion of the arm bone (humerus). **These four muscles** (supraspinatus, infraspinatus, subscapularis, teres minor) are the principal **dynamic shoulder stabilizers**. They carry out this job by drawing the head of the humerus into its socket. Failure of these muscles to properly perform this function leads to damage in the muscles themselves, the socket, static stabilizers, as well as adjacent soft and bony tissue. It is important, then, that these muscles be properly strengthened (Chapter 8), and employed with flawless mechanics (Chapter 2).

The pitcher strains and stresses the rotator cuff muscles, and invites impingement problems in the following four situations:

1. Failure to bring the throwing arm into the "cocked" position in a relaxed manner (supraspinatus and subscapularis).

2. Use of an exaggerated overhand delivery (supraspinatus).

3. Initiation of forward movement (acceleration) before the aiming foot is firmly planted (infraspinatus and teres minor).

4. Failure to **correctly align** shoulders, trunk and extremities along the pitcher plate-home plate path (all the rotator muscles).

5. Failure to completely and correctly "follow through" after release (all the rotators).

**SOUND FAMILIAR?**

**Coaching Significance**: Pitchers experiencing pain (not soreness) in the shoulder require referral to a medical provider to determine the exact nature of the injury, initiate proper treatment and supervise adequate rehabilitation. Once the "rehab" has restored the shoulder to its preinjury status, the coach's role is to study and correct the flawed mechanics.

If not corrected, impingement syndrome can often lead to a partial or complete rotator cuff tear.

---

**Coaching Pearl**

Teach correct mechanics and save an arm, maybe a career.

---

**Caveat:** Do not change the mechanics of a pitcher who is comfortable with his motion, performing well, and has no symptoms.

# Bicipital (Biceps) Tendonitis

The biceps is located on the front of the arm. It flexes the arm and forearm and turns the palm upward (supination). This muscle has two muscular bellies (or heads) and two tendons. The tendon of the long head runs within a groove over the head of the humerus. This tendon is one of the body's longer tendons, and because of its length and position in the groove, it is easily rubbed and frayed. So common is this fraying action that, even when a pitcher experiences no symptoms, finger pressure on the tendon causes substantial discomfort.

The repetitive rubbing on this tendon (**MOI**) frequently induces an inflammatory condition called tendonitis. The cardinal symptom is pain in the upper front part of the arm and within the shoulder. The biceps tendon is vulnerable at any time it performs its actions.

**Coaching Significance:** Biceps tendonitis can accompany other impingement symptoms, or it can appear alone. Most often, it is difficult to differentiate the two problems. A pitcher with signs of bicipital tendonitis and/or impingement needs the attention of a medical provider.

163

# Shoulder Dislocations

There are two kinds of shoulder dislocation: anterior and posterior. The anterior dislocation is much more common. Both these injuries result from falls, collisions or certain forceful stresses placed on the arm. Dislocation is a medical term that means the head of the arm bone (humerus) is separated out of its socket.

A base runner who overslides a bag — feet first — and reaches out with a hand to catch the bag, can force his arm to rotate upward and outward and away from the trunk (**MOI**), thereby creating an anterior dislocation. A head-first slider (see below) who "late-slides" can force an arm to rotate violently inward and toward the trunk (**MOI**), and create a posterior dislocation.

The cardinal manifestation of a dislocation is severe pain and complete loss of function in the shoulder. With an anterior dislocation, the ballplayer positions the injured arm so that it hangs with a slight rotation **away** from the trunk, supported usually by the uninjured upper extremity. The appearance of the injured shoulder differs remarkably from that of the healthy shoulder. The injured shoulder assumes a "squared-off" appearance. The tip of the shoulder is very prominent and an indentation appears below the "tip." The examiner can feel the humeral head as a ball in the front portion of the shoulder. Movement is not possible due to pain. The posterior dislocation often lacks definitive signs, except that the player commonly holds the injured arm close to, and rotated toward, the trunk. Both dislocations require prompt reduction by a medical provider. Yanking maneuvers or application of brute force by well-meaning lay bystanders is discouraged.

**Coaching Significance**: Forces sufficient to cause shoulder dislocations can also cause fractures, rotator cuff tears, AC injuries, biceps tendon ruptures and/or later impingement problems. This injury requires the attention of experts to make a correct diagnosis and initiate proper treatment with rehabilitation.

# AC Arthritis

This disease follows a blunt injury to the "point" of the shoulder where a bony protuberance from the shoulder blade (scapula) unites with the end of the collar bone (clavicle) to form a bony arch. Hence the jargon: AC or acromioclavicular joint. Arthritis denotes an inflammatory process. Occasionally, this arthritis appears without a history of blunt injury, and the inflammation apparently results from repetitive subtle movements in the joint from throwing or weight lifting.

The cardinal symptom in this condition is shoulder point pain with throwing or lifting overhead. The "AC sign" is a localized "pain in the point" brought on by the pitcher's reaching across his chest to grasp the opposite arm. At times it is difficult to differentiate AC pain from impingement pain. However, with AC arthritis even gentle pressure on the AC joint is very painful.

**Coaching Significance**: This pain in the shoulder, like all shoulder pain, requires the attention of a medical provider. Pure AC arthritis does not appear to be associated with flawed mechanics, but we continue to study this problem from a mechanical point of view.

## Prevention of Shoulder Injuries

Knowing the causes of the injuries is the first step in prevention. For those not in possession of sophisticated monitoring devices, plain home videos will provide assistance to discover improperly executed mechanics. Proper conditioning, sufficient warm-up and correct mechanics all fall within the coach's purview.

## Arm Bone (Humerus) Fractures

This injury can appear during the act of throwing. Usually, the injury is the end result of a flawed acceleration phase mechanic during which the thrower makes a violent throw before setting his feet (**MOI**). This type of pitch is likely to occur with a runner on base. If the hurler thinks the runner may "go," he correctly "slide steps," or "quick kicks" but improperly launches the ball toward the catcher before setting his feet. In this flaw, "the arm gets ahead of the body" and acts like a bullwhip. The snap of the bullwhip, as the arm rotates violently inward, can impose sufficient stress to fracture the arm bone (humerus).

Dave Dravecky fractured his arm after returning from cancer surgery and radiation therapy on his arm. Somehow the stresses of surgery and radiation caused the arm in its weakened state to fracture from the torque induced by the throwing motion.

## Elbow Injuries

Overview: Like shoulder injuries, elbow injuries are usually the result of subtle damage inflicted over a period of time (chronic). Occasionally, an acute injury may crop up (see Little-Leaguer's elbow below).

The most serious elbow injuries occur mainly during acceleration. Unlike the ball-and-socket shoulder joint, the elbow is a hinge joint. Consequently, the elbow is a more stable joint than the shoulder.

During the acceleration phase the elbow bends **outward** (valgus) as it passes the head (Fig. 2-18), then **inward** (varus) as it **approaches extension** (Fig. 2-19). This bending places repetitive stresses on the inner (medial) and outer (lateral) elbow structures (**MOI**).

At the **end of acceleration** the arm and forearm forcefully extend (straighten forward) at the elbow under the influence of the triceps. To temper the force of this extension, the flexor muscles (the biceps and brachialis) contract in a balanced fashion. When these muscle contractions are unbalanced, they become additional **mechanisms of injury** during extension. If extension is not completely decelerated, overextension occurs and pain is felt within the elbow and in the triceps. If elbow extension is decelerated too rapidly, unbalanced flexion forces stress the biceps, and pain appears in the front of the arm. Flawed deceleration also commonly leads to a condition known as valgus extension overload (VEO). Muscle imbalance is the result of improper muscle conditioning. (See Chapter 8).

Incompletely tempered extension at the elbow can also cause wear on joint bone and cartilage on the outside (lateral) elbow parts. The lateral injury can progress in persons under 18 to create a condition known as osteochondritis dissecans (old-timers referred to this as "bone chips") in which a piece of bone and cartilage separate from the end of the arm bone. When this condition arises, the player needs to be a spectator for the rest of the season and attend periodic medical follow-up. Surgery to remove "bone chips" may be required.

Coaching significance: Elbow injuries are acceleration phase injuries and require prompt referral to a medical provider.

## Little-Leaguer's Elbow

Two U.S. Air Force orthopedic radiologists, Brogdon and Crow, coined the term "little-leaguer's elbow" in 1960. They described an avulsion (tearing away) of the inner (medial) ossification center in the elbow. This structure is part of the immature arm bone not yet firmly united with the main shaft. If you examine your elbow you can feel three bumps: One on the outside (lateral), on the back (point of elbow) and inside (medial). The inside bump is the medial epicondyle in the adult and the medial ossification center (epiphysis) in the youngster under age 16. We point this out because if the inside bump hurts there is a good chance the youngster is experiencing "little-leaguer's elbow." This condition requires prompt referral to a physician.

How does this condition arise? **Excessive throwing, and not the type of pitch thrown, e.g., curveball** (see Chapter 1)!. It is usually a chronic condition in which subtle injury occurs during the **acceleration** phase when the elbow **bends outward then inward** and the wrist and hand flex forward to release the ball – **MOI**. The common tendon for hand and wrist flexors is attached to the inside "bump" (ossification center) at the elbow! Throwing invariably makes this condition worse, and its cardinal symptom is **pain**. Sometimes the elbow swells over the inside bump. **Occasionally the pain appears suddenly** (acute injury). This is worrisome and may indicate an abrupt tearing away (avulsion) of the medial ossification center.

**Coaching Significance: Prevention is the best treatment. Proper warm-up, correct pitching mechanics and limitations on number of throws per day and per week are required**. Little-league rules wisely prescribe the **number of innings** a pitcher may throw per week. It is also necessary to limit **number of throws**. What if a pitcher throws 30 or 40 pitches in a single inning?

## Ulnar Collateral Ligament Injuries

Reportedly the "pop" that Tommy John heard, and felt, in his elbow – an injury which caused him to exit abruptly from a game – was a ruptured ulnar collateral ligament (UCL). This ligament spans the space between the medical epicondyle (see above) and the ulnar bone in the forearm. This is a thick, tough triangular ligament that supports the inside (medial) portion of the elbow joint.

During acceleration tremendous forces bear upon this ligament, as the elbow bends inward – (MOI) Improper warm-up, fatigue and **failure to align the trunk and shoulders** along the pitcher plate - home plate path (for faulty alignment, see Figure 2-12) all combine to produce chronic, and at times, acute stresses that exceed the strength of the ligament. The ligament then develops tears, or it may eventually rupture.

## UCL Instability and Ulnar Nerve Injury

During the acceleration phase, as the elbow bends outward then inward, a stretch is placed on the ulnar nerve! The ulnar nerve passes the elbow through a groove at the back of the elbow. In this location, the nerve is referred to as the "crazy bone" by non-anatomists. During the outward bend of a normal elbow joint, the ulnar nerve may stretch 4 to 5 mm. When the UCL is weakened by small rips and tears, the elbow joint becomes unstable. In this situation the nerve stretches even farther and may become compressed in its groove.

The symptoms of nerve stretching and compression are uncomfortable, often painful, needlelike sensations running down the inside (medial) surface of the forearm into the little finger, and part of the ring finger. Weakness in some hand muscles may accompany the sensory changes.

The **MOI** of UCL instability and nerve injury is excessive outward and inward bending of the elbow brought on by poorly conceived mechanics – **failure to align**!

**Coaching Significance**: Inside (medial) elbow pain has at least two sinister causes: UCL strain (or rupture) and little-leaguer's elbow. Pain in the outside parts of the elbow may indicate serious damage to bone and cartilage (osteochondintis dissecans). Both are preventable, or at least remedial with correct mechanics. A youngster who cannot straighten his arm at the elbow may have a flexion contracture due to osteochondritis dissecans. This is serious. These conditions are preventable with correct mechanics. **Pain** in these parts requires referral to a medical provider; **prevention is within the province of the coach.**

# Prevention of Elbow Injuries (In General)

Understanding the **MOI** is the first step in prevention. The other preventive measures include adequate warm-up, proper conditioning and correct mechanics.

Pearl: A sidearm pitcher is more likely to injure his elbow, because the inward bending during acceleration is much greater than that experienced by the pitcher who "comes over the top." These latter pitchers are more likely to injure the shoulder. Walter Johnson spent his entire career pitching with a sidearm motion, and there have been at least two very good "sidearmers" since: Ewell ("The Whip") Blackwell and Don Drysdale.

# Wrist and Hand Injuries

"There is no such thing as a wrist or hand sprain," so spoke my professor of orthopedics when I was a medical student.

What did the professor really mean? He meant that hand and wrist injuries are "sprains" only if the presence of a fracture or dislocation has been ruled out. Fractures and dislocations are most properly identified by X-ray.

Acute trauma is the principal cause of wrist and hand injuries. Repetitive use (chronic) injuries to the wrist, e.g., carpal tunnel syndrome, are uncommon in baseball, unless the athlete is performing repetitive tasks with the wrist and hand in another setting (typing long dissertations on a computer keyboard – maybe writing a book like this).

The **MOI** of two common traumatic injuries – fracture of the scaphoid and radius bones – is a fall onto an outstretched hand with wrist bent backwards. The radius fracture occurs at the end of the forearm on the thumb side. The scaphoid fracture occurs in a bone located less than an inch from the end of the radius. This bone can also fracture when striking an object (opponent's head) with the heel of the hand.

**The cardinal manifestation of a fracture in either bone is pain, accompanied by swelling that may be minimal**. Hence the temptation to dismiss the injury as a "sprain." Fractures left unattended can lead to chronic pain, and later, to an arthritic condition known as "post traumatic arthritis." If this occurs in your throwing hand, you may have to take up accounting.

The immediate first aid is RICE – rest (immobilization), ice, compression (with an ace bandage) and elevation. A trip to your medical provider on the day of the injury is mandatory.

## Gamekeeper's Thumb

This is a catching injury. The **MOI** is forcible outward movement of the thumb away from the hand (abduction) as the ball is partially caught or deflected by the thumb. The main symptom is pain in the inside part of the joint between hand and thumb.

The injury here is a partial or complete tear of the ulnar collateral ligament (UCL). Remember: there is an elbow ligament with the same name. This ligament spans and supports the first – thumb – joint (MCP). This ligament is an important support, because when the thumb pinches against the other fingers to hold an object, the MCP joint must remain stable or the pinch grip will fail.

The first aid is RICE. This injury must be evaluated by a medical provider for definitive diagnosis, to check for fracture and for treatment.

## The Mallet Finger (Baseball Finger)

The **MOI** is a direct blow to the extended finger tip(s) from a poorly caught ball. The blow causes a backward bending of the finger tip at the joint (DIP). This bending disrupts the extensor tendon and other joint structures leaving the athlete with a finger tip that bends downward toward the palm and that will not straighten. Commonly the ballplayer or coach attempts to straighten the finger tip in an effort to reduce the pain. It is best that a medical provider attempt this maneuver and search for a fracture.

# Finger Dislocations

Occasionally, a finger tip, or the joint in the middle of the finger (proximal interphalangeal joint – PIP joint), will dislocate through the same **MOI** as a simple mallet finger. The malalignment of the two parts is obvious. One attempt at reduction by the trainer may be reasonable; a failure at reduction needs the attention of a medical provider.

**Coaching Significance**: The player who incurs a mallet finger or a finger joint dislocation should be removed from the game and referred to a medical provider. Too often these apparently simple injuries involve finger fractures.

# Hamate Fracture

Recently, two famous major-league sluggers disappeared from their lineups into the disabled list (DL) because they had sustained hamate fractures. Where the devil is this infernal bone? The hamate is a small wrist bone. If one were to draw a straight line along the palm from the web space between ring and little fingers, back toward the skin fold of the wrist, the line would pass over the hamate about 2 cm before reaching the fold. Expert clinicians are able to locate, by careful pressure, a portion of this bone referred to as the "hamate hook."

One **MOI** for a fracture of this bone is direct blow(s) to the bone from the bat itself. Hold a bat in your hands in the manner of Ken Griffey Jr. or Jose Canseco. The nub (knob/base) of the bat does not strike the wrist until full extension is achieved. It is conceivable that this is the point in the hitter's swing when an encounter between bat and hamate occurs. Given the right amount of force supplied by bat and ball, a fracture ensues. This is not a common occurence, and its prevention (if that is possible) is left in the hands of the hitting coach.

# Head-First Sliders

For those who desire to emulate Pete Rose or Ricky Henderson, take heed. Those two ballplayers were masters at their trade and came by sliding "noggin first" very naturally.

This base pilfering technique has its hazards! First, the injury I see most often arises from the closed, or partially closed, fist hitting the bag. When the fingers flex to make a fist, the knuckles, powered by the trailing, flying body, smash into the anchored bag. The base was not intended to function as a boxer's punching bag – it does not move in response to a blow. The result is an all too often jamming or fracture of the knuckles.

When the fingers are extended, they tend to "surf" across the ground and slide up onto the bag instead of smashing into it.

Second, heads frequently encounter hard parts of the baseman's anatomy, and noses are occasionally "smooshed" by a firmly applied tag.

Third, I have seen several fractured forearms in "noggin-first" base bandits. Lower extremity "bone ware" tends to be more rugged. **Best to slide feet first, unless your name is Henderson or Rose.**

The first aid is RICE. If there is any doubt about the magnitude of an injured hand, head, wrist or forearm, refer the player to a medical provider.

## Referred Pain

Do not assume that upper extremity pain necessarily arises in the part that hurts. It is not uncommon for shoulder, elbow, even wrist and hand pain, to be referred pain whose origins lie in the neck, where vertebrae, nerve roots, spinal cord and/or disc problems may be the culprit.

## Back Injuries

Back pain in the little-leaguer that lasts more than several days needs the attention of a physician, because it might signal that a small stress fracture has occurred. The part involved is a segment of the bony arch surrounding the spinal cord in the lower (lumbar) spine. This segment is called the **pars interarticularis**. If this fracture is detected early, it is potentially reversible (will heal).

For the adult pitcher the **MOI** of back injuries fills a lengthy list. However, most commonly the **MOI** is defective deceleration: failure to correctly flex the spine (forward) at the pelvis. Consult Figures 2-20, 2-21 and 2-22. Notice that these pitchers have flexed the spine fully forward at the pelvis during deceleration. Except for knuckleball pitchers who "chuck" the ball at the batter, deceleration properly terminates only when the pitcher is nearly fully flexed forward. Pitchers who "reign up short" distribute the remaining untempered acceleration forces throughout the body, including the spine. In some respects, pitchers who fail to fully flex forward (follow through) become a **human bullwhip**, the snapping end of which is the spine and shoulder.

There are two general categories of back pain: Mechanical and structural. **Mechanical pain** is produced by excessive repetitive spinal movements, appears with certain positions or postures and is muscular in origin. **Structural pain** is produced by derangement of the bony parts of the spinal column. Fracture of the pars interarticularis discussed above is an example of structural pain.

**Coaching Significance**: Regardless of its origin, back pain in the adult that persists longer than two weeks in spite of rest, ice, mild analgesics (ibuprofen, etc.), active-passive exercises, calls for an evaluation by a health provider.

## Trauma Followed by Neck Pain

Rare in baseball, but it can happen. In the 1940s, Pete Reiser, a great outfielder for the Brooklyn Dodgers, crashed into a wall while chasing down a fly ball. He may have briefly lost consciousness. His head and neck hurt immediately after the collision. What he needed was immobilization of his neck (C-spine) and transport to a medical facility for X-rays of the neck. Pete was never the same after this injury. He was plagued with constant pain in neck and arms for many months.

---

### Coaching Pearl

Any injury above the clavicle followed by neck pain, especially if there has been a loss of consciousness (LOC) — however brief — requires C-spine immobilization and transport to a medical facility properly equipped to evaluate the injury.

---

## Hamstrings

Hamstring injuries are one of the most common and frustrating athletic injuries. **These muscles flex the knee, extend the thigh and help to decelerate knee extension.** There are at least two MOI. The first is a sudden knee **extension** improperly tempered by the flexor hamstrings. A second **MOI** occurs when a fully extended knee is violently flexed. Both these **MOI** commonly appear during sprints, e.g., the pitcher's sprint to cover first on an infield hit to the first baseman, or the pitcher's scramble to gobble up a bunt. Too violent an extension of the aiming knee fits the first **MOI**. The ballplayer with a strained hamstring will not want to continue in the game. Remove him. First aid: RICE. Refer this player to a medical provider.

The short head of the biceps femoris – the hamstring that attaches to the outside (lateral) surface in back of the knee – is the hamstring most frequently injured. It is a design flaw. The nerve that signals this hamstring to decelerate knee extension apparently fires too early – in some people – and the powerful extensor muscles (quads) literally tear this hamstring's tendon.

Hamstrings carry a well-deserved notorious reputation, "once strained, always strained." Why this? Hamstring strains tend to recur. Reason: Inadequate rehabilitation of the injured muscle(s), and failure to strengthen the hamstrings before the injury. Watch athletes warm up. Stretching the hamstring occupies a large part of the menu. This exercise is well-advised, but before and after the season, and between games, supplement stretching with strengthening. A strain weakens the muscle, and weak hamstrings are prone to further strains – the proverbial vicious cycle.

**Coaching Significance: Hamstring strains deserve expert treatment and expert rehabilitation.**

# Knee Injuries

The knee: Appears to be a simple hinge joint, but it is really a complex entity. **The injured knee is more likely to fail rehabilitative treatment than any other joint.** The result: Progressive, residual instability and greatly diminished athletic ability.

Fortunate for the pitcher, but not his running-fielding teammates, is the fact that serious knee injuries occur infrequently to pitchers. The usual scenario surrounding knee injuries – the **MOI** – are blows to either side of the knees (hard slide into a baseman), running-decelerating-cutting (rounding a base), unanticipated knee thrust (stepping in a hole or on a sprinkler), falling and twisting the knee (slip on wet surface), mislanding a jump (infielder leaping to avoid hard-sliding base runner) and the list goes on. The key elements to knee injuries are sudden twisting, bending or extension – usually in a weight-bearing knee.

The twisting motion of pitchers like Hideo Nomo causes me to worry. Why? Watch Nomo's power leg and note that when Nomo opens his hands (especially in the windup), his power knee nearly faces second base. From this position he executes a twisting movement through a horizontal arc of more than 90 degrees as he properly aligns himself with home plate. Nomo has succeeded for years with this motion, but it is wise not to teach this move to young pitchers.

**Coaching Significance**: Like hamstring problems, knee injuries require expert help. After a knee injury if the ballplayer is unable to run without pain or limp, remove him from the game. First aid is RICE. Second aid is a medical provider.

# Gastrocnemius Strain
## ("Gastroc pull" or "tennis leg")

This injury is described because (1) it can be confused with Achilles tendon injuries, and (2) if not properly treated, results often in months of disability.

The "Gastroc" is one of two large muscles located on the back of the leg. Its partner is the Soleus muscle. Both muscles share the Achilles tendon and cause the foot to flex toward the ground (plantar flexion).

The "Gastroc pull" usually involves only the inside (medial) half of the "Gastroc" and not the lateral side or soleus. The most common **MOI** is a sudden, violent flexion of the foot, e.g., during the pitcher's sprint toward first. Some experts believe that the injury is more common in female persons over the age of 30, but I have seen at least two cases during 1996 in young pitchers. The pitcher frequently hears a "pop" and experiences instant pain in the upper leg. Soon after the injury, the pitcher finds that he can walk only on the toes of the injured member. Why? The injured muscle goes into spasm and causes the foot to plantar flex continuously. Occasionally this injury is confused with an Achilles tendon rupture. However, a ruptured Achilles tendon cannot plantar flex the foot. Swelling and dislocation (purple) over the injured "Gastroc" occurs within hours and prompts a visit to a medical provider. The first aid is **RICE**.

**Coaching Significance**: The injury occurs in the fatigued pitcher who has improperly conditioned his leg muscles. This equation's solution lies within the purview of the coach.

# Achilles Tendon Rupture

In Chapter 1, Achilles, the Greek's star pitcher (he hurled spears), eventually ended his career after a devastating injury. Paris, a Trojan hitter, shot an arrow into the back of Achilles' heel – the tendon which now bears his name.

The Achilles tendon is the large, very firm tendon which joins the gastrocnemius-soleus muscles to the heel bone. The rupture (total or partial) occurs while jumping and landing. The **MOI** is usually a rapid knee extension accompanied by a forceful dorsiflexion (upward bending) of ankle and foot. The player, and often those standing nearby, hear a loud pop as the tendon rips apart. The player experiences a sensation of being kicked in back of the ankle. Nearly always the player goes down. When he stands, he is unable to move his foot downward. The only clue to tendon disruption other than pain may be a definite defect ("notch") in the tendon.

**Coaching Significance**: Do not allow the player to walk or stand on the injured extremity. The tendon tear may be incomplete. Attempted walking may tear the remaining tendon. A medical provider needs to evaluate the injury at once.

---

### Coaching Pearl

When in doubt, take him out. Do not allow injured players to continue in the game if there is any doubt about the significance or severity of an injury.

---

It is important for the coach to understand mechanisms of injury (MOI). Many MOIs have their origins in faulty mechanics and improper preparation. Correction of these flaws lies within the coaching expertise.

## Ankle-Foot Injuries

The number of injuries to the ankle and foot is legion. An attempt to describe each injury would fill a volume. No sport is spared ankle injuries. Unlike knee injuries, nearly every ankle injury responds to rehabilitation. The majority of ankle injuries are sprains, and most of these injuries affect the lateral (outside) ligaments of the ankle.

The most common **MOI** of lateral ligament injury is forceful turning in (inversion and supination) of the ankle and foot. First aid: **RICE.** The ankle is invariably painful after this injury and the ballplayer should be assisted from the field such that he does not walk on the affected limb. Because some ankle injuries represent fractures, high-grade sprains or ligament/tendon disruptions, a medical provider should be consulted.

**Coaching Significance**: Do not allow the player with a painful, swollen ankle to continue in the game. The magnitude of injury is unknown until medically assessed.

## Referred Pain

Just as pain felt in the upper extremity may be referred from the neck, so also can pain in the lower extremity be referred from the lower (lumbosacral) spine.

# Turf Toe

This is a repetitive use injury which causes variable amounts of pain and swelling over the ball of the foot (the metatarsophalangeal joint of the large toe). It is more commonly incurred on unyielding, artificial turf – hence the name. The **MOI** is repetitive bending on the ball of the foot as the ballplayer correctly pushes off on his toes while running. This ailment can be very disabling and requires referral to a medical provider. A stiff-soled shoe fitted with a rigid plate in the toe will prevent a recurrence. Great runners do not enjoy wearing this type of shoe, so expect a protest!

# Foot Arch Pain (Plantar Fascitis)

This is also a repetitive use injury induced by **new, excessive** activities such as sprints or hill running. These activities invite a visit by the pain devil in the arch of the foot and/or the heal.

The plantar fascia is a thick, canvaslike sheet of tissue which extends deep inside the foot arch from heel to base of the toes. Its role is to maintain the foot arch. First aid for plantar fascitis is ice and elevation. The trainer can often provide dramatic relief with "Low-Dye" taping technique. **Caveat**: Athletic activities must cease until the foot is totally painless. A heel cup and orthotic arch support may help prevent recurrences.

**Coaching Significance**: Avoid well-intentioned, but excessive new training, conditioning and practice techniques. Remember: nature brings changes about slowly.

# Eye Care

Some young players unaccountably deteriorate in performance. While players, coaches, trainers, managers – and even physicians – sort through biomechanics, the musculoskeletal system and the social life of the afflicted player, the problem grows inexorably worse. After weeks of searching for a source to the problem, someone – usually the batboy – casually remarks, "Does he need glasses?" Well, out of the mouths of babes, etc... The player often does not recognize changes in his visual acuity because the changes evolve subtly. The unexplained problem may lie in the eyes of the afflicted. Enough said.

# Summation

We could fill thick volumes with discussions of baseball injuries. Sports medicine experts have already done this for us. Our goals were (1) to describe the more common injuries; (2) to discuss the significance of these injuries for pitcher and coach; (3) to present coaching methods to prevent injury.

# 8
# Pitching Physiology

*George A. Jansen, M.D.*

## In a Nutshell

1.  Baseball muscles
2.  Muscle size, strength, power, endurance
3.  Resistance training
4.  Coaches must be scientific
5.  Curls and little-leaguer's elbow
6.  Balanced weight training
7.  Build your own gym
8.  Muscle microcomputers
9.  Dehydration can be disastrous
10. Wholesome food is the only drug needed

> *"The young men sometimes do not listen to their elders, because they want to rebel, or because they do not understand the wisdom of the elders."*
> **Cheyenne chief at the signing of the Treaty of 1851 – Fort Laramie**

Substitute the words "young ballplayers" and "young coaches" for the chief's "young men," and you will understand the points developed below. Like **Chapter 7, Baseball Injuries,** this chapter is not intended to be a complete text on its subject. The intent is to present basic, thought-provoking material to the coach and ballplayer. They will undoubtedly expand on this topic by consulting supplemental texts like those cited in **Appendix B.**

# Muscle Endurance

Most pertinent to pitching activities is the topic of endurance. **Endurance** is the length of time muscles continue to contract until fatigued. Endurance depends chiefly on muscule glycogen stores. Glycogen breaks down to glucose which supplies energy for muscle contraction. A ballplayer builds his glycogen stores with a high-carbohydrate diet.

The amount of glycogen stored in muscle by the ballplayer on a high-carbohydrate diet is about twice the amount stored on a mixed diet and more than six times the amount stored on a high-fat diet. "Carbos," preferably the **complex type** (pasta, other starches), need be the ballplayers' most frequent bill of fare – pay attention, Mom! (Guyton, 941)

When physiologists study marathon runners (some ballgames are just that), endurance is defined as the time the marathoner can continue to run until total fatigue occurs. Amazingly, those on a high-carbo diet can go three times as far as those who consume a high-fat diet, and twice as far as those on mixed diets.

The ancient poet, Horace, cautioned: "Anything or everything, but in moderation." No one should **limit** his/her diet to carbohydrates alone. **A balanced diet is required to grow and maintain health**. "High carbo" means that at least 65 percent of daily caloric consumption is taken as carbohydrates.

**Caution:** Avoid gas-producing and spicy foods on game days. While these foods may provide JATO (jet assisted takeoff) on the base path, the amount of propulsion is negligible. In some persons these foods produce mild stomach cramps. Cramps tend to subtract from one's concentration. Baseball lore recounts a story about Babe Ruth who once indulged himself in a dietary indiscretion. Reportedly, he consumed a large number (some say 30!) hot dogs several hours before a game. He soon found himself unable to play that day because of stomach cramps. What most historians fail to mention is that it was the spicy mustard that got the Babe! **Even so, don't eat like that**.

**In addition to proper diet, low-resistance and high-repetition exercise improves endurance.** For baseball players, bike riding is an inexpensive and highly efficient method to enhance endurance. Ballplayers carried to and from the park in cars, trucks and buses are rendered a disservice. Sitting adds nothing to endurance. If the park is at least five miles away, ride a bike, and not one with gears! Use a mountain bike. If it is all uphill, so much the better. If riding the streets is dangerous or impractical, use a stationary bike. Stationary bikes are excellent, because the loads and resistance are adjustable, and you're off the streets.

Bike riding provides **aerobic** training, a not to be underestimated – or neglected – part of a pitcher's development. Recall, however, that baseball is principally an anaerobic sport (see below). **Pitching endurance is important** in getting to – and beyond – the sixth inning, and through (heaven forbid) the 30-pitch inning.

## Muscle Strength

**Muscle size determines muscle contractile strength. Contractile force** is the most useful measurement of muscle strength, and in a healthy adult male this force equals about 3 to 4 kilograms per square centimeter of cross-sectional area. The larger the cross-sectional area, the greater the strength. Large muscles can bring good news, and bad. An Olympic weight lifter whose quadriceps muscle* has a cross-sectional area of 125cm$^2$ can generate 1,100 pounds of force in his quads. During a lift the quads transmit this force over the kneecap to the patellar tendon**. No wonder, then, that this tendon occasionally ruptures in weight lifters (Guyton, 941).

After each contraction a muscle needs to relax, lengthen or stretch in preparation for the next contraction. Contraction and stretch actions whip-saw muscles, tendons, adjacent joints and ligaments with forces commensurate with muscle size. Consequently, the athlete should increase muscle size in a gradual, progressive manner under expert supervision, because if this muscular activity is overdone, severe joint, muscle, tendon and ligament inflammation and injury may occur.

**Most importantly: Pitchers must develop lean, strong – not bulky – muscles! Bulk subtracts from the flexibility and fine muscle motor control necessary to pitching.** More on this later!

---

*Muscle in front part of thigh - often referred to as "quads."
**Spans the gap between kneecap and leg bone and attaches to leg bone.

# *Muscle Power*

**Muscle power** is a commodity different from **muscle strength**. Power is a measure of the amount of work a muscle performs per unit of time. The speed of a sprinter in a dash or a base runner running the bases depends on muscle power.

Human muscles disburse power according to a strange schedule. A well-trained ballplayer during a maximum power surge, e.g., running out a triple, will attain more than 55 percent of the total power **attainable** by his muscles in the **first 10 seconds** of his run. After the first 10 seconds, his power falls off drastically. In the next 10 seconds, he will be able to achieve only another 15 percent. The distance, home to third (via second), is 270 feet – nearly 100 yards. An excellent sprinter can cover 100 yards in 10 seconds. Considering that the hitter has to turn two corners, how long does it take a speedster (Ricky Henderson or Ty Cobb) to get to third? "Cool Papa" Bell, legendary speester of the old Negro League, reportedly made it around all four bases (120 yards) in 13 seconds.

So what is the point? When your coach directs you to do **"wind sprints,"** thank him. **You are improving power** – the amount of work that muscles can perform per unit of time. Pitchers occasionally hit triples! Ask Tom Glavine (NLCS 1996).

# *Anaerobic and Aerobic Capacities*

Another benefit derived from "wind sprints" is an enlargement of the ballplayer's **anaerobic capacity.** Active muscles obtain energy from two metabolic systems: aerobic and anaerobic. The **anaerobic system** provides short-term energy for brief, explosive movements, e.g., dashes to steal a base, to field a hit or to charge a bunt. **Most – but not all – baseball muscular activities are anaerobic.** In spring training, daily wind sprints of 90 to 270 feet, repeated 20 to 30 times – after appropriate warm-up and stretches – is one acceptable method to enhance anaerobic capacity. The number of daily wind sprints should exceed by at least 20 percent the number of explosive movements a player is expected to perform in a game.

The **aerobic system** provides energy for sustained activity, e.g., all the work performed in a game between explosive movements. Aerobic training is best provided by 20- to 25-minute jogs, swims or bicycle rides.

Both anaerobic and aerobic training must be on the physiological menu for pitchers. The specific regimen depends on team policy and the conditioning coach's philosophy. During the playing season, the number of anaerobic repetitions and the duration of aerobic exercises are reduced, appropriate to the pitcher's physical condition and work load with special care to avoid fatigue, exhaustion or overtraining.

**Caution: Most exercise-related injuries occur during the final repetitions or minutes of an exercise!**

# *Increasing Muscle Size with Resistance Training*

In the healthy male athlete, muscle **size before** starting a training program is determined by two factors outside his control: genetics and testosterone levels. **Caution-Caution-Caution: Do not use anabolic steroids, including testosterone, to build muscle size. The dangers to health are very serious.** See discussion of "rhoid" abuse later in this chapter.

**Resistance Training**: Muscles that function against no resistance (load) develop insignificant increases in strength, even when exercised for long periods of time. The corollary to this principle is that muscles that contract to near **maximal force of contraction** (against a load) build strength rapidly. Muscle physiologists have shown that maximal muscle contractions accomplished in three separate sets, six to eight repetitions per set, three times a week, produce efficient strength increases (and muscle size) without creating **chronic** soreness or muscle or tendon injury.

It is possible to enlarge muscles 45 to 65 percent through resistance training. This enlargement is due either to hypertrophy (simple enlargement of individual fibers), or due to hyperplasia (some fibers split in two and both fibers separately enlarge). Weight lifters refer to this phenomena as "muscle ripping." Every time a pitcher hurls a ball, he works against some resistance. It is precisely in this way that he develops his pitching muscles (Guyton, 945).

**Baseball muscles must be "lean and strong," not "bulky!"**

For a century and a half, baseball pundits have preached this doctrine. What is the basis of this claim? Does it have a scientific basis? Cast your eyes upon the photos and persona of the great hurlers of yore and today: Cy Young, Christy Mathewson, Walter Johnson, Bob Feller, Carl Hubbell, Nolan Ryan, Gaylord Perry, Juan Marichal, Roger Clemens, Greg Maddux, Orel Hershiser and others. None of these greats had bulky muscles. Careful observation is the basis for the claim cited above! Now, a word about observation from Edward Jenner.

# *Smallpox and Baseball*

In 1796 Edward Jenner looked into a common English belief that milkmaids who had acquired cowpox, a minor disease, never caught smallpox, a serious and often fatal disease. Jenner did not know why this happened. He just knew it did. So Jenner put his observations to work. Jenner removed "matter" from a fresh cowpox sore on the hand of a milkmaid, Sarah Nelmes, and applied the "matter" to two scratches he had made on the left arm of James Phipps, an 8-year-old boy. The boy contracted cowpox over the inoculated sites. Six weeks later, Jenner inoculated Phipps with material gathered out of the sores of a smallpox victim. Phipps did not contract smallpox. This became the first recorded successful vaccination.

Jenner lived before Pasteur (1822-1895) who discovered that "germs" (bacteria and viruses) can cause infections. Try as they may, scientists of Jenner's time could not explain his findings. In fact, some scientists were convinced that Jenner was "crazy," or at least incorrect. Jenner successfully inoculated thousands to prove his theory.

What has all this to do with baseball – other than the fact that James Phipps was a right-hander and that is precisely why Jenner inoculated his left arm? This tale is meant to teach the reader something about observations and science. **Conclusions derived from observation can be correct even though the conclusion cannot be explained scientifically**. Over the 150 years of its existence baseball has acquired more observers than most other athletic events, and most of these observers repeat the refrain: "Pitchers need long, lean, strong – not bulky – muscles." Bulky muscles lack the flexibility needed for pitching. Consult also **muscle efficiency, microcomputers** on page 187.

Professional baseball coaches, players and managers since 1846 have turned their observations into solid, reproducible theory. To dismiss such theory as unprovable, or, as the mindless mutterings of curmudgeonly "old school" pundits, is to render grave disservice to the human intellect.

On the other hand, new data extracted by sophisticated technology can assist "old school" curmudgeons to understand and prove, or disprove, the product of their observations. The problem with data extracted by advanced technology is not the data itself; it is the interpretation and application of the data. The problem is also with experimental design. Jenner's observations were valid, his experimental design simple, and the results reproducible in many different individuals.

It isn't all that simple when you coach pitchers. Why? Because it is difficult with even the most sophisticated "modern" technology to account for **individual differences in anatomy, physiology and most importantly, attitude, intellect and spirit.** Tom House in his book, *The Pitching Edge,* comments on a discussion between himself and Nolan Ryan in 1989. Apparently Tom, the Rangers' pitching coach, had pondered Nolan's high leg lift – as compared with other pitchers. Reportedly, Nolan answered his coach's questions about the leg lift with: "Tom, I throw harder when I lift my leg higher. Go put that in your computer."

Tom consulted his associates at Bio-Kinetics in Orange County, California. Using computerized motion analysis the scientists at Bio-Kinetics determined that by lifting his left leg six inches higher at the balance point (see Figures 2-4 and 2-5; add six inches to the lift shown there!) Ryan increased his fastball velocity at least two miles per hour. Lowering the lift by six inches reduced the speed accordingly.

Now think like a scientist! We make **a single observation:** the enormous Ryan leg lift. We analyze the phenomenon using high tech methodology and conclude that our pitchers can increase the speed on their fastballs by imitating this leg lift. Correct? No! **The phenomenon is unique to Nolan Ryan.** This pitcher's great strength, flexibility and balance permitted him to translate the high lift into added velocity. Rare is the pitcher who can emulate Ryan. Furthermore, scientists seldom rely on a single observation to develop a theory.

Unique to him? What do you mean, Doc? I mean that even identical twins possess nerves, muscles, bones and brains that no one else, not even the identical twin, possesses. The millions of nerves and cells in each body all act in unique ways within different persons. Presently, there is a pair of twins in professional baseball. One is a major-league star, the other is "stuck" in the minors. How do you explain that? Unique individual differences.

Recently, a high school player pitching batting practice had just fallen on his face after firing a fastball while imitating Nolan Ryan. The boy looked up from the ground at his pitching coach standing above him on the mound and asked, "What happened, coach?"

"Nolan Ryan is a mutant, kid. Forget about trying to imitate him!"

# Introducing Novel Ideas on Strength and Conditioning

Whether the coach makes decisions based on technology, or observation, or both, he needs to use caution while introducing new strength and conditioning methodology. Do not hurry away from coaches' clinics anxious to apply novel theory and thought on these subjects. Think about what you "learn" from others before bringing the new concepts to your own pitchers. Larry has pointed out an axiom, "If it ain't broke, don't fix it." I add there is an ancient warning issued by Hippocrates to physicians: "First of all, do no harm!"

What do the utterances of these two sages mean? Coaches are anxious to see their players succeed. Every high school coach is forever proud to see one of his boys make it to major-league baseball. **Consequently, there may be a temptation to overcoach. Resist the temptation.**

# Useful Axioms Related to Muscle Conditioning

1. **Nature is slow to render change**. Consult those who diet to lose weight! Conditioning a pitcher's legs, back, shoulders and arm is a slow process. An unconditioned pitcher – one who has loafed all winter – may not entirely shape up in spring training. Resist the impulse to accelerate pitcher conditioning.

2. **The muscle performance required of a weight lifter is different from that performance required of a pitcher.** Weight lifters train with weights in a manner calculated to increase holding strength (see page 181) – bulky muscles.

3. **Baseball pitchers train with weights using movements specific to the throwing motion.** The bench press may improve strength in certain muscle groups, but not those groups **specifically used in throwing.**

4. Pitchers must train under the aegis of those who are expert in coaching the art and science of weight lifting.

5. Improper training methods can lead to unbalanced muscle development (see p. 185) and injury.

# Curls and "Little-Leaguer's Elbow"

The most common elbow injury in adults and youngsters arising from weight lifting is "medial epicondylitis." Some refer to this as "little-leaguer's elbow," regardless of patient age, but this term is properly applied only to youngsters with immature skeletal structures (see chapter 7, **Injuries**). In adults, the correct term is "flexor/pronator tendonitis."

How does this medial epicondylitis happen? It occurs when the athlete of any age curls with weights too heavy, and/or with excessive repetitions. These are mechanisms of injury (**MOI**). The anatomy of the injury: wrist flexors resist the force of gravity as they "curl" the wrist, hand and weight backward and inward. The tendons of the wrist flexors attach to the medial epicondyle (adult) or medial ossification center (youngster up to age 14-16). As the wrist flexors contract, they tug on the tendons. This tugging, when performed with weights too heavy, and/or excessive repetitions, creates small tears in the tendon and its attachment to the medial epicondyle or ossification center.

In the adult an inflammatory process sets in around the medial epicondyle. In the youngster the inflammatory process is often accompanied by an avulsion (tearing away) of the ossification center from the arm bone (humerus).

**Coaching significance**: Stop curls (and throwing) until all symptoms resolve. The ballplayer must be evaluated by a medical provider. When the medical provider returns the ballplayer to full activity, use lighter weights, fewer repetitions per set and per week. Make sure that the ballplayer is completely warmed up before committing him to the game.

## Muscle Balance

It is important to develop muscle size, strength, power and endurance in a balanced manner because muscles always work in association with one another. When a ballplayer enters the gym to begin weight training he must place himself under the supervision of the person skilled and educated in weight training who understands the pitcher's peculiar needs. Correct muscle training for pitchers should be based on **an integrated progressive specific program.** For example, one cannot work on shoulder deceleration muscles this week, and acceleration muscles next week. The training must be balanced such that muscles, which work together in a given activity, develop together. Over-under development in opposing muscle groups is unacceptable and can cause injuries during a game or practice.

The whole concept is even more complicated than the simplistic view discussed above. When a group of muscles contracts to move any joint, not only does the opposite muscle group go to work, but nearly every muscle around the joint is doing something. The entire group of muscles around the joint act like the elements of a correctly tuned racing engine. Anyone who has worked with motors knows that to tune an engine properly, one must balance all the variables including fuel flow, ignition, timing – the list is long.

How do we handle this complicated subject, Doc? One of two ways: (1) place the ballplayer in the hands of a muscle development expert, or (2) if a gym is not affordable/available, help mother nature (she's an expert) to develop musculature correctly in a balanced manner.

Fortunate for the human, nature has sculpted the body to perform work, and the mind to reason. **Strenuous physical work** has within it the capacity to develop muscle size, strength, power and endurance in a **balanced manner**. The performance of work does not require consideration of what muscle groups need to be balanced. The act of working takes care of that, provided the work is strenuous, performed against resistance, uses most of the body's muscles, and **is not overdone**.

Why not build your own gym to fill in for those circumstances when expert gym instructors or a gym is not available or affordable? Perhaps a gym and coach are available and affordable but you would like to take a break and go outside to enjoy a blizzard (Minnesota/Montana?) or an oppressively hot day (Arizona/Nevada?). Should you be of that ilk, here is a low-cost, easy (it's the 1990s) proposal.

The first ingredient is a radio, CD or cassette tape player of some sort to play cool tunes and reduce boredom. Most young athletes already have these anyway. The second supply is enough 2x6 lumber to fashion two simple rectangles 4 feet by 6 (same dimensions as the batter's box). Third trick is a yard of "heavy" (wet) sand. (Doc's goin' crazy, you say). Fourth fixture is a coal shovel (has a broad, flat lip) and two five-gallon buckets.

Lay the two rectangles flat on the ground, **three feet apart**. Place the sand in one of the rectangles. Shovel the sand from one rectangle to the other. Very important: if you are a right-hander, the sand is placed in the box to your right, so you turn right to left as you move the sand from one box to the other – same way you turn when you pivot to face the hitter. The opposite is true for the southpaw. **Caution: Warm up before going through this drill. Jog, stretch and perform calisthenics in a manner similar to prepitching.**

After you have shoveled all the sand from one box to the other, haul it back to the first box by loading the pails and carrying each (don't throw it!) from box two back to box one. Then repeat the entire routine several times.

"Wax on; wax off; wax on; wax off." Mr. Miagi to the *Karate Kid.*

What we have created here is a form of work that enlists in a **symmetrical, natural and balanced manner** all the muscles the pitcher will rely on.

Think about the act of shoveling, transferring and carrying a load. Pantomime the movements. The back and shoulders flex forward. Note: "Real tall dudes" need to have longer shovel handles to prevent overstooping. If you are a right-hander (my prejudice, because I am right-handed), the right hand grasps the shovel handle; the left: the handle shaft. **Step forward with your left foot toward the sand in the right box, and push with your right foot.** Sound familiar? Consult Chapter 2, **Mechanics.**

Using this motion, scoop up sand in the shovel, small scoops at first as you continue to "warm up." The secret to any shoveling activity is to restrict the amount of load on the shovel. Step back with the loaded shovel until the feet are close together and the body balanced. Pivot at about a 45-degree angle, step toward the left box with your left foot, push with your right and unload. Make sure that when you scoop and unload you fully extend the elbows. And also make sure that after you scoop, and after you unload, you flex the elbows back toward the trunk and straighten the spine. Follow through (decelerate) when unloading by flexing the back fully forward. **Note:** When turning the shovel to unload, the elbows must be comfortably flexed, and the elbow of the throwing arm elevated to shoulder height.

Analyze briefly the principal muscle groups and biomechanics involved in these activities. **Each muscle group and movement used is specific to the pitching motion.**

"Mr. Miagi, I want to learn karate. All I do is wax on, wax off." *Karate Kid.*

The similarity between the sand box and Mr. Miagi's drill should be apparent. Miagi was creating subconscious and conscious movement control in his student using those movements specific to karate.

"OK, Doctor Miagi, what about the pails and sand hauling?"

**Answer:** Pantomime the act of filling, lifting or carrying pails of sand. The same muscle groups involved in shoveling from box to box are activated plus, when the pail is lifted, feel those biceps, shoulder muscles and wrist flexors at work in the lift, and the forearm pronators/supinators when the pail is emptied. **Caution:** Loads that are too heavy, or excessive repetitions lead to the injuries already discussed in Chapter 7, **Injuries**, and in this chapter.

## *Muscle Efficiency: Muscle Microcomputers*

Muscle efficiency is the fourth measure of muscle performance. It is controlled by an ingenious system of microcomputers. Muscle fibers incorporate thousands of microscopic computers which instantaneously and continuously furnish real-time information to the spinal cord, cerebellum (lower brain) and cerebral cortex (main brain) on (1) muscle **length** and **rate of change** in length; and (2) muscle **tension** and **rate of change** in tension. Length data is furnished by muscle spindles and tension data by Golgi tendon organs.

The spindles, about 8-9 millimeters – or less – in length, are built into skeletal muscle fibers in generous numbers, and are connected to the spinal cord with special nerve fibers. When a muscle fiber **stretches,** the spindles send positive signals to the cord. This increased neural traffic "prompts" motor nerves leaving the cord to fire and activate a muscle **contraction**. When the muscle **contracts**, the opposite occurs. Reduced nerve traffic headed to the cord dampens activity in the motor nerve and relaxation occurs. The spindles, thereby, constantly "tune" muscle fiber length.

While the spindles look at and adjust **muscle length** and rate of change in **length**, the Golgi tendon organs sense muscle **tension** and rate of change in **tension**. The positive/negative nerve traffic emanating from the Golgi bodies, located in all muscle tendons, functions in a manner opposite to that from the spindles. Increased tension elicits heavy neural traffic to the cord which dampens motor nerve activity thereby reducing muscular tension. This constitutes a negative feedback system to prevent excessive muscle tension. Occasionally, when severe muscle tension develops, the Golgi-spinal cord traffic becomes so intense that an instantaneous relaxation of the entire attached muscle group occurs. This event is known as the **lengthening reaction** and is probably a survival mechanism to prevent extensive muscle tears or avulsion of the tendon. This reaction may account for the rare instances in which competitive weight lifters suddenly drop enormous weights or suffer a collapse of the lower extremities. The "Golgis" continuously tune muscle fiber tension.

The spindle-Golgi system is designed to prevent overstretch and excessive tension. The system also promotes balanced muscle performance. Balanced performance leads to **efficient activity** in which the muscles function with precise amounts of contraction/stretch and tension. When the muscles perform efficiently, they consume the least amount of fuel (glycogen-glucose) and oxygen and avoid production of excessive lactic acid and carbon dioxide.

**These microchip computers are adjustable and trainable**. Anaerobic exercise repetitions and aerobic training are the tools for adjustment and training. Through mechanisms not entirely understood, the spindles and Golgi bodies "learn" and adjust to repetitive activities. If the anaerobic repetitions and aerobic durations are not excessive, the spindles remain "healthy" and constantly pour useful information into the spinal cord. When the repetitions are excessive the spindles and Golgis may temporarily, or chronically, malfunction – probably because they are physically or chemically (excess lactic acid) damaged by overtraining.

Common human experience contains many examples of normal microchip muscle tuning. The soreness and stiffness that appear and re-solve in spring training is an example of microchip muscle adjustment and resolution. The entire system does not have it right at the onset; con-traction-stretching accompanied by lactic acid accumulation account for the disagreeable symptoms. When fully on-line, the symptoms resolve and the system works efficiently.

Spindle and Golgi-organ training, performed correctly, is the final determinant in how strong, powerful, long-enduring muscles will efficiently serve the ballplayer. With every practice, every game, every weight train-ing (or sandbox session!) the spindle and Golgi bodies adjust, refine and tune muscle performance. Next time you marvel at Tony Gwynn's bat control or Greg Maddux's perfect placement, think about those players' spindles and "Golgis."

**Some sports medicine experts feel that the spindles and "Golgis" in bulky muscles fail to function in a way that allows muscles to perform with the finesse and precision demanded by pitching – another argument against "bulking up."**

## Muscle Training Summation

Muscle training with weights, or the sandbox, or on the field seeks to increase muscle size, strength, power, endurance and efficiency in a bal-anced, unhurried, progressive manner. Do not isolate and train selected groups of muscles. Get the whole body involved in training. Put yourself in the hands of an expert if you train with weights. Hard physical work is good training. **Avoid excess. Do not create bulky muscles in pitch-ers.**

## Dehydration Can Be Disastrous

Until the 1960s, consumption of fluids and foods during a game was vehemently discouraged. Nowadays, fluids are encouraged and snacks (granola bars, sunflower seeds, etc.) allowed.

The old edict proscribing fluids – unwritten but enforced with taunts and epithets – was based on a **false conclusion, drawn from observa-**

**tion**, that the fluid drinker became "waterlogged." As he ran, said some old-timers, the fluid sloshed around his innards, added useless weight to his corpus, unbalanced him and taxed his energy. What was lacking in this theory was an accounting for the alarming weight losses pitchers and catchers experienced during a nine-inning game. It was not unusual for Larry, and pitchers before the 1960s, to lose eight to 10 pounds in a nine-inning game on a hot day. That loss equates to four to five quarts of fluid.

The weight loss was almost entirely due to **dehydration** from unreplaced sweat excretion. It required two or three days to restore the fluid losses. The restoration came just in time for another start on a four-day rotation. Abstinence from fluids was taxing the energies of the battery. It surprises me that more pitchers and catchers did not experience muscle cramps, nausea, dizziness, high/irregular pulse rates and a host of other problems that accompany dehydration. The boys of yesteryear were pretty tough!

## Prevent Dehydration

In the unacclimatized athlete, sweat contains large amounts of salt (sodium chloride). After the ballplayer acclimatizes himself with graduated exposures to heat and exercise, the amount of salt in sweat decreases because the body learns to meet the salt loss by excreting a special salt-saving hormone (aldosterone). Supplemental salt tablets are not necessary, because acclimatization occurs rapidly in healthy persons.

Alas, nature's perversity! Aldosterone, while saving salt, increases loss of potassium in the urine. The solution is a solution – drinks which contain correct amounts of sugar, salt and potassium. Many are commercially available and tout their usefulness to the athlete. (Guyton, 949).

How much fluid is enough? The kidneys will tell, provided the ballplayer does not use caffeine (coffee, tea, colas, chocolate). **Caffeine** is a diuretic – it promotes urination and subsequent **loss of fluid**. If the ballplayer who abstains from caffeine needs to urinate every two to three hours, he is usually well-hydrated. The correctly hydrated person produces **at least** 50-60 milliliters of urine per hour (about two ounces). The average adult person is aware of urine in the bladder with the presence of 100 ml or more. Lack of awareness usually means less than 100 ml, and a "huge urge" to void occurs after 400 ml has accumulated. Within the framework of a well-pitched, 2½-hour game, drink enough fluid so the presence of urine is felt during the game and at least a cupful is discharged after the game. Any less is dehydration.

# Too Much Heat!

When muscles work, they use nutrients (glycogen → glucose). This metabolic process, even in the most efficient, well-conditioned muscles, produces heat. The amount of heat produced is directly proportional to oxygen consumption, and oxygen consumption in a well-trained athlete can increase as much as twentyfold. That's a lot of heat! It comes mainly from the metabolism of glucose in the presence of oxygen. (Guyton, 948).

The body must dissipate this heat somehow. Dogs pant and pitchers sweat. The sweat evaporates and cooling occurs. The efficiency of cooling by evaporation is diminished and heat discomfort increased on humid days. Somewhere in the dim past, when man started shearing sheep and using wool fibers to make clothing, he learned that certain weaves of wool not only protected him from the cold, but also efficiently cooled him in summer. What? Why? Because wool (flannel especially) quickly picks up the sweat and brings it to the outside surface of the garment where it evaporates. This knowledge prompted armies for centuries to issue only woolen clothing to soldiers. The uniforms on both sides during the Civil War and in World War I were wool. And yes, you guessed it, that is why baseball uniforms were made of flannel until baseball valets fell into the hands of fashion marketers. So, who is the "really cool dude?" The guy in flannel or he who wears polyester?

Refer to Chapter 3, **Placement,** for a discussion on the use of and precautions with warm-up (starter) jackets. Advice to wear the jacket between innings must be tempered by the climatic conditions during the game.

# Drugs

> *"The teaching, not preaching, approach to drug education... (is the most effective prevention)... scare tactics are not only ineffective, but worse, they create a credibility gap..."*
>
> ***Darryl Inaba, Pharm. D., Director,***
> ***Drug Detoxification, Haight-Ashbury Free Medical Clinics, San Francisco***

Within Doctor Inaba's modus I provide a factual portrayal of the adverse reactions to several commonly abused drugs and allow the reader to draw his own conclusions. Authoritative references are cited after discussion of each drug, e.g., *Uppers, Downers, All-Arounders*, D. Inaba, Cinamed Inc., P.O. Box 96, Ashland, OR, 1989.

# Anabolic or Androgenic (testosterone) Steroids ("rhoids")

These substances are used by some athletes to increase muscle size and strength. The adverse effects most commonly associated with these steroids are irritability, impaired judgment, impulsiveness, mania, paranoid delusions (pitchers are justifiably paranoid – see Chapter 4, **Rules** – but rarely delusional!). Steroids possibly cause acute cardiovascular events (a medical euphemism for "heart attack"). R.W. Rockhold, *Annual Review of Pharmacological Toxicology*, 33: 497, 1993. Withdrawal symptoms have been reported. S. E. Lukas, *Trends in Pharmacological Science*, 14:61, 1993. Strangely, androgens can cause low sperm counts. Further, certain androgens have been associated with liver cancer when used over several years. K.S. Ishak, *Recent Results Cancer Research*, 66:73, 1979. "Rhoid" use has been associated with tendon rupture due to sudden forceful contractions of muscles that have enlarged under the influence of steroids without concomitant bolstering of tendon fibers. Genetics determine testosterone levels in each individual. If the ballplayer has a problem with his testosterone legacy, he needs to speak with his parents.

# Cocaine (Freebase, Crack, Rock)

This substance can be "snorted," swallowed, smoked or injected intravenously (IV). Its adverse effects are summarized in the acronym "C-C-C": Cardiac, convulsion, coma. The cardiac effects are dramatic and include rapid heartbeat, explosive hypertension (very high blood pressure), irregular cardiac rhythm. Cocaine constricts coronary arteries and has caused myocardial infarction (heart attack) in persons without pre-existing coronary artery disease (a real bummer!). Heart failure followed by pulmonary edema (water in the lungs) is not uncommon. D.Y. Haim, *Chest*, 107: 233, 1995.

The adverse effects to the central nervous system are as dramatic as those in the heart -- paranoia, delirium, convulsions, stroke and coma often occur. K.J. Beckman, *Circulation*, 83:1799, 1991 and R.W. Derlet, *New England Journal of Medicine*, 334:534, 1966. **In coma, all stress disappears**.

# Amphetamines (Crystal, Crank, Speed, Met, Ice)

Street amphetamines are related to several prescription drugs: Dexedrine, Ritalin and ephedrine. These substances can be swallowed or injected (IV). "Ice" or "crystal" can be smoked. The adverse effects are similar to cocaine, but last longer. A.K. Cho, *Science*, 249:631, 1990.

## Heroin, Opioids

Opioid is a pharmacological term that means any synthetic narcotic that has opiatelike (like opium) activity, but is **not** derived from opium, e.g., Demerol and Darvon. Opiates and opioids, also known as O, Op, smack, junk, hope, H, Mexican brown, China white, skag, rufus, the list is endless, all are "downers" usually with prolonged effects (hours to days). Overdose leads to respiratory depression, low blood pressure, slowing of the heart and occasionally coma. J.E. Smialek, *Journal of Forensic Science*, 39:159, 1994. Withdrawal in a habituated person is a well-known phenomenon portrayed in television and movie drama. It is not a pretty sight. In San Diego, amphetamines abused with crack cocaine is called "Croak." How appropriate!

## Caffeine

Finally, **the diuretic effects of caffeine** were discussed above. Taken within four to five hours of a ballgame, caffeine can give the pitcher a false notion of his hydration status. Caffeine in some individuals predisposes lower extremity muscles to severe cramps, apart from its diuretic – dehydration effects. My argument is weakened by evidence that in *one* experiment a marathon runner reduced his running time seven percent by ingesting caffeine equivalent to a couple cups of coffee. However, this runner had been abstinent from caffeine for months before the race!

## Gamma Hydroxy Butyrate
## (liquid ecstasy, liquid X, GHB)

In recent years GHB has "...become a staple in the underground scene, especially in... 'rave clubs.'" Certain individuals in the body-building community have touted the substance as an adjunct to accelerated muscle growth. Untrue! The FDA has classified this drug as a narcotic. The substance even in minimal overdose "...can easily cause seizures, coma, even death." Michael Greenberg, *Emergency Medicine News*, February 1997, pages 18-19.

## Smokeless Tobacco

In 1988, physicians and dentists from the University of California at San Francisco Medical School and University of British Columbia, Vancouver, Canada, studied the effects of smokeless tobacco (ST), also known as snuff, dip, chewing tobacco, plug, wad and chew, in 1,109 members of major- and minor-league professional baseball teams during spring training. The major health effects of using ST were oral leukoplakia (white lesions on mouth tissues) and periodontal (gums) disease. Emster, V.L. et al, *Journal of American Medical Association*, 1990, 264 : 218-224. The International Agency for Research on Cancer in its publication *Evaluation of the Carcinogenic Risk of Chemicals to Humans*, Lyon, France, 1985 : 37, and the Surgeon General of the United States in its publication N086-2874, National Institutes of Health, Bethesda, MD, April 1986 : *The Health Consequences of Using Smokeless Tobacco* both concluded that ST increased the risk of leukoplakia and cancer.

# Heart and Lungs

After initial muscle glycogen-glucose burnoff, additional glucose (from the liver) and oxygen (from the lungs) must arrive at the muscle cells to keep them working. These arrivals are dependent on heart and lung performance.

The needs of the exercising muscle for nutrients and oxygen are enormous and have to be matched by adequate blood flow and oxygen supply. In the well-trained athlete, resting blood flow to muscles averages 3.4 to 3.8 ml/100 gm of muscle per minute. During maximal exercise this can increase to 87-93 ml – a 25-fold increase. The heart, which is itself a muscle, must increase its pumping capacity (cardiac output) to furnish the added flow. The average young man at rest has a cardiac output around 5.3 to 5.6 liters/min. A well-trained athlete can easily increase that up to 30 liters/min. A young untrained, but otherwise healthy, "couch potato" (alternate politically correct spelling is potatoe) "maxes" out around 20 liters/min with his best effort. (Guyton, 947).

How does one train heart muscle to perform so well? Answer: By inducing a modicum of heart muscle hypertrophy. "Modicum" is used advisedly, because we are not training marathoners whose heart size may increase as much as 40 percent. Hypertrophy increases the heart's pumping capacity.

The medical literature is replete with papers showing the cardiovascular benefits of bike riding. This training not only improves heart-lung performance and induces a modicum of hypertrophy, but also trains and develops the lower extremity muscles – with small chance of injury. Remember: "A pitcher throws with his legs." – an Old Adage.

The nice part about outdoor bike riding is that it is not nearly as boring as some other forms of endurance training. On a bike the athlete is out "in the air" and going somewhere: to the park where he practices or plays the game he loves, or home to supper that mom or wife (or maybe he) cooks. Next to being outdoors working and playing, pitchers love to eat. **After all, wholesome food is the only drug a body really needs.**

For further reading, consult the reference section.

# 9

# Baseball Psychology

*With George A. Jansen, M.D.*

## In a Nutshell

1. *Counterproductive controversy*
2. *The ballplayer's mouth*
3. *Anger control*
4. *The squanderer*
5. *Deference to umpires*
6. *Be cool*
7. *Practical jokes*
8. *Confidence is contagious*
9. *Stay within yourself*
10. *Relationships*

> *"I try never to be controversial."*
> **Cal Ripken during a TV interview, 1996**

# *Counterproductive Controversy*

This chapter is better entitled: **Personal Behavior**. *Tactical psychology* is discussed in Chapter 5, **Tactics**. In this chapter I describe the expected norms of a ballplayer's personal behavior -- on and off the field. This behavior nearly always involves his relationships with the human race surrounding him.

What did Cal Ripken mean when he stated that he tried never to be controversial? He made this remark during an interview for television when a reporter questioned him about a heavily publicized plan by the manager to move Cal from shortstop to third base. Ripken opposed the move, but rather than arguing his case before the media, he chose to persuade his manager privately. Ripken prevailed in those private discussions with his manager, and remained at shortstop.

Had Ripken chosen to air publicly, and negatively, the differences between himself and his manager, he undoubtedly would have prevailed. However, the fallout on his team and manager would have been considerable as the fans, who witnessed the case reported in the media, took sides. It is human nature for "side-takers" in a controversy to paint one side black, the other white, even when the entire problem calls for a light coat of gray.

Ripken prevented a **polarized politic**. Instead he opened to view the sensitive and rational behavior which pervades most – but not all – baseball relationships. What if Ripken had decided to launch a public verbal assault on his manager? Ripken's constituency is enormous. This superb all-star performer had recently stepped out from Lou Gehrig's shadow to surpass the great man's endurance record (most consecutive games played). In many ways, Ripken's behavior resembles Gehrig's – quiet, laconic, self-effacing and tirelessly competitive. With Ripken's constituency marshaled behind him during the debate, what is the manager's next move? He has but two choices: (1) quit (Davey Johnson is not the type); (2) stand his ground and argue that it is his prerogative, and his alone, to position his players. He cannot, and will not, abdicate this responsibility. Ripken's teammates, if not in public, certainly in private, would have chosen sides.

It is hard enough to stay on top in baseball even when the team's cohesiveness is so intense that the organization resembles a giant live organism whose every part moves in concert with the whole. So who needs controversy?

Those with a historical bent argue: Washington, Jefferson, Lincoln and the Roosevelts were controversial. So were Patton, MacArthur and Martin Luther King. When the debated question involves morals, ethics, rights or truth, a person is often compelled to proclaim his/her beliefs and logic. Ripken recognized, and the fans understood, that the problem of a position shift was not a matter of profound moral gravity; rather it was a debate between two intelligent humans who chose to disagree on what was best for the team. To have degraded the problem with public vituperation would have been counterproductive. Counterproductive controversy is not confined to professional baseball. Ask any little-league parent.

## A Player's Mouth

If it is mind and muscle that bring success to a baseball player, it is his mouth that will eventually make him better than best – or less than he could be.

Ty Cobb and Babe Ruth were the best hitters of their era with lifetime averages of .362 and .342, respectively. How much better could these great men have been had they made better use of their mouths. The histories of both these immortals are replete with recountings of their rantings, rages and vitriolics. Some allege that the "Georgia Peach" was a mean-spirited bully who announced his intent to intimidate, shred and bloody opposing basemen with his meticulously sharpened spikes. Others hold that Cobb was merely acting out a charade to unnerve the timid infielder, or to interrupt the pitcher's concentration.

Some authors portray the Babe as a jovial, good-natured braggart. Others recount how Ruth voiced a calculated meanness toward young Gehrig as Lou gained in stature as a star. Periodically, the Babe boasted to opposing hurlers how he would destroy even their best pitches.

Utterings like those attributed to Cobb and Ruth only wake up sleeping lions. There is nothing a pitcher likes better than to face characters like this and finish them off with a **"Sit down!"**

Similarly, the threatening, taunting, boastful, mean-spirited pitcher is live game, prey for a hunter hitter – at short range (60 feet, 6 inches). Enough said.

## Anger Control

Chapter 1, **Preparation,** contains specific advice on this problem with particular emphasis on how anger shatters concentration. Everyone handles anger differently and puts on a unique anger mask. With some,

197

the most virulent anger lies behind a placid face. With others the anger mask includes reddened skin, bulging neck veins, widened eyelids and unmistakable body language.

In some respects anger mimics weather phenomena. The thunderstorm that heaves up suddenly, accompanied by brilliant lightning and crashing thunder, often dissipates as quickly as it arises. On the other hand the monsoon comes to stay for a sustained time period and features prolonged downpours interspersed with thunderstorm activity. Leo Durocher was a thunderstorm – quick to anger, soon to forgive, forget and return to the task at hand. John McGraw was a monsoon who indulged himself with tedious tirades.

The pitcher must ask himself: "Am I the thunderstorm or the monsoon type?" The difficulty with the monsoon type is that this individual **ruminates**. He cannot shake off his frustration and return to his work. He frets, pouts and ponders with less than perfect concentration while he invites "black thoughts" to roll around inside his mind. **Example**: During a June 1996 game between two major-league clubs, an otherwise excellent pitcher confronted a no-out situation with runners on first and second in the sixth inning. The score was tied at zero. The third batter, a left-hander, laid a hard, one-bounce bunt down the third-base line. The pitcher pounced on the ball, turned, and threw short to the third baseman who stretched like a first baseman to snare the throw. The third base umpire, standing behind the baseman, called the runner safe. TV replays from the infield side of third base showed clearly that the throw had beaten the runner.

The pitcher vehemently protested the umpire's call which, of course, was final, irrevocable and without appeal. The pitcher now faced a bases-loaded situation. Returning to the mound, he snatched the rosin bag, slammed it down, repeatedly shook his head, mumbled (the TV camera showed facial close-ups), called time and shuffled in small circles behind the mound. Finally, he indicated readiness to pitch, shook off two signs and threw a ball to the hitter, followed by two more balls – each well outside the strike zone. Behind in the count, the pitcher sailed a pitch into the sweet zone (5-spot), watched the ball carom off the left-center field wall, and, as he backed up the catcher at home, took note of three runs scorching the plate – the last on a close play after an excellent rifle shot from the left fielder. The hitter went into second standing up.

Still betraying the body language that preceded the three-run double, this pitcher threw two balls to the next (weak) hitter. That was enough!

The pitching coach arrived at the mound. Undoubtedly the coach spoke with words similar to this:

"There is nothing you, or I, or anyone can do about the bad call at third. The ump knows he made a mistake. So what's he going to do? Get down on his knees and beg forgiveness? Settle down. Put this guy away. The two after him have been sawin' air all day with you out here. Bullpen's quiet. I'm countin' on you."

Humor, firmness, practicality and confidence in his pitcher all wrapped up in a 30-second coach's monologue! I would have been out there sooner talking with this monsoon type to turn off his dribbling ruminations and redirect him. Do you recognize yourself in this scenario? Now you know what you have to do.

This pitcher finished the game, losing 3-2. Behind him was the best infield in the league. What if he had gotten the fourth hitter to hit a pitch sharply on the ground to an infield playing "in," thereby creating a force at home? And what if this out were followed by a double play to end the inning?

You must look ahead to see and create opportunities to solve the present problem. You are the leader, and as such, **you control the outcome**.

> *We all create our own problems; others only help make*
> *the problem worse. We all develop our own solutions;*
> *others only help make the solution better.*
> ### *The authors*

# *The Squanderer*

In a different vein, we now study a person whose flaw emerges only after he starts to earn a substantial salary. Occasionally, overnight a young player will find his pockets bulging with more money than all his ancestors before him had collectively earned. Big money can bring big problems: taxes, bad investments, theft, lawsuits.

## Taxes

If the ballclub does not withhold taxes, hire an accountant to advise you. Do not allow yourself to end the year owing taxes and all your money spent. If you have to borrow to pay taxes, you have entered the field of gross fiscal mismanagement. Leave that sort of debacle to the government.

# Bad investments

An endless stream of big-idea promoters and obfuscates will harass you at home, outside the locker room, in your hotel room. If the idea presented sounds too good, avoid it! There are large corporations whose assets exceed many times what you will ever earn. Observe how they enter into investments and deals. Note how they investigate and research every move – and sometimes still lose out. How could a "big-idea" individual, whose credentials are undocumented, assure you that your money is secure with him or her? Exotic animal ranches, undeveloped oil and mineral ventures, land development schemes, clothing lines featuring your name, soft drinks, candy bars – the list of harebrained ideas is endless – are but a few of the ways unscrupulous persons will try to separate you from your money. Investigate thoroughly, and do not rely on referrals from other ballplayers. They also may have been duped.

# Endorsements risk-free?

What if a manufacturing flaw leads to a serious injury in a consumer? You may not be liable, but if your borrowed name is sewn on those parachutes that failed to open, what then? Besides, what does a ballplayer know about parachutes anyway?

# Theft

Not really the masked robber with a gun in your face kind. It's the theft that happens inside your business: the money misappropriated by an agent, bookkeeper or attorney you hired. An ethical CPA can show you how to set up **internal controls** to avert this problem. The squanderer mindlessly drops his guard, fails to establish controls and acquires victim status.

# Lawsuits

Association with persons of dubious character reflects upon you as a person. An old saying goes: "You are known by the company you keep." When persons of unsavory character become embroiled in lawsuits, you may innocently, or deservedly, be swept into the suit. The sports pages over the last 20 years are replete with stories about sports persons (high school level and up!) who have fallen into hard times because of ill-advised relationships.

Establish yourself as a straight shooter, a person with strong family ties, sensitive to the needs of your community; witness the esteem that persons like Roberto Clemente and Michael Jordan have earned. Enjoy yourself, be cool, be gregarious, but look around at those who stand at your side.

# *Deference to Umpires*

Have you ever wondered what it's like to be an umpire? Nearly every pitch and every play is an **implied or spoken** dispute as to outcome. When a batter (not under orders to do so) takes a called strike, he does so because his judgment proclaims (usually) the pitch is a ball. True, some excellent hitters will take a called strike, because, although they know the pitch is a strike, it was not **the pitch** they wanted. Ordinarily, no hitter wants to fall behind in the count. When the batter's eye says "ball" and the umpire's voice bellows "strike," the situation becomes a black-white difference of opinion. Parties to the event, defense and offense, are alternately elated or dejected. It can be said with reasonable certainty that it is humanly impossible for the umpire to make both parties simultaneously happy. This is unlike the common arbitrator whose job is usually to find a compromise to which both disputants can agree.

Without an umpire, chaos reigns, as those of us who were fortunate to play sandlot appreciate. Without an umpire sandlotters with the loudest voices, most threatening demeanor or largest bodies prevailed. In spite of the fact that the "pax baseballum" exists only because of the umpire, the man in blue is rarely acknowledged by cheers or applause. In fact, the umpire's *modus operandi* is to remain unnoticed and obscure until the moment of decision. The deep blue clothing and absence of prominent lettering, numbers or name enhance the obscurity of their persona.

In spite of their studied self-effacement, umpires are not insensitive automatons! They hear the rails and ranting, the boos and bellowing; they see the gestures and gesticulations. No more than any other human can they ignore the taunts. Like other persons, they appreciate courtesy and humor. Consequently there are practical rules of decorum for the pitcher who wants to survive.

The first of these rules is to never "show up" an umpire either with abusive words or body language, such as shakes of the head on called balls. Umpires do miss calls, and they often recognize their error immediately. Ask the umpire "what the count is" after a call that goes against you. This act sends a signal that you disagree with the call. "Good" and "bad" calls have a way of balancing out in a game, as long as you do not "show up" the umpire.

Secondly, do not look up at the scoreboard after an adverse call. This act is interpreted by the umpire as a put-down. Thirdly, avoid whining. Even when a whiner has a legitimate beef, the tendency of most humans is to ignore the complaint. Fourthly, there are certain foul words, which,

201

when directed at an umpire, will prompt the umpire to remove the pitcher from the game – forthwith!

Jocko Conlin was a great National League umpire. In my rookie year, I was convinced Jocko was not giving me the corners of the plate for called strikes. This spells death for a breaking-ball pitcher. In one game with Jocko behind the plate, I was coming to bat for myself. As usual, I passed **behind** the umpire on my way to the batter's box (passing behind the umpire in this situation is an act of respect). The catcher had gone out to talk with the pitcher, so I had Jocko all to myself.

"Jocko," I began. "That black border that runs around the plate."

"Yes, Jansen," Jocko interrupted. "What's your question?"

"Well, sir," I smiled, "isn't that black border a part of the plate?"

"Of course," Jocko harumphed in a very judicial manner.

"Then, if I can get a part of the ball over the dark border, it's a strike, right?"

Jocko roared with laughter at this rookie pitcher sheepishly attempting to rest a point of law from the bench.

"Yes, Jansen; it's a strike!"

Jocko never failed to call strikes on the corners for me after that.

## Be Cool

Pitchers are sensitive persons, so I've been told. Sensitivity is healthy, but becomes unhealthy if you take yourself too seriously. Example, veterans and opponents invariably discover some foible, anatomical oddity or habit in a young ballplayer, and taunt him about this discovery. If you show resentment, or overreact to the taunts, the taunters continue to search for additional innovative insults.

## Practical Jokes

When I first reported to the San Francisco Seals in the old Pacific Coast League (1941), Tony Lazzeri (Hall of Fame, 1991) was finishing out his career as a player for the Seals. Tony liked mischief that did no harm. We had a shortstop who nearly always showed up at the locker room late and hurriedly dressed for the game while an "understanding" coach briefed him. Tony did not much care for these late arrivals, so he decided to anoint this player's jock strap with an odorless, colorless liniment.

One day, the shortstop showed up late as usual, quickly donned his uniform and went out to take infield practice. After about 15 minutes of practice, the poor dupe began to experience a tremendous burning discomfort in his groin which quickly crescendoed. As he ran to the locker room howling, Lefty O'Doul, the manager, inquired about his problem.

A coach sitting nearby O'Doul responded, "Think someone might have put liniment on his jock strap, Lefty!"

"Now, who on earth would ever do something like that?" An obviously flabbergasted O'Doul replied.

Lazzeri, seated at the end of the bench responded solemnly, "I don't know who would do such an awful thing, but when they catch him, he ought to catch hell."

Boys will be boys. No harm was done.

**Caution: Do No Harm.**

# Confidence is Contagious

Without a show of cockiness, a pitcher can convey an air of confidence that spreads out on the field like a virus to infect the entire team. How do you accomplish this? It is the sum of many factors: Facial expression, body language, verbal utterings. A smile, a wink, a placid face after a terrible error all convey the impression that whatever problem is out there, you know how to manage it. Review the situation presented in Chapter 5, **Tactics. Pitchers do not react to problems; they solve them**.

Gloominess is the antithesis of confidence and is equally contagious. When the pitcher pulls the sad mask on, the other players subconsciously react in negative ways, and the game tactics begin to unravel.

# Stay Within Yourself

The ball field is not a laboratory where new theories and ideas are suddenly brought under study. Every pitcher should know what his pitches can do. If he accurately places his best pitches and the hitters are "taking him downtown," the pitcher must remind himself that there will be another day, because every pitcher is "roped" occasionally. When experiencing a shelling, resist the temptation to experiment with new pitches, or to try "new things" with your best pitches. Stay within yourself. Do what you do best until the manager says he's seen enough.

As a corollary to the above, the relaxed player, pitcher or hitter, invariably performs more efficiently than the excessively nervous individual. Hitting and pitching depend on eyesight and muscle/eye coordination. The overly anxious player is subject to hyperventilation (too many breaths per unit of time – **in excess of physiological needs**). Hyperventilation reduces blood flow to the brain and subtly affects vision. Hyperventilation can also acutely affect blood calcium levels to a point where muscular spasm in hands and feet occur. Ironically, hyperventilation can cause a mild constriction of the small bronchials and produce an ache in the chest. Persons suffering with this acute malady are often unaware of the origins of the problem. The treatment: slow down the breathing, relax – "chill out."

What does **breathing at a rate in excess of physiological needs mean?** When a base runner sprints to steal a base or hustles to run out a triple, his body needs to breathe in more oxygen. The body also produces extra carbon dioxide which must be excreted. To fill this physiological order, the brain signals the lungs to breathe faster and deeper. Forty breaths a minute upon arrival at third on a triple is not unexpected and will not ordinarily produce the symptoms of hyperventilation, because the body is excreting excess carbon dioxide and taking on required oxygen. However, 40 breaths a minute while standing quietly represents a 100 percent increase in breathing over what is needed in a resting adult and can easily bring on the symptoms described above.

## *Magical Thinking and Rituals*

There was once a minor-league pitcher who drove himself to the ballpark every day when the team was at home. Not unusual, you say! It was unusual, because it took him two hours to drive 30 miles in light traffic. Reason: He made only right-hand turns to get to the park; compulsively, he acted out a repetitive ritual. He harbored a belief that his performance would deteriorate if he did not perform this ritual. **To him, careful and exact ritual performance was an assurance of success**. This belief system is called **magical thinking**. The pitcher did not make it to the major leagues. Undaunted, he replied when questioned about the apparent contradiction between his faithfulness to the ritual and failure to make the majors: "Had I not done my ritual every day, I would not have done as well as I did."

A major-league relief pitcher in the 1990s was given to brushing his teeth while his team was at bat. He also, using a very stylized pirouette maneuver, repeatedly leapt across the foul line while walking to the dugout. These rituals emanated from this pitcher's magical thinking: "The ritual protects against failure." When his behavior began to attract public curiosity (questions from the media), and to take on an obnoxious quality (brushed his teeth in the dugout drinking fountain), the managers and coaches asked him to "knock it off." His manager suggested that his behavior smacked of unprofessionalism.

Magical thinking and ritualized behavior arise out of unfounded fears and anxieties. The individual suffering with these problems **calmly** points out that, when the ritual was neglected or abandoned in the past, "things got worse" or failure ensued. Failure may have been simply a **coincidence** or a **self-fulfilling prophecy.** When a person believes firmly that the "situation is going to get worse," the negative thought infects his whole being, and, sure enough, things do get worse. No scientific evidence has ever shown that rituals do anything but consume time and irritate others.

More importantly, the rituals of both pitchers above needlessly consumed vital mental and physical energy required to perform efficiently. This behavior interferes with concentration and assumes an importance greater than throwing the next strike. A pitcher infected with this mental "virus" may not get beat by a more talented hitter. He may beat himself.

Treatment of this disorder is best left to professionals who specialize in psychology. In the case of the tooth brusher, his manager – turned therapist – broke the cycle quickly. Not all "patients" are so easily cured and may require special "behavioral therapy." Coaches who detect ritualistic behavior developing in young men must act quickly and positively to discourage it. Failure to terminate the problem may call for prompt referral for medical, or paramedical, counseling.

## Relationships

Friendships made in times of stress tend to run deep and long. Nothing quite brought the Giants together like the 1951 season. We trailed Brooklyn by three games going into the last week. Three victories for us matched with three losses for Brooklyn meant a tie for the pennant. That is exactly what happened, and a playoff ensued capped by Bobby Thomson's ninth-inning three-run homer in the last game. My friend and teammate, Sal Maglie, started the game. I relieved him and was credited with the win.

The electricity that ran through the club and pitching staff that season began when Sal Maglie and I started our climb in early June toward a total of 23 wins apiece. When we needed runs, our hitters responded. When our hitters were down, our pitchers held the opposing offense. When we needed great defense, our fielders delivered. Everything seemed to fall into place. The chemistry was right. Most of us had been together as a "family" for four or more years. We were more than team-mates, we were friends pursuing a common goal. To this day my wife and I have kept up correspondence with the wives and players of that team. We are still family, unseparated by the miles between us and the years that have passed. Give yourself fully to both your families; they will be a joy to you forever.

# 10

# The Pitcher's Wife

*Eileen Jansen (nee Vandehey)*

The United Airlines stewardess (they were not called "flight attendants" in 1951) smiled quizzically at me as I climbed the stairs to the airplane cabin followed by a "duck line" of six small children: five girls, one boy.

"Are these all your children, Mrs. Jansen."

"Every last one."

"To Portland?"

"To Portland."

"I see you are expecting. Can I help you with your bag?"

"No, I'm fine, thanks. My daughter Kathleen may need your attention; she's a bit inquisitive and tends to be an explorer."

"Kathleen? You're Kathleen?"

"Yes, ma'am, and I'm four years old."

*Larry Jansen during his days as a pitcher for the New York Giants.*

"Why don't you come with me Kathleen. You can help me pass out snacks and napkins while I serve the drinks before the plane takes off. Our takeoff has been delayed 30 minutes."

"Can I? Really? Mom, is it OK?

"Yes, Kathleen. You've said you wanted to be a stewardess. " I quietly prayed that her usual highly charged enthusiasm would not lead to a cup of coffee in a passenger's lap.

"Hooray! Show me what to do, ma'am."

"This way to the galley, Kathleen."

Kathleen, holding the stewardess' hand, vanished up the passenger aisle toward the front of the plane. It was just after Labor Day 1951. My husband, Larry, a pitcher for the New York Giants, was having another successful year. The children and I had spent June, July and August in New York so we could be close to Larry. Since 1947 we had trekked to New York each summer and settled into a rented house at New Rochelle, not far from New York City and the Polo Grounds where the Giants played home games. After Labor Day we endured the 18-hour flight back to Portland near Forest Grove, our Oregon home. In 1951, the children and I repeated our homeward migration, a migration that proved to be different from those past. Nearly three weeks after the flight home our second son, Gregory, was born on September 22, the day that Larry won his 20th game. Greg has never let us forget it!

1951 was a great year in Giants history, because on the last day, the Giants tied the Brooklyn Dodgers for the pennant. The Giants and Dodgers engaged in a three-game playoff, the last game of which was won by Bobby Thomson's ninth-inning "shot-heard-round-the-world" home run hit off Brooklyn pitcher Ralph Branca. Larry, pitching in relief for his friend, Sal Maglie, was the winning pitcher.

Now after 57 years of married life filled with 10 children, 21 grandchildren and 22 great-grandchildren, Larry and Doctor Jansen thought it reasonable to assume that I had formed some opinions on the life of a "baseball wife." Never did I crave public attention during Larry's career. Had I done so, disappointment would surely have followed. It is not a baseball tradition to spotlight the ballplayer's wife. Rarely do sport pages run feature articles on any athlete's spouse. Larry and "Doc" felt the time had come to feature the wife of a baseball player. It required but a modicum of persuasion to gain my assent.

The format is my own, a breezy narrative because as I reflect on my life with Larry – baseball pitcher and coach – there is much laughter,

*Eileen and Larry Jansen on their wedding day in 1940 (left) and 50 years later at their golden wedding anniversary (below).*

many smiles and few tears. My family questioned my sanity when, at age 17 (1939), I announced my intent to marry a 19-year-old semipro baseball player. After Larry and I celebrated our 50th year together, there was no question that I had passed the family Rorschach.

Just kids we were when the wedding bells rang, but we had helped ourselves to an enormous serving of American-Dutch tenacity (a euphemism for hard-headedness). Historians have reflected at length on this Dutch trait. Legend makers have given us the stories of the "little Dutch boy" stanching the leak in the seawall during a night-long vigil and Hans Brinker with his silver skates. Holland, half the size of Maine, is a country of farmers, shopkeepers and seafarers who have had the temerity to push back the wild North Sea with a series of dikes and reclaim the land from the briny water.

Youth tends to be myopic when it looks at hazards. Unwarranted optimism is the prevailing tone. Nevertheless, Larry and I appreciated that enduring marriages are anchored on a bedrock equation: mutual mental and emotional support equals the best chance for success in the marriage and careers of the partners. So two youngsters from the farm joined in marriage at the Visitation Roman Catholic Church in Forest Grove, Oregon, and less than a year later (April 1940) found themselves traveling through the night on a Greyhound bus to Salt Lake City. This desert place was home base for a Class C minor-league team, the Bees.

"Minor league" is a phrase suitable to describe both the level of play and the conditions of the environment. The bus ride occurred during my first pregnancy. A long, lurching, bumpy bus ride does nothing to enhance the comfort needed by a pregnant woman. The discomfiture did not end with the bus ride. We rented a flat in the same apartment complex as the team's player-manager, Tony Robello, and his wife, Ann. The Salt Lake team paid Larry $125 per month; $28 of this went for rent. Air conditioning was not a common commodity in cheap rentals at that time, and in 1940 the summer temperatures frequently exceeded 100 degrees. We had no car, so Larry rode to the ballpark in Tony's car.

Tony and Ann were superb human beings. Tony introduced Larry to the complexities of professional baseball and Ann became my surrogate older sister and confidant. I needed this support during my first time away from home. It was all so new, even frightening. Other players' wives formed a support and empathy klatch. Ann was a genuinely concerned friend to all the wives. We spent many hours sipping lemonade, fanning ourselves and talking about our girlhoods, our lives and our plans.

"How did you come to meet and fall in love with Larry," Ann asked one day.

Larry and I were both born at home in the farming village of Verboort, Oregon; he in 1920 and I two years later. We attended the same school in Verboort, but took little notice of one another. The two years' difference in age was a broad chasm separating our interests and social activities.

I never knew my mother. My dad lost two wives in about five years' time. I have a half-sister, six years older than I. My mother died of peritonitis when I was 22 months old and my younger sister was eight months. So my Dad raised us three girls with some help from two of his sisters until they married. Then we were on our own. My older sister was Dad's "tomboy." She helped him milk the cows and had her own riding pony, so my younger sister and I were in charge of the household duties. When friends and relatives looked at Dad with his three girls and asked where his boys were, he'd tell them he figured if he had the girls, the boys would come along. And after we three were married, he'd add, "and they did." I was very happy and proud to take my dad with me to the World Series in 1951.

The local high school did not have a baseball team so the boys of Verboort and Forest Grove formed a semipro baseball team. "Semipro" was one of those arrangements where the hat is passed around during the game and fans drop "donations" into the "collection." Larry made this team at age 14, a remarkable accomplishment considering that most of the players were 17 to 30 years of age. My dad was a rabid fan, and his idea of family entertainment was a jaunt to the ballpark.

The year was 1934, and I was age 12 – a time for the normal girl to develop crushes. Here was this 14-year-old phenom dazzling the older players – the perfect person for a 12-year-old's crush. Awkwardly, I probed my two uncles and a cousin, players on this team, for more information about Larry. They were quick to recognize my apparent foolishness, and I wrung very little input from any of them. Fortunate for me, my dad went to nearly every game. Dad did not have to prod me into going out to the games. I was the first one in the car when Dad bellowed out, "Time to play ball, sports fans!"

Girlish infatuation deepened into friendship with Larry when he began to notice me at the games. We began to date frequently when I turned 15. Our idea of a date was going to the game together. I watched; he "performed." Our first upgrade in the dating scenario occurred when Larry invited me to a Sunday evening movie. This was now becoming serious business. After all, I was 15, and he, 17! My cousin borrowed his dad's car and the four of us – the cousin and his girl, Larry and I – embarked on a double date. The movie was Jean Harlow's last, and probably best, film. It was very romantic and exciting. Thereafter, we courted steadily for two years. The more I knew Larry, the more I wanted to be with him. In time, our friendship evolved into love. We were kindred spirits so close that we nearly always anticipated the other's thoughts and feelings. A permanent commitment was approaching.

A tragedy befell the family in 1937 when an aunt died in childbirth leaving behind seven boys, including her newborn infant. My uncle faced the prospect operating his farm and raising his sons alone. I volunteered to help out. With my dad's consent, I served as cook, nanny and housekeeper in my uncle's household for two years. Another of his nieces relieved me in 1939 so I could marry Larry.

When we announced our intent to marry in 1939, my family's reaction took me aback. Thoughtful, considerate they were as they offered advice. They pointed out that Larry, invited by the San Francisco Seals to "try out" with them in the spring of 1940, was destined to be a professional ballplayer. To my "advisors" this meant – even under the best of circumstances – long separations and a disjointed family life, quite unlike the staid, predictable life of a farmer in Verboort, Oregon.

I argued that, whatever the circumstances of his chosen career, I wanted to be with him. This was to be my husband. Quietly the family withdrew its objections and we married as planned.

In April 1940 Larry returned to Forest Grove from spring training with the Seals. The Seals, a Triple-A team in the Pacific Coast League, had a working arrangement with the Class C Salt Lake City Bees. The Seals wanted Larry to play at least one year at the Class C level for "seasoning." Fortunately, the Bees had allowed him to return to Forest Grove to pick me up so we could travel together to Salt Lake City.

For a minor-league wife, childbirth is a rude summons to reality. The doctor's bill and hospital fees were to be paid out of Larry's $125 salary. At the time, mothers and their infants customarily remained in the hospital for 10 days postpartum. Dutch-Americans have a reputation for frugality, but Larry and I were fast approaching the envelope limits of our thrift. The financial situation was not the only problem. Yet to be dealt with was the question of what to do if I went into labor when Larry was on the road. Tony had left his car and Ann could drive. That solved the transport problem. Unanswered was the question: "What is it like to labor alone with your husband many miles away?"

Babies know exactly when to come on stage: middle of the night when Dad is away and the car won't start! The only piece of scenery missing in this scenario was a blizzard. So it came to be that Larry was in Boise, Idaho, pitching a night game when word was brought to him that I had begun labor. Boise was 12 hours by road from Salt Lake. Larry made short work of the Boise team and hopped a Greyhound bus for Salt Lake. All night he traveled while I labored. Next morning I was ready to deliver. Larry, running all the way from the bus depot to the L.D.S. Hospital, made it to the delivery suite just before our first daughter, Darlene, was born.

The Salt Lake team had a glorious season in 1940, winning the pennant. Larry was the ace, winning 20 games while losing only seven. At the end of the season in September the little Jansen family returned to Forest

Grove feeling pretty good about themselves. Larry's parents were excited about their first granddaughter; my cousins and uncle were proud of Larry's pitching accomplishments.

My sisters and Dad, a grandfather for the first time, delighted in my success as a new mother. Many households in Verboort were aglow with our good news.

The bad news was the minor-league salary, which had provided us a hand-to-mouth existence in Salt Lake City, did not continue into the fall and winter. Larry found work wherever he could: farmhand, "filling station" attendant and store clerk. In spite of a lingering national hangover from the depression of the '30s, Forest Grove farms continued to bring produce to market and many small businesses remained solvent. The Forest Grove folks gave Larry and other young men whatever work was available. Our family roots held firm, and we were invited to live in my father's house until the following spring. We jumped at that opportunity. Larry and I acquired shelter, and my dad gained a willing winter cook and housekeeper.

In February 1941, Larry left for spring training with the Seals who now were considering the prospect of moving him up to San Francisco. Larry did well in the spring and the Seals added him to their roster. Now I could live in a city definitely cooler, and far more exciting, than Salt Lake. We enjoyed an "enhanced" housing arrangement in a rented apartment on Steiner Street – heated, furnished, with a good stove, "icebox" and carpeted flooring, no less.

Larry and the Seals had a good season. Larry's record was 16 wins against 10 losses: superb for the first season in Triple-A ball. We returned to Forest Grove even more exhilarated than the year before. Some couples might consider our family burdens excessive considering the circumstances. But one must study the context in which these scenarios evolved. Both Larry and I were, and are now, Roman Catholics. Our families had been Catholic since that epoch in history when our ancestors ceased to worship stones and trees. Catholic tradition and teaching encouraged large families. Children were considered immense blessings. Larry and I considered carefully our anticipated earnings in baseball, and alternative plans for a farming career should Larry not be able to continue in baseball. My dad was enthusiastic about our striving and unabashedly offered his home each winter until we could buy our own place. Triumphantly, we returned to Forest Grove in the fall of 1941. However, unforeseen disasters in the world, and in our lives, lurked immediately ahead.

The entire community and country turned topsy-turvy on December 7, 1941, "a day that will live in infamy" (Franklin Roosevelt). Boys already in the National Guard and the Reserves were called to active duty and the draft spooled up. Farms were quickly stripped of male laborers. Larry reported to spring training in 1942 and was again selected for the Seals roster. The joy of the previous years was absent. Larry returned from a road trip in May suffering with a cough and fevers up to 104 degrees. Immediately he was hospitalized with pneumonia in San Francisco and given multiple injections of penicillin (not commonly available in 1942). He recovered after 14 days, but was quite weak for nearly two months afterward.

If the pneumonia were not enough, as he recovered, Larry developed a serious problem in his right heel – Achilles tendonitis. He consulted a team physician who advised that he rest the heel and not pitch until all symptoms were gone. Larry considered this unacceptable. He proceeded to cut away the back of his shoe, wore two pairs of socks and continued to pitch in major pain. His performance began to slip and at the end of the season his record stood at 11 wins and 14 losses. I have been advised by physicians in later years that Larry was fortunate that he did not rupture his Achilles tendon, because continued competition with Achilles tendonitis is considered an invitation to this catastrophe.

Another summertime baby (our second) was due to drop in during the season, just to provide us a diversion from other problems. A July baby, this second child was to be. Again, Larry was scheduled to be away on a road trip in spite of the fact he was too weak to pitch more than a few innings. The Pacific Coast League teams at that time included cities as close as Portland and as far away as San Diego. The Seals traveled by train. An aunt of mine lived in Martinez (across the Bay from San Francisco). At her behest, I stayed with her as the due date closed in. Our second child, a boy, Dale, was born in the Martinez Hospital while Larry was still in town. Shortly after Dale's birth, Larry left on a road trip while my aunt and I managed a two-year-old and a newborn infant. Family ties again proved to be a very important aspect in our lives.

Larry and I returned home in the fall of 1942, more wealthy in spirit, if not in pocketbook. We now had two children, and Larry had begun the season with a substantial increase in pay. The Seals, as did many Triple-A clubs, paid by the month and in the warm environs of the West Coast the season was nearly eight months long – a welcome boon to the family purse! However, Larry's hospitalization and the arrival of our latest child had cut a wide swath through our earnings (health insurance was a rarity), but we were able to purchase our first car, a used Dodge, and rent a house from my sister and brother-in-law. We lived there until we were able to build our house in 1947. This house remains our home today.

Now, Larry's thoughts were directed toward the war. With his tendonitis, the military recruiters were unwilling to take a chance on him in spite of Larry's argument that the heel was better, and that he was, after all, an otherwise sound athlete. In addition, draft boards were not calling men with two or more children. Because he insisted on being allowed to do something for the war effort, the draft board finally offered him an alternative – work in a "war critical" job, e.g., coal miner, ship building, agriculture. Larry knew agriculture and chose accordingly. Furthermore, the western Oregon farms were by now desperately short of help.

Larry worked on a nearby dairy farm for two years: 1943-45. The farmer kept a herd of Holstein cows – known for the large quantities of milk they produce. Holsteins are also known for the fact that they cannot tolerate not being milked promptly each night and morning. Failure to expeditiously milk these cows leads to inflammation of the udder called mastitis. Larry helped milk the cows by hand, morning and evening, and worked in the fields during the day helping cultivate and harvest the farm's many crops.

Ever the optimist, Larry's only comment was: "look how my hand and arm strength are improving." This went on day in, day out for "the duration" (war years).

Larry's Achilles tendon healed very slowly (if at all), because the farm chores were taking their toll on that heel. Our family doctor repeated the advice given in San Francisco, but Larry just cut the backs out of his shoes and boots and trudged on like a "good little Dutch boy," keeping that finger in the seawall. His only response to my questions of concern about the heel: "I've got to do something for the war effort, Eileen." Oh, well.

Finally, in August 1945 Japan was brought to its knees and the "shooting war" ended. The Seals, ever watchful of world events, called Larry to check on his status. His heel was nearly well, and he was eligible for release from his dairy assignment. The Seals sent him a ticket to San Francisco, and Larry, the backs of his shoes (baseball spikes) still cut away went to work on opposing batters. He ended the season with four wins and one loss, and that was a 1-0 loss.

The following year, 1946, was an amazing year: Larry won 30 games, the last San Francisco pitcher – major- or minor-league – to do so. Now

216

we had four children: Three girls, one boy. An unexpected delight occurred in spring training. Paul Fagan had bought a half ownership in the club. Mr. Fagan had vast interests based in Hawaii and thought it only natural that the club perform its spring training there. I remained home in Forest Grove during the spring training – by now my customary practice – while Larry lapped up the rays on Waikiki (just a little humor because I had my hands full with the children and our eldest was in school).

In May, after the close of school, the children and I trekked down to San Francisco so we could all be together with Dad. At the end of the season, now richer by far in children and savings than we had ever imagined, the family returned to Forest Grove. New opportunities were about to come into view.

Both parties in this marriage were feeling pretty good about themselves ("self-realization," I believe, is the current term). Another major event thrust itself upon us in the fall: the New York Giants bought Larry's contract from San Francisco. After a short haggle over salary, we began a relationship with an organization (the Giants) which would endure until 1971 – more than 24 years. I was excited for Larry, because to play in the major leagues is the top rung in baseball. But Larry was concerned about me. New York was an enormous distance from our roots in Forest Grove. Two of the children would be in school, followed not far behind by two more and I was pregnant with our fifth child, Kathleen. She was born in August 1947. The problem seemed gargantuan. How would we two, no longer just country kids, meet the new obligation?

Larry had an expression: "When you're in a jam, go with your best pitch." My best pitch was to keep the family close together. To me this equated to remaining in Forest Grove until school was out in May, then joining Larry with the children until the new school year opened after Labor Day. Larry liked the idea, and this was to be our "M.O." until 1955 when Larry signed with Seattle. Why this "M.O.?" Why not take up residence in New York or Connecticut or New Jersey?

In baseball, trades and transfers are an inevitable nastiness. With our roots secured in Forest Grove we were continuously in a position to deal with a known quantity. Our children would grow and be schooled where Larry and I had developed. Although it was our good fortune to remain with the Giants during Larry's major-league career, we could have experienced another fate – that of the vagabond player who bumps from team to team.

Eventually, Larry and I were to have 10 children. In the livestock industry, eight animals is considered a "herd." Luckily this was an orderly and quiet "herd," most of the time. In my role as the family recreation director, I was often asked how I managed to entertain 10 children. My answer: "I don't! They amuse one another." The two older girls were eternally anxious to care for the babies, and the three younger girls were close enough in years to cooperate in playing "house" or "school." Our other five children were boys, four born consecutively after the first six children (5 girls, 1 boy). In pediatrics, four consecutive boys are known as a "critical mass" – the immediate forerunner to an atomic explosion. Fortunate for all, our first son was the second-born, so when the last four boys arrived, he assumed the role of "junior scoutmaster." When his first brother was born in 1951, he said he was going to spoil him rotten, and proceeded to do just that. The trick of the trade for the burdened mother is to recognize and utilize auxiliary talent.

The Giants held their 1947 spring training in Phoenix, Arizona. Larry called home at frequent intervals, so when I went to answer the phone one day in March, I expected to hear Larry. Instead, the hospital in Tucson called to say that Larry had been hit with a line drive in an exhibition game against Cleveland. According to the hospital, Larry was in surgery to repair damage to his face. This was a dreadful moment. My husband, injured, in surgery, circumstances and his condition unknown. I asked that his doctor call me as soon as the surgery concluded.

The specter of injury haunts every athlete. In a single moment, an injury can snatch away a career; even worse, it can create permanent, disabling damage. It was a hand-wringing several hours I endured, punctuated by seemingly incessant demands from the children. The call finally came: Larry would recover uneventfully from multiple fractures in his facial bones.

When the season opened in New York, I followed the Giants in the Portland newspaper. Larry's name appeared only occasionally, and then only as a relief pitcher. It appeared as though his appearances were not going well. Larry called home often and he seemed optimistic, but I knew better. I knew he was not performing up to "Larry Jansen standards."

Larry did not start a game until mid-May. In that game, Larry beat Boston (Braves) 2-1. Four days later he beat St. Louis (Cardinals). That season would end with Larry the league leader in won-lost percentage (.808) and 21 victories. In June, the children and I boarded the airplane in Portland for the first of eight trips to the "Big Apple."

The Giants' families, like those in Salt Lake and San Francisco, formed enduring, supportive friendships. Not only did the ballplayers feel a part of something larger and cohesive – their team – but also the wives and

Larry and Eileen Jansen take time to enjoy their children in New Rochelle, N.Y., in 1953. The Jansens made their home in New Rochelle during the summer months and then headed back to Oregon when school began while Larry finished the season with the Giants. (Photo from the Jansen family collection)

children enjoyed a familylike environment. My children looked forward each year to returning and renewing relationships with the other players' children in New York.

With our family approaching herd size (five by 1947), I found it difficult to attend many of Larry's games. Although he appeared to perform better when I attended the game, we both agreed that our emphasis was to be the children. That meant that the family "activities director" needed to be close to the children. Some might argue that women today no longer live their lives as I did. The woman's role has changed. True, but dig deeper. I chose to be a mother of as many children as God would grant me. This was to be my career. Other wives may choose different paths, but as for me, I am completely happy. The importance of our relationship was that we agreed before our marriage on the pathway, and we maintained the marital equation of mutual support.

When I did attend Larry's games, the other wives often commented upon my apparent serenity in the face of Larry's trying moments. The wives could not perceive how I churned inside when, with a one-run lead in the ninth, and a man on base, Stan Musial stepped up to bat. I was truly "smiling on the outside, crying on the inside."

The tribulations of minor-league ball, finally making it to the "bigs," remaining in the big leagues, and being successful, all take their toll. When finally the wife and her ballplayer husband realize that the major-league career is at an end, how do you deal with it? Realistically! You turn toward new opportunities. Our religious faith furnished us much solace as we believed earnestly that the Lord would look after our family, and open new paths. By 1954, Larry's major-league career was winding down.

During Larry's years in the major leagues I did not realize how much he loved to teach. In 1955, his career in the majors over, Larry signed on with Seattle in the Pacific Coast League as a player-coach. Until 1961, Larry served in this capacity first with Seattle (1955-1957), then Portland (1958-1960). This was interrupted just briefly in 1956 for a short stint with Cincinnati as a player-coach. Larry loved this work and was now close to our Forest Grove home. The onerous trips to New York were over.

After the 1960 season, Portland wanted to elevate Larry to team manager. During the days he pondered this opportunity, a call came from the Giants, now ensconced in their new home: San Francisco. The Giants' manager, Alvin Dark, wanted Larry to be his pitching coach.

Alvin had played shortstop and was team captain for the Giants from 1950 to 1956. Larry and I had become close friends with Alvin and his wife, Adrienne. Both our families were anxious to be reunited around a common purpose. That was the good news. The bad news was that San Francisco is 12 hours by road from Forest Grove. Do we perform a modified version of the New York shuttle, or become the occasional roadster to bring the family together in San Francisco?

Decision time again. Larry and I weighed the alternatives, and the effect each would have on the family unit. The Giants' organization and Alvin were familiar with our family attitudes. Quite in jest, Chubb Feeney, a part owner of the Giants, offered me a fur coat to convince Larry that this was a favorable opportunity., "If that's your offer, Mr. Feeney, he's as good as in your pocket now," I replied (tongue in cheek). I hate fur coats! Mr. Feeney was another fine person we had the honor to know. We welcomed his friendship, but I never did accept his offer.

Finally, we configured a plan. When the team returned from San Francisco from road trips back East, Larry would receive a ticket to Portland instead of San Francisco. On some of these occasions all of us Jansens

Larry and Eileen Jansen were joined by all 10 of their children at their 50th wedding anniversary in 1990. From left are Sandi, Gregory, Kathleen, Dale, Larry, Eileen, Keith, Darlene, Robert, Shirley, James and Alynn. (Photo from the Jansen family collection, ©Muir Studio)

drove to San Francisco and remained during the "home stay;" then we would return to Forest Grove with "Mom" at the wheel. When Larry couldn't arrange that ticket home, I drove both ways.

A baseball wife is continuously bombarded with having to sort out alternatives. The new San Francisco plan seemed viable, and once again, no forecast was available regarding the longevity of this arrangement. As it turned out, the relationship lasted 11 years (1961-71)! These were some of Larry's best years in baseball. By 1963, our "little family" had grown to 10 offspring. That was it for child bearing. We did not feel that the Lord wanted us to re-create the "12 apostles."

"Turn the lights out, the party's over!" After the 1971 season, the Giants and Larry parted company. Larry had enjoyed one of the longest tenures ever in baseball as a pitching coach with a single team. His pitchers accumulated an 11-year record of 1,001 wins, 777 losses – an amazing accomplishment. I viewed Larry's departure from the Giants with mixed feelings. After 11 years, the 12-hour drives to and from San Francisco were getting "a bit old," but visiting friends and relatives in the Bay Area brought us all a lot of happiness.

Larry was not ready to leave baseball after the 1971 season. His manager from the 1950s, Leo Durocher, had become the manager of the Chicago Cubs. He had inherited some serious pitching problems and wanted Larry to help him. We decided against a shuttle this time; the family was too unwieldy to be traveling back and forth to the Windy City, a' la the New York, later the San Francisco, shuttle. Now Larry would be away an entire season. It was not workable. Larry resigned after two years in Chicago. The final four children, all boys, had entered the vulnerable stage of their growth and maturation process, and Larry knew these youngsters needed his year-round presence. He settled into selling real estate in the Forest Grove area. Now at last we had Dad all to ourselves, a willing captive at the house we built after the 1947 season in our beloved Forest Grove.

Were our baseball years excessively arduous, destabilizing or were they fruitful and fulfilling? Everything is good or bad by comparison. Let's examine the products of our labor: our marriage and our children. Three more years until Larry and I celebrate our 60th anniversary! We are still friends, still in love, still happy. All 10 of our children are successful. Their vocations range from banking to distributors to sales managers to housewife to electronics engineer. None of our children went into professional baseball, but each of us knows that we gave our best to the game, and the game treated us well.

# 11

# Baseball as a Career

## In a Nutshell

> *Problems are to be solved; questions to be answered.*
> *Issues are merely divisive.*
> **The Authors**

# *Attitudes*

The foundations for the present discussions were laid in general form throughout the text. Now it's time to be more specific.

**All careers are built around attitudes.** Attitudes toward what? Let me name the situations: student toward teacher; worker toward work; employee toward employer; ballplayers toward teammates; players toward society.

# *Attitudes Toward Teachers*

My first baseball teachers were my older brothers. They showed, suggested and encouraged my game. From the start, I understood that their sense of accomplishment was found in my learning to play the game. Never did they leave me the impression that their comments were given for the purpose of ridicule or to "show me up." Beyond the satisfaction they felt from teaching, there were, of course, several secondary gains: it's more fun to play with three than two; three makes a third of a team. After I turned 10 years of age, my brothers were continuously busy organizing a "town team." That team would eventually represent our community, Verboort-Forest Grove, in the Oregon semipro tournaments. Perhaps I learned the principal teaching attributes from my brothers: patience, repetition, encouragement. As a student, I returned their gift of teaching by **trying out their suggestions**. Some suggestions I kept as useful tools; some I later discarded as not helpful. **But I tried everything**. Pragmatically, I enlarged my list of options.

> *"I believe the best decisions are made when a person seeks out the maximum number of options available, then selects the best option."*
>
> **Attributed to Dean Rusk,**
> **former secretary of state**

The best way to discover options is to listen carefully and try to understand what the mentor offers. Then try the suggestion. If the idea is useful, keep it; if not, lay it aside.

My high school had no baseball team! Playing on my brothers' team took on special significance. We invited our cousins and several neighbors to join us to form the nucleus of our first team. I was 12 at the time, and all of us were too young to form a semipro team. So we decided to enter an American Legion league. We convinced a man named Bud Houston to be our manager.

What a stroke of luck! Mr. Houston decided I should come off short-stop and learn to pitch. He taught me how to throw a curve and a hard slider. Once I learned to spin the ball correctly, I possessed two of the pitches that would earn me a ticket into professional ball. Thank you, Mr. Houston.

When I was 14, my uncle organized a semipro team to represent Verboort. Naturally, I had to join this team, and I brought with me Mr. Houston's pitches plus my own native fastball (a four-seamer). At that time, I had little appreciation for the importance of changing speeds. The semipro hitters in our league included a few men who had once played minor-league ball, in addition to some very talented youngsters who could pick up the spin on the ball early in its flight.

I learned in a hurry that a pitcher cannot expect to throw a fastball past a skillful hitter (see Chapter 5, **Tactics** where I discuss my handling of Eddie Mathews). My fastball did not run faster than 87 to 89 mph, so I had to learn to use this pitch for a "purpose" (see Chapter 3, **Fastball** section). My uncle taught me to appreciate speed changes, but I learned most from watching other pitchers.

In Chapter 10, **The Pitcher's Wife**, Eileen describes me as a 14-year-old "phenom." I considered myself a struggling **student** of the game, trying hard to listen and learn from everyone. (Oh well, Eileen just had a crush on me then!) It turned out that every pitcher around the league unwittingly became my teacher. Thanks, guys. When I wasn't sure how another pitcher accomplished something, I asked him after the game how it was done. Generally, humans are flattered by being asked to show and teach and help. Pitchers are no different.

## Attitude Toward Work

Verboort-Forest Grove, Oregon, about 30 miles west of Portland, as the crow flies, is where I grew up – a farm boy. Before the reader becomes all misty-eyed about the wholesomeness of farm life, the odor of new-mown hay, the rooster's predawn call, the opportunity to commune with nature, let me explain a few things.

Our family kept a few dairy cows, raised chickens, planted grains and alfalfa. In-house and field chores began as soon as a farm boy could toddle. It is said that a farmer has no boss, and the livestock join no unions. Don't believe it! There was no shortage of bosses on our farm: parents, relatives, brothers. Mother nature is an exacting executive and president of a vast natural union. Not even a brief procrastination does she permit. When rain soaks cut hay, it rots. Cows not promptly milked develop "mastitis," a condition in which the udder becomes inflamed and tender. It takes days for the cow to recover, while the farmer applies packs and poultices and performs around-the-clock frequent small milkings (it was the 1920s and '30s).

Farm work, even in the era of high-tech mechanization, is bone-banging, muscle-ripping hard. The hours aren't that good, either: often pre-dawn to beyond sundown in every season. The good news is that the farmer (and others who work this hard) need not join a health club to stay in shape.

No question about where the farmer's duty lies. If the cows are sick and the hay rots, he goes broke. How does this relate to other jobs? Whatever the job, the job is where the worker's duty lies during working hours. Failure to perform can mean lost customers, late schedules, faulty production. Such happenings are as bad (if not worse) as losing a cow or field of hay. If the organization goes broke, where does the job go? Where does the employee go?

## Attitudes Toward Employers

The dutiful worker wants the employer to succeed. It goes without saying: no boss, no job. My brothers and I had to help Dad succeed. Without the farm, we had nothing.

What about employer exploitation of the worker? Or inadequate pay? It happens, and when **injustice** creeps in, the workers may need to voice their displeasure – individually or as a group. Nineteenth-century America saw lots of exploitation, low pay, poverty and misery.

While we respected my father as the farm's prevailing authority, we boys could still muster a chorus of complaints when we felt overworked. Dad listened as we "reasoned together." If the relief we sought did not seriously affect the farm, Dad conceded and we could "tear off to town" to catch a movie, do some shopping or just "horse around" (boy fun). The work relationship between sons and Dad was based on the fundamental, generally unspoken, concept that the sons needed Dad as much as he needed them. Naturally, deep family love strengthened the bond.

So, what has this to do with baseball? At **all levels of the game** (little-leaguer to majors) a boss-job-worker situation develops. Before "signing up," the ballplayer needs to listen and understand what the boss expects and what the boss will provide in return. If the terms lay in doubt, both boss and worker need to ask questions. If the terms are unacceptable to the player or boss, the deal should not consummate. Once consummated, both parties owe their best efforts to each other and the job.

*Larry Jansen pitched for the New York Giants from 1947 through 1954. He appeared in the 1951 World Series, pitched five innings in the 1950 All-Star Game and was selected to the 1951 National League All-Star team.*

My first experience with a potential employer came when a Boston Red Sox scout signed me to a contract in 1939. Somehow, the contract never arrived at Fenway Park. As the spring of 1940 approached, no call or letter came from Boston. At that time the San Francisco Seals were approaching me with offers to try out for their team. I asked the Seals to wait because I had a contract (but no follow-on exchange) with Boston. After several of my inquiries to Boston went unanswered, I decided to write Judge Landis ("Kennesaw Mountain" Landis), Commissioner of Baseball. I had long admired the grizzled old "savior of baseball." This just and wise jurist became commissioner after the 1919 "Black Sox Scandal" threatened to kill baseball. The firm, but even-handed, demeanor of the judge restored public confidence in the legitimacy of baseball dealings. I asked the judge for guidance, and he gave it. The judge decided that because I had received no response to my inquiries after a reasonable period of time, I was free to sign with any team.

In 1940, the Seals trained at Boyes Springs in Sonoma County, California. I reported nearly a week late because I had waited for Judge Landis' response. At the end of spring training the Seals' offer went as follows: (1) The Seals have a working agreement with Salt Lake Bees (Class C, minor league). (2) The Seals assign my services to Salt Lake for one year. (3) After one year, the Seals take me back for spring training. (4) If I make the Seals' team at that time, the Seals owe Salt Lake nothing. (5) If I fail to make the Seals' team, Salt Lake gets me for three years (if they want me – an option). The exact legal language is paraphrased because the original document is lost.

There was no doubt in my mind about my duty – pitch well for Salt Lake, and try hard next spring to make it to the Seals' roster. I was thankful I had a job! Eileen has related information on our salary – meager, but a paycheck! No thought of whining and sniveling once we got to Salt Lake. Had to do my best for my job, and let the job do well for me.

When I was "optioned" to Salt Lake, that team still had a week of spring training left to complete. They had started later than the Seals, possibly to work over some "option possibilities" offered by the Seals. Salt Lake trained on the grounds of the Napa State Hospital near the ballfield now used by Napa Valley College. Some of us speculated, briefly, on whether we too should be committed to the State Hospital on the basis of our irrational choice of livelihood. Time would be the judge of our sanity.

The job and I did well by each other in Salt Lake. The Bees won the Pioneer League championship. My pitching record was 20-7; so my contribution to the team was substantial. Most importantly, Tony Robello, the Bees' manager, taught me a great deal about professional baseball. This first experience at playing for a living was an eye-opener! The professional batter at this level (Class C minor league – no longer in existence) watches every little thing a pitcher does. It is a matter of survival! The hitters constantly search for "giveaways." Does the pitcher "give away" the type of pitch, placement, throwovers? Some of the "old-timers" are so good at spotting pitcher foibles that one would swear they are mind readers. Tony taught me how to fool them. How to use a "foible" to make the hitter think I would throw a certain pitch; then I threw another. He taught me how to "...weave a tapestry of deceit (Angell)..." around my pitches. Thanks, Tony.

The spring of 1941 found me training with the Seals. This team signed me to a contract for the 1941 season. I had jumped from Class C to Triple-A. Lefty O'Doul managed the Seals in 1941 and was one of my very best instructors. Lefty had been a truly great major-league hitter (.349 lifetime batting average; in 1929 he hit .398 with the Phillies). The gift of knowledge Lefty gave me was a diagnostic skill. He showed me how to analyze the hitter by his stance, by the direction he moved his feet, by the way he took his practice swings. He insisted on my watching the other team's batting practice. We had few "films" to watch in 1941, and no radar guns! Lefty was a very cerebral person with an almost crystal-ball approach to each game situation.

Fortunate for all of us who played Triple A ball was the presence of numerous former major-leaguers, now in the autumns of their careers. Tony Lazzeri (Hall of Fame, 1991) played with us. From such elder statesmen we gleaned an enormous amount of information. Also, young pitchers had an opportunity to try out their ideas and skills on those who had been "at the top." I ended the 1941 season with a record of 16-10.

## Attitudes Toward Adversity

The following season (1942) brought a reversal of fortune – I won only 11 games and lost 14. What happened? Eileen has described the case of pneumonia that earned me a trip to the hospital for two weeks, followed by two months of incredible weakness. Much as I tried, it took all I had left to pitch a few innings. I learned from mother nature on this one! The team had traveled north to Seattle and Portland on a road trip early in the spring – a time of year that these two cities experience frequent episodes of cold, rainy weather. I pitched a complete game in this weather and awoke the next day with a fever, chills and a cough. I thought the symptoms would pass. Not so! The illness only grew worse, and when we arrived back in San Francisco I was a "mess." Lefty sent me to the hospital where I stayed two weeks. I am not sure I even remember most of the first week. The Lord was with me! The hospital rounded up some penicillin, and the bacteria finally struck out. **Sit down, bugs!** What I learned from this episode is that an illness with fever and cough, even in a healthy athlete, needs to be taken seriously. I gained zero from "toughing it out."

Another illness beset me in 1942. This problem was unrelated to the pneumonia, maybe. I developed Achilles tendonitis – a serious inflammation – in my right (power) heal. My author colleague says he is sure it had to do with my mechanics. In an attempt to cope with my after-pneumonia weakness, I was stressing my Achilles tendon by extending my power knee too violently and pushing too hard with my power foot – maybe.

I approached this problem incorrectly by failing to follow medical advice to rest my leg. Instead, I cut out the back of my shoe to reduce the irritation. I firmly believed that this was completely adequate treatment that would allow me to continue pitching. I was wrong. Worse yet, the military doctors spotted the problem during an exam to enter the service and rejected me. As it turned out, I worked on the farm from 1943 through V-J day in 1945. Even though this work was arduous, I was able to avoid repetitive stresses on the heel by varying my gait and stance at work. The tendon healed very slowly. I was surprised how long it took.

Warily, I rejoined the Seals in September 1945. During what remained of that season, I had five decisions: four wins, one loss. Apparently my four wins helped put the Seals in the playoffs and earned the players an extra bonus. Although I was not eligible to pitch in the playoffs, the team voted me a full share of the prize money. They reasoned that were it not for my four victories, they would not have been in the playoffs. Oh well, they were entitled to their opinion. Who was I to argue? That event taught me that among themselves, ballplayers possess a strong sense of fairness and justice.

1946 was a banner year. The Seals captured the playoffs. My contribution was 30 wins. After the season, the Giants purchased my contract from the Seals. I was thrilled, but then came talks about a salary. The Giants wanted to pay me less than I had earned in Triple A ball! I "held out" for five or six days to allow the Giants time to adjust their thinking. The salary **question** (not "issue") was **answered** by the Giants with a salary offer slightly greater than my Seals salary: $12,000 with a "bonus" of $7,000 if I showed the Giants I could win. What a windfall!

Injury is a terrible specter that haunts all athletes. Eileen described my smashed face in spring training, 1947. In retrospect, I am somewhat amused by the whole affair, but at the time, I was not amused – not at all. Within minutes of my "decking," a Cleveland outfielder fell and broke his arm. The ambulance called for me was reallocated to the outfielder, because he was in tremendous pain. I was still benumbed, and not fully aware of the extent of my injury.

The first ambulance left with the outfielder, and about 15 minutes later (so my teammates later told me), the second ambulance carted me off. My ambulance arrived first at the hospital. The other ambulance crew had "gotten lost" en route!

As both of us ballplayers lay there in the emergency room, my face swelled. This, of itself, made my caved-in face appear "normal"," or perhaps, slightly swollen. "No sweat," right? Once the outfielder had been attended to, the surgeons returned, and they too inquired about my condition. I replied that my face felt like there was a large hole in my cheek. The surgeons finally agreed to x-ray. The "films" surprised them. My left cheek bones and part of my jaw were, in fact, severely fractured and caved in. I was taken immediately to surgery where the surgeon expertly restored my facial bones to their proper location. After I awoke from the anesthesia, the surgeon stated that it was not necessary to "wire" my facial bones, because he had gone inside my sinus and "pushed everything back into place." He cautioned me not to roll over on my left cheek that night to prevent disruption of his repair. "I'll have to go back and wire the bones, if you roll over on your face during the night," he admonished.

I was in a private room, and there was no one there to warn me had I rolled over. All night I fought sleep to prevent my rolling over. The next day the surgeon repeated x-rays of my face, and announced that my bones were "aligned correctly." I didn't have to worry about rolling over after that. I still do not understand why the surgeon wanted me off my face just one night. All in all, I am pleased with my "facial" job.

I returned to spring training several days later, but the Giants would not allow me to throw a ball for two weeks. After that they used me sparingly: one or two innings at a time. When the season opened, I did not start a game for six weeks. The sum total of my pitching was several relief appearances in which I did poorly. Mel Ott, the Giants manager (Hall of Fame, 1951), was leery of pitchers from the Pacific Coast League. In 1946, two pitchers came to the Giants from the "coast." One had been a 30-game winner! Both were big-league disappointments. In fact, Ernie

Lombardi (a Hall of Fame catcher, 1986) commented derisively when I first walked in to the Giants' locker room, "Well boys, here's another coast leaguer." Between Ott and Lombardi the heat was on.

Immediately, I went out of my way to gain the "Schnozz's" (Lombardi's nickname) friendship. Lombardi respected hard work and talent. Before long we were close friends. He was the first teammate to visit me in the hospital. "Bocci" (Lombardi's other baseball nickname) and Hank Gowdy, our bullpen coach, taught me how to set up the major-league hitter "to put the ball in play" – to the infield!

After the first six weeks of the 1947 season, Mel Ott was ready to ship me to Minneapolis, the Giants' Triple A club. My relief appearances had been notably unimpressive. Hank Gowdy, and perhaps "Bocci," approached Mel Ott and said something to the effect that "Jansen needs a chance to start." Ott acquiesced. In mid-May 1947, I started against the Boston Braves and beat them 2-1. Four days later, I beat St. Louis 4-2. I was on the way to a 21-5 season. Thanks, "Bocci" and Hank, both now somewhere in catcher's heaven.

By now it must be obvious to the reader that a job – mine was pitching – requires an interest in learning and special attitudes. Also, friends and teammates help "make" the job.

## Attitude Toward the Fans

Several highly respected studies have shown that the persons most respected by many Americans are sports celebrities. A substantial segment of Americans have chosen athletes over political, theater, military, scientific and business leaders as persons who they would most like to emulate. That choice brings with it both honor and responsibility. It is the athlete's responsibility at all levels to act as a role model through pursuit of a moderate, intelligent and giving lifestyle.

Exactly what is meant by **moderate, intelligent** and **giving**? The moderate athlete is best described by what he/she **does not** do. A **moderate** individual does not indulge in illicit drugs, barroom brawls, **high-speed** auto chases, misuse of firearms, slander and other misdemeanors, felonies and torts. The moderate person does not associate with persons of ill repute (gangsters, felons and the like). An **intelligent** person uses his money wisely and honors his/her family. A **giving** athlete is generous with his time and positively participates in community functions ('a la Roberto Clemente). The giving athlete extends a helping hand to the disabled and others far less fortunate than himself/herself.

Fans, like faithful old dogs (meant respectfully), trudge along behind us, loyal to the last, even when we lose. **They are our true employer and enablers**. Their ticket purchases provide the fuel that fires the owners' and players' engines.

Accordingly, as much as we are able, when not occupied by the team or our families, we need to answer letters, appear for interviews, provide **free autographs** and endorse healthy social programs.

## Attitudes Toward Family

The 1948 and 1949 seasons brought more successes and more friends. Most important was the role my wife played. Eileen would have been a success at any career she entered. She chose to be an at-home mother and homemaker. I concurred in her choices. She was, and is, eminently successful in her career as a wife, mother, grandmother and yes, a great-grandmother. Eileen and I decided before our marriage that family and children, rooted in our community of Verboort-Forest Grove, Oregon, was our top priority, whatever the job.

Eileen developed routines and techniques to maintain consistency and predictability in our children's lives: school and a permanent home in Forest Grove; summer migrations to New Rochelle; fall flights to Oregon. After 1947, we had enough money to make a down payment on our home in Forest Grove – a house we have occupied ever since. Eileen prided herself on being "the fastest valise packer in the West." Sometimes I wonder how she did it – traveling with our children, as many as seven or eight at a time! There is no question in my mind that Eileen was, and is, the sustaining spirit and rock foundation in our family and in my career.

## Attitudes Toward the Team

A big-league surprise occurred in 1948. Halfway through the season Leo Durocher came over from the Dodgers to become manager of the Giants. His style of leadership was very different from Mel Ott's. In a nutshell, Leo was very expressive. So badly did he want to win that it was not uncommon for him to "blow his stack" at players only to come back the next day and pat the offended player on the back. Leo's use of the English language was a wonderment to behold. He was able to convey complex concepts in a single sentence. I found that when he barked at me without good cause, if I barked back, he pulled his horns in, often with a smile. I really believe he wanted my kind of response from his players.

Nothing spectacular occurred in the Giants' performance under Leo during 1948 and 1949. In 1949 our record was 73-81 and a fifth-place finish. In 1950, things began to happen. Sal Maglie, another breaking-ball pitcher like myself, joined the team. Sal showed he was an invaluable asset and ended the season 18-4. My record was 19-13, and another new pitcher, Jim Hearn, ended 11-3. Our infield also had new faces: Alvin Dark, shortstop; Eddie Stanky, second base; Hank Thompson, third base. Whitey Lockman would move from the outfield to first base in 1951. In 1950, we finished third behind the first-place Phillies (the great "Whiz Kids" team) and Brooklyn. Our overall record was 86-68. The Giants were now poised for the great event – the pennant year of 1951.

Eileen has related to you some of the ecstasy of that year. The **attitudes** of all the Giants players could not have been more favorable. Our pitching had spooled up to "max thrust." Sal Maglie and I each won 23 games, and Jim Hearn 17. Sal posted 22 complete games! Two charismatic outfielders had joined the regular lineup -- Willie Mays and Monte Irvin. Mays hit .274 and Irvin .312. Monte won the RBI title with 121.

Pertinent to our discussion of attitude, it is important to note that in 1951 every Giant player – reserve and regular – every coach, and our manager, Leo Durocher, felt good about the specific contribution each was making toward the total effort. The chemistry was perfect. We just knew we would win, even when we trailed the Dodgers in the ninth inning of the third playoff game. The Yankees beat us in the World Series, but that loss did not dim the pride we had in ourselves.

In 1952, the team's purpose and spirit were there, but the pitching diminished. I finished 11-11, Jim Hearn 14-7. Sal had a good year at 18-8. Willie Mays hit .236 before he answered a call from his draft board to serve a two-year hitch in the army. We finished 92-62, second behind the Dodgers (96-57). A few more victories from Jim and me, and the pennant would have flown over the Polo Grounds again. My attitude was optimistic as I looked forward to the 1953 season, and to a better year. I knew the team counted on me and that Sal had done his best to shoulder more of the load. Sal was the league's second-best winner behind Robin Roberts who won 28 games.

Unfortunately, 1953 was not to be a better year for me, or for the team. The Giants (70-84) had a losing season and finished fifth. I also had my first losing season (11-16). Sal did no better with an 8-9 effort. Willie Mays was still in the Army. On the bright side, we had four .300 hitters: Alvin Dark, .300; Hank Thompson, .302; Don Mueller, .333; and Monte Irvin, .329. Whitey Lockman hit .295 and David Williams .297. This tells you something. Connie Mack said it best: "Pitching is 80 percent (an exaggeration!) of the game!"

*New York pitchers Jim Hearn, Hoyt Wilhelm, Larry Jansen and Sal Maglie show their pitching grips during 1953 spring training. The four Giants pitchers had combined for 58 wins the previous season. (From the Jansen family collection, ©United Press)*

After the 1953 season, I developed major problems with my back – probably disc disease. Actually, the problem may have been there on several occasions before 1953. As I favored my back, I began to injure my arm. I was becoming a wreck. What should my attitude now be? I resolved to continue my struggle to help the team and to keep my job.

The Giants were good to me. They offered several alternatives early in the 1954 season after I struggled to a 4-4 record. The alternatives: 1) Removal from player status and assignment as a coach in New York; 2) go to Nashville (Southern league – Triple A) as a manager; 3) go to Minneapolis (American Association – Triple A) as a player-coach. I chose the first, because the family had come east again at the end of the school year. Also, our friends (teammates and families) were in New York and I wanted to be close enough to contribute to this team which now sparkled with the fire of 1951.

In 1954 the pitching was there. Our new pitcher, Johnnie Antonelli (acquired from Milwaukee), won 21 games. Ruben Gomez won 17; Sal was 14-6 and Hoyt Whilhelm 12-4! Willie Mays came back with a bang, hitting .345; Mueller hit .342 and Alvin Dark .293. The Giants' record rose to 97-57. We won the pennant and swept the Indians in the World Series.

## *Attitudes Toward Teaching*

After the Series, New York released me and I signed with Seattle in the Pacific Coast League (Triple A) as a player-coach. This situation represented a new role for me in baseball. After the 1954 season, I considered leaving baseball altogether. I decided against that alternative because as a coach with the Giants I realized the joy of teaching and helping others "make it."

Seattle is only two hours by road from our home in Forest Grove, so I had the best of all worlds: my family close by in our home, and the opportunity to develop young ballplayers. Seattle did expect me to pitch from time to time, and in 1955 I had a record of 7-7; in 1956, 11-2. Lefty O'Doul had come up from San Francisco to Seattle as the hitting coach under manager Freddie Hutchinson. The three of us enjoyed one another, and I felt as though I was definitely making a contribution, especially in my coaching duties.

During the 1956 season, Cincinnati called Seattle and asked for my services as a player-coach. The Reds were locked in a tight pennant race with Brooklyn and Milwaukee. Eventually, the teams ended the season within two wins of each other: Brooklyn 93-61, Milwaukee 92-62, Cincinnati 91-63!

I returned to Seattle in 1957 as a player-coach. From 1958 to 1960 I undertook a similar role in Portland in the Pacific Coast League.

During the winter of 1960-61 Portland offered me a job as manager. While I pondered this offer, the (now) San Francisco Giants called and stated that Alvin Dark, the new manager and my old teammate, wanted me to be the pitching coach. Eileen has described in some detail the events occurring during the negotiations for that job, and how later our family maintained its cohesion during our 11 years with San Francisco. Eileen was by now not only the "fastest packer in the West," but also (though she won't admit it) the "fastest driver in the West" (ask the California Highway Patrol!).

For 11 superb years, the relationship with San Francisco endured. To be close and contribute to the likes of Gaylord Perry and Juan Marichal – both superb human beings, friends and Hall of Fame inductees – as well

*Eileen and Larry Jansen pause during a layover at Salt Lake en route home from the 1951 World Series. (From the Jansen family collection)*

as totally excellent pitchers like Jack Sanford, Billy Pierce and Don Larsen was a singular honor. The Giant teams of that era (1961-71) were filled with talented players. During that decade we had ten 20-game winners, one pennant (1962) and one division title. The Giants were a force to be reckoned with because hitters like Willie Mays, Orlando Cepeda, the Alous and Willie McCovey crushed opposing pitchers while our pitchers dazzled hitters.

In seven seasons we won 90 or more games. In 1962, the Giants garnered 103 victories. Over my 11 seasons as coach our pitchers racked up 1,001 victories against 777 losses. The overall percentage was .563 without a single losing season. In 1971 the Giants captured the Western Division title.

After the 1971 season the Giants and I parted ways. Again, I confronted the end of a baseball career. Then Leo Durocher called from Chicago. He had managed the Cubs since 1966 and now needed a new pitching coach. Leo was my friend, and I wanted to help, but there was a kicker. Eileen has discussed how this job meant separation from family, spring training to October. Not a pleasant prospect.

In 1971, the Cubs had finished third in their division with a record of 83-79. Ferguson Jenkins (24-13) was their ace and Milt Pappas was second (17-14). My estimate of the Cubs' staff was that, because they failed to get into shape during spring training, they ended up with too many losses early in the season. My goal: get them in shape to win early in the season, and continue winning! In 1972 Chicago advanced to second in its division. "Fergie" Jenkins garnered 20 wins (20-12), Pappas another seventeen (17-7) and a superb ERA (2.77) – all without a bunch of early-season losses. Jenkins was later inducted into the Hall of Fame (1991), eight years after he left the majors.

## Attitudes Toward Retirement

1972 was my last year in baseball. The Cubs, with Whitey Lockman at the helm (my friend and former teammate on the Giants), had an "off" season (77-84). Neither the hitting or the pitching was there. "Fergie" struggled to notch 14 wins (14-16) and Milt picked up only seven (7-12). Eileen and I were still raising the last four (all boys) of our 10 children at home in Oregon. I was now in my 53rd year. It was time to bid adieu to baseball and turn back toward the Oregon hills. The Cubs were disappointed and tempted me to stay by doubling my salary, but I knew what I had to do.

Never have I or Eileen regretted any of the decisions we made regarding baseball or our family. As Eileen so beautifully put it, "we gave our best to the game, and the game treated us well."

My deepest feeling of satisfaction in baseball is knowing that I contributed in a very special way to the careers of those who surrounded me as teammates. My fondest wish is that this book will enlarge upon the nucleus of student pitchers as well as bring knowledge to other players, coaches, and, perhaps best of all, the fans who provide us with the support, spiritually and financially, to pursue this truly American game – baseball.

NOW, I WILL SIT DOWN – AND WATCH!

# APPENDIX A

## *Selected pitching records*

**Larry Jansen**

| Year | Team | League | W | L | BB | SO | ERA | CG |
|------|------|--------|---|---|----|----|-----|-----|
| 1940 | Salt Lake City | Pioneer | 20 | 7 | | | | |
| 1941 | San Francisco | P.C.L. | 16 | 10 | | | | |
| 1942 | San Francisco | P.C.L. | 11 | 14 | | | | |
| 1943-44 | | Out of Organized Baseball | | | | | | |
| 1945 | San Francisco | P.C.L. | 4 | 1 | | | | |
| 1946 | San Francisco | P.C.L. | 30 | 6 | | | | |
| 1947 | New York | National | 21 | 5 | 57 | 104 | 3.16 | 20 |
| 1948 | New York | National | 18 | 12 | 54 | 126 | 3.61 | 15 |
| 1949 | New York | National | 15 | 16 | 62 | 113 | 3.85 | 21 |
| 1950 | New York | National | 19 | 13 | 55 | 161 | 3.01 | 21 |
| 1951 | New York | National | 23 | 11 | 56 | 145 | 3.04 | 18 |
| 1952 | New York | National | 11 | 11 | 47 | 74 | 4.09 | 8 |
| 1953 | New York | National | 11 | 16 | 55 | 88 | 4.14 | 6 |
| 1954 | New York | National | 2 | 2 | 15 | 15 | 5.98 | 0 |
| 1955 | Seattle | P.C.L. | 7 | 7 | | | | |
| 1956 | Seattle | P.C.L. | 11 | 2 | | | | |
| | Cincinnati | National | 2 | 3 | 9 | 16 | 5.19 | 2 |
| 1957 | Seattle | P.C.L. | 10 | 12 | | | | |
| 1958 | Portland | P.C.L. | 9 | 10 | | | | |
| 1959 | Portland | P.C.L. | 1 | 0 | | | | |
| 1960 | Portland | P.C.L. | 3 | 0 | | | | |
| **MAJOR LEAGUE TOTALS** | | | **122** | **89** | **410** | **842** | **3.58** | **107** |

- Pitched in 1951 World Series, 0-2
- Pitched five innings 1950 All-Star Game, gave up one hit and no runs, struck out six.
- Selected to 1951 All-Star Team
- Won two playoff games, 1945 S.F. P.C.L.
- Pitching coach San Francisco Giants, 1961-1971
- Pitching coach Chicago Cubs, 1972-1973

# *Coaching Record*

**San Francisco**

| Year | Won | Lost | 20-Game Winners | League/Division Standing | Comments* |
|---|---|---|---|---|---|
| 1961 | 85 | 69 | 0 | League: 3rd | NERA: 3.77 |
| 1962 | 103 | 62 | 1 | League: 1st<br>World Series: Lost<br>to Yankees<br>4 games to 3 | NERA: 3.79 |
| 1963 | 88 | 74 | 1 | League: 3rd | NERA: 3.35 |
| 1964 | 90 | 72 | 1 | League: 4th | NERA: 3.19 |
| 1965 | 95 | 67 | 1 | League: 2nd | NERA: 3.20 |
| 1966 | 93 | 68 | 2 | League: 2nd | NERA: 3.24 |
| 1967 | 91 | 71 | 1 | League: 2nd | NERA: 2.92 |
| 1968 | 88 | 74 | 1 | League: 2nd | NERA: 2.71 |
| 1969 | 90 | 72 | 1 | Division: 2nd | NERA: 3.25 |
| 1970 | 86 | 76 | 1 | Division: 3rd | NERA: 4.50 |
| 1971 | 90 | 72 | 0 | Division: 1st<br>NLCS: Lost<br>to Pittsburgh<br>3 games to 1 | NERA: 3.33 |

**Totals:**

| | Won | Lost | 20-Game Winners |
|---|---|---|---|
| **League:** | 999 | 777 | 10 |
| **World Series:** | 3 | 4 | |
| **League Playoff:** | 1 | 3 | |
| | **1,003** | **784** | **10** |

*NERA — Net Earned Run Average (team ERA)

# APPENDIX B

## References

1. Adair, R.K., *The Physics of Baseball*, New York: Harper Perenial, 1990.*

2. Andrews, J.R., G.L. Harrelson, *Rehabilitation of the Injured Athlete*, Philadelphia: Saunders, 1991.*

3. Baker, Dusty, *You Can Teaching Hitting*, Masters Press, 1993.

4. Blomquist, C.G., B. Saltin, "Cardiovascular Adaptations to Physical Training," *Ann. Rev. Physiol.*, 45:169, 1983.

5. Brengelman, G.L., "Circulatory Adjustments to Exercise and Heat Stress," *Ann. Rev. Physiol.*, 45:191, 1983.

6. Brogdon, B.S., M.D. Crow, "Little Leaguer's Elbow," *Am. J. Roentg.* 83:671, 1960.

7. Commissioner of Baseball, *Official Baseball Rules*, St. Louis, Sporting News Publishing Co., 1996 edition.

8. Fisher, A., C. Jansen, *Scientific Basis of Athletic Conditioning*, Philadelphia: Lea & Febiger, 1989.

9. Guyton, A.C., *Textbook of Medical Physiology*, Philadelphia: Saunders, 1991.

10. Garrick, J.G., D.R. Webb, *Sports Injuries*, Philadelphia: Saunders, 1990.

11. Gourtzke, B., M. Milner, *Scientific Basis of Human Movement*, Baltimore: Williams & Wilkins, 1988.*

12. Hocky, R., *Stress and Fatigue in Human Performance*, New York: John Wiley and Sons, 1983.*

13. Mercier, L.R. et al, *Practical Orthopedics*, St. Louis: Mosby Year Book, 1991.

14. Neer, C.S. "...Chronic Impingement Syndrome in the Shoulder," *J. Bone Jnt. Surg.*, 55:41, 1972.

15. Nemac, David, *The Rules of Baseball*, New York: Major League Baseball, 1994.

16. Nordin, M. and V.H. Frankel (eds), *Basic Bio-Mechanics of Musclo-Skeletal System*, Philadelphia: Lea-Febiger, 1989.*

17. Ryan, Nolan, *Kings of the Hill,* New York: Harper Collins, 1992.

18. Schumacher, H.R., et al, *Primer on Rheumatic Diseases,* Atlanta: Arthritis Foundation, 1993.

19. Sisto, D.J., et al, "An Electromyographic Analysis of the Elbow in Pitching," *Am. J. Sports Med.,* 15:260, 1987.

20. Thomas, J.A. (ed.), *Drugs, Athletes and Physical Performance,* New York: Plenum, 1988.

21. Thorn, J., J.B. Holway, *The Pitcher,* New York: Prentice Hall, 1988.*

22. Will, G.F., *Men at Work,* New York: Harper Perennial, 1990.*

23. Wolff, R., *The Baseball Encyclopedia,* New York: Macmillan, 1993.

* Indicates "Jansen Hall of Fame" references.